In The Footsteps of The Anasazi

EXPLORING THE FOUR CORNERS' BACKCOUNTRY

Howard L. Smith

IN THE FOOTSTEPS OF THE ANASAZI

Exploring The Four Corners' Backcountry

Acknowledgements

Each chapter of *In the Footsteps of the Anasazi* begins with a wonderfully lyrical haiku written by long-time friend Terrye Bullers. As you will see, Terrye has great sensitivity for wild places and an astonishing ability to capture the spirit of land, sea, sky, forest, mountains, rivers and wildlife in a few breathtakingly vibrant words. Terrye and soul-mate Bill Bullers collaborated on the poetic verse preceding *Hidden Hot Springs* (Chapter 13) and Bill wrote the short prose introducing *Indian Summer* (Chapter 11). Others should be so lucky to have such gracious, caring friends who are as talented in penning poems as they are in dancing through wild lands with kayaks, skis and hiking boots.

The front cover of this book incorporates copyrighted art from Ward Hooper of Ward Hooper Gallery in Boise, Idaho (wardhooper.com; 208-287-8150). An immensely talented artist, Ward is renowned throughout the Northwest for his iconic historic and vintage renditions.

Lesley Van Foster's considerable creative talents assisted in the production of this book. Without Lesley's esprit, talent and encouragement, this book would only exist as an electronic document.

*Buttes, mesas, sage, dust, vestiges of
the ancients mark the sacred ground.*

*Ranging far and wide connecting with
the ancients, we walk in beauty.*

TERRYE BULLERS

1

Ancient Paths

On a brittle November day twelve-hundred years ago in the mountains of southeast Nevada a close-knit family gathers within their cozy pit house, a crude home by today's standards, fashioned from toast colored mud, plastered over a woven mesh fabricated from brush, limbs and stones.

Phissssstttt.......ssnnaaapppp.....ffuuttthhh.

POPppppp.....*phiss.......*

Pooooffffffffffffff.....

Sssspppplllaaaattttttttt....

Rabbit is sizzling on the spit, a few meager fat droplets flare on hitting yellow-orange flames dancing off crackling cedar

1

branches. Ambrosia fills the dense air inside this abode; seared rabbit's cloyingly gamey scent, a delectable reminiscence of sweet sage, odoriferous zephyrs of stale sweat, and musty damp earth.

Squinting in soft golden light, gnarly old grandmother – twisted as the juniper and piñon trees outside – places finishing touches on a simple but elegant crimson clay bowl destined to hold next season's scrumptious pine nuts. Two feet away her granddaughter grudgingly weaves a sturdy yucca fiber blanket. She's been at it for a week now and her mother is none too happy about how slow it's going.

The rest of the family shares light banter concerning events around the village today. They're intimately embracing the fire's flickering flames and buoyant by this afternoon's lucky catch. Tomorrow holds promises of even better fare; portents of full bellies. Father will embark on a hunting trip to the large river – the Muddy River as it will be called several centuries later – where game abounds.

This scene is unfolding near the Moapa Valley of Nevada. Parallel events are happening this fall evening in literally thousands of villages sprinkled throughout this shared nexus of the Southwest – southeast Nevada, southern Utah and Colorado, Arizona and New Mexico. Many Southwest communities share ancestors stretching back thousands of years. It's a vibrant, yet delicate, network of life spreading like crisscrossing arteries and veins over desert mesas, up lonely canyon arroyos and past richly forested mountains.

No matter where you turn in the Southwest vestiges of the ancient ones remain reminding us that a long succession of cultures inhabited these magical lands. Controversy continues about the use of the word "Anasazi." Some authorities suggest that an appropriate substitute term is "Ancestral Puebloans;" an expression that is seemingly more sensitive without pejorative connotations. Despite the debate, "Anasazi" continues to be widely used by Native Americans, scholars and the public.

From Moapa Valley, head south to gravel-strewn floodplains sixty miles outside of Phoenix. Hohokam settlements flourished there from 700 AD until the mid-1100s. They were followed in the 1300s by a culture known as the Salados — people who built masonry villages that still can be found today resting patiently in sharp hills overlooking the Salt River.

South of Phoenix and snug against Tucson's rugged foothills the Hohokam culture left hundreds of rock art effigies and pictographs. Saguaro National Park, west of Tucson, is renowned for picturesque cacti with up-reaching arms. Saguaros are quintessential desert icons that visually pop into mind whenever we think about desolate arid wastelands baking under unrelenting sun. However, beyond these alluring cacti are more indelible mementos — petroglyphs and pictographs — of those who went before. The often mysterious images are hidden among boulder fields, but prominent once you know what to look for.

Some two-hundred miles east from Las Vegas as the crow flies to Flagstaff settlements proliferated in the Flagstaff-Phoenix corridor: Palatki in Sedona; Tuzigoot and Montezuma Castle in the Verde Valley; Walnut Canyon's cliff dwellings; the prodigious Wupatki and Wukoki pueblo villages; and, thousands more resting where ancient people left them, slowly melding into the earth but resolutely preserved by an almost waterless climate.

Approaching the heart of the Southwest's Anasazi country, geography intensifies into gigantic proportions — the Grand Canyon, Painted Desert and Petrified Forest, Monument Valley, Canyonlands, Bryce Canyon, Capitol Reef, Arches and Zion.

Seemingly by design, the scale of ancient human settlements kept pace with the land – Canyon de Chelly, Mesa Verde, Chaco Canyon, Lowry Pueblo, Nine Mile Canyon, Ute Mountain, and Hovenweep, among so many other sites. This rich legacy and imprint of ancestral peoples rests like a massive blanket over the region.

What finer backdrop could enhance explorations in the Southwest? This heritage takes center stage whenever setting foot along any path in the region. There's no way of knowing whether I'll intersect the trail of that Muddy River hunter who centuries ago went out looking for venison, bison, antelope or anything better than a scrawny rabbit. Perhaps the track was originally pounded into existence by him and his progeny. That piece of lovingly shaped clay resurfacing alongside the pathway may be a remnant of grandmother's precious crimson-colored pine nut bowl.

Few backcountry discoveries are more thrilling than unexpectedly coming upon Indian ruins and artifacts. Pottery shards and arrowheads suddenly appear when I'm not looking for them. A petroglyph emerges on a volcanic rock in a spot that is totally unanticipated; completely unpredictable. A faint mound of tuff blocks comprising former walls materializes beneath a sheltering juniper. Tangible reminders of the ancient ones add great value to wilderness walks and reinforce that any of us are only one in an achingly long line of explorers who have trod these somewhat obscure trails.

Once my eyes opened to traces of the ancients, it was difficult *not* to see prevalent ancestral shadows, especially in the backcountry. Realization hit that the majority of the wilderness trails I chase originated with deliberate footsteps by long-forgotten Indian predecessors. They created paths that many sojourners religiously followed over the centuries. This knowledge enriches such rambles. It also makes me pause to reflect about what they saw or what they experienced at any particular spot; introspection that usually leads to more questions than answers.

Was a twisting cherry sandstone canyon no wider than outstretched arms valued for its beauty, or was it feared because danger lurked within its dark recesses? Did the ancients appreciate the sensuously graceful drop of a melodious stream into a tranquil pond or did they only think about whether that inviting pool held dinner? Did they locate their homes on a subdued vanilla-yellow butte solely because of defensive advantages, or did they also factor in the view to distant snow-capped mountains stretching like a blazingly white saw blade? Was a flourishing meadow simply a potential grocery store or did they enjoy walking across it as feathery grasses swished, tickling their calves?

Answers to these questions may never surface. But does this really matter?

Ancient paths on lands covered in ancestral shadows beckon with intriguing possibilities. After having walked these byways; after observing the old ones' physical reminders; and, after living under their spiritual influence, the connections are vividly apparent. We are not the first, nor will we be the last to enjoy life in this remarkable corner of our planet. We all share a place in the continuing stream of humanity, thereby adding richly to these enduring ancient shadows.

Outside of the Southwest's rough and rugged backcountry, ancestral shadows also hover over frenetic life unfolding in our teeming cities and towns. Modern distractions tend to blunt our recognition of ancestors past. Electronic gadgets keep our brains engaged in banal conversation. At work and home, steel and glass and stone buffer us from the Southwest's harsh environments.

Modernity ensures that we are tucked safely away from the brutally honest interaction ancient ones maintained with an oftentimes unforgiving Mother Earth.

Despite society's best efforts to distance itself from a past of pit houses, jacales, stacked stone pueblos or crude caves, reverberations of the ancient ones endure. They had their global climate change and we have our looming environmental challenges. The old ones gradually confronted new technologies while we pathologically pursue the latest scientific discoveries. Past denizens of the Southwest left indelible marks of their passing gouged in stone. We also mark our territory in ways that make petroglyphs and rock art seem ephemeral by comparison.

This book, *In the Footsteps of the Anasazi,* drills down into the very marrow of what it means to live in and explore places the old ones and similar precursors called home. The implications are deeply rich. No matter where we dwell or travel, our passing is foreshadowed by those who went before.

The ancient ones' intriguing heritage is literally everywhere to the point of being inescapable. Regardless of where I turn, where you turn, reminders of the Anasazi surface whether in contemporary icons or prehistoric artifacts. Walk through any phone book in the Southwest; the names of businesses, organizations and people ring with a legacy of indigenous people. Drive down a street and observe road names; chances are the old ones emerge in name and spirit. Take a hike up an arroyo; scan the scattered sand for detritus washed down from ruins resting in the hills.

With omnipresent ancestral shadows serving as an overarching theme, several corresponding findings arose during the course of living in the Southwest and of persistently exploring its backcountry over ancient paths. These supportive points flesh out the skeletal framework of this book.

In some respects these corollary discoveries may appear to be almost naturally evident to the point of being truisms; modern denizens of the Southwest usually take them for granted. However, in my mind what we fail to register is the less obvious connections of these conclusions to ancestral shadows

First, a *palpable spiritual energy of this region is impossible to ignore.* The land resonates with a natural spirituality that engenders sanctity among its people. A person has to be pretty shallow to avoid being touched deeply by the sight of a mid-winter sunset over the Sangre de Cristo, Virgin, Wasatch or Organ Mountains. Multi-hued serpentine canyons take your breath away leaving you muttering epiphanies and focused on holy thoughts. Soaring mountain ranges represent the central symbol of people's lives, acting as perceptual anchors and emblematic touchstones. Although Santa Fe and Taos, New Mexico may be the most famous power vortices, the entire Southwest vibrates with a divine and utterly contagious sacred vitality.

Next, *the Southwest's pervasive wildness inexorably shapes life in ways we don't understand or sometimes care to acknowledge.* Sheer acreage comprising the region is instrumental in protecting wildlife and wilderness. In even the most civilized areas wildness lurks just over the fence line; mere yards beyond the city limits. The old ones witnessed startling growth of their populations, but even as their numbers increased vast uninhabited mountain ranges, deserts, mesas, canyons and all other manner of geological features continued to hold sway. Wildness inevitably shaped who they were and how they thought – similarly as it does to us today.

As Ancestral Puebloans realized, *the land has a remarkable capacity to renew and invigorate people.* Perhaps this is due to the relatively sparse number of people per square mile allowing opportunities to escape civilization's oppressive blanket swaddling cities in the Southwest. Some would argue that being surrounded by untrammeled land to the horizon line naturally leads to pristine cleansing of the human spirit. Alternatively, it may be a richly super blessing of natural beauty that soothes and heals those who live there. Whatever the explanation, this region offers abundant avenues for people to restore their souls.

Time and time again I found that *magic happens off the beaten path*. Exploring a wide variety of areas in the Southwest convinced me that the simple act of going where others don't serves as a prelude to the supernatural. Inexplicably once I head into the backcountry all sorts of little enchanted events occur: I continually encounter shabby black bears on feral high country trails when no one else is around; sauntering down a trail-less wash inevitably turns up an arrowhead or pottery shard; and in other cases, casually exploring a little side ravine to its farthest reach will often reveal a delicate seep surrounded by ferns bracketing a natural grotto as perfect as the Sistine Chapel. Eventually I came to accept that magic was all part-and-parcel of exploring behind the scenes.

Finally, *the past seemingly repeats itself – our future is informed by the past*. Continually tugging at the back of my mind as I tuned into the conspicuous presence of the Anasazi was a compelling question: what does the future hold? The more that I tried to formulate answers to this question the more that parallels surfaced between the 21st Century and the 13th. In some respects it appears that like the ancient ones, our civilization may be destined to merely evaporate leaving few indelible reminders for those who quizzically shuffle over our remains a millennium from now. This makes me wonder what the old ones would say about our future.

Throughout the following chapters, the preceding ideas are examined in a series of tales recounting special experiences that enriched my life. These stories derive from some three-decades-plus years of field research throughout the Southwest. When all was said and done, I could only conclude that the 700-1,300 year gap between me and the old ones is not all that prominent. Indigenous shadows seemed to literally hover everywhere I went – their existence was unassailable and definitely palpable.

As far as the Anasazi are concerned, I believe I found what they found. There is little question that we both discovered beautifully wild lands and a preternatural spirituality embracing their home and mine. I also believe their experiences and mine possess startling parallels. It is probable that we both were able to recognize and enjoy rejuvenation from the unique nurturing qualities of this region. Undoubtedly we mutually reveled in mystical experiences – those little, but highly vital, magical events that inexplicably accompanied our daily lives and far flung adventures.

The sum of these findings is sobering. When it comes to the question of what the future holds for us, we need only glance back to the old ones. They grappled with social, technological, economic, political and spiritual changes like we do. They endured wild climatic fluctuations like we are suffering. Their civilization disappeared despite the phenomenal resources of the Southwest. Will our society follow suit?

Considering the gravity of this question, *In the Footsteps of the Anasazi* has far reaching connotations. This book is more than a compilation of stories about how people find the Southwest to be so engaging. It is also a metaphor for all who live in regions with a vibrantly rich ancestral legacy. By the time readers turn the last page my hope is that all will come away with a greater appreciation for this heritage and how it continues to influence life today – just as generations hence will examine our lives and contemplate whether they are destined to repeat our experience.

Omnipresent
Heritage

Coyote listens
as drums call buffalo, deer.
Only Wind replies...

2

Ancestral Shadows

THUMP, THUmp, thump, thump.

THUMP, THUmp, thump, thump.

Buffalo Clan dancers dressed in riveting ceremonial finery hold onlookers' rapt attention at Acoma Pueblo's centuries old church in Sky City. A lead drum group pours its very soul into a hypnotizing cadence reverberating off ten-foot thick adobe walls, trampled chocolate-colored earthen floor hard as concrete, carved charcoal-black wooden corbels and viga beamed ceiling above. Ancestral spirits sway in time with the beat and look down from Mission San Estéban del Rey's sky-scraper interior with two massive bell towers.

This pulsating tempo washes over somber spectators bundled from head-to-toe against stupefying cold. Young ones swaddled claustrophobically to fight-off Acoma's twenty-degree temperature with colorful red mittens, sun-yellow caps and sky-blue mufflers peer from narrow slits in their armor. Late December days are only just beginning to lengthen after winter's solstice. Sky City's mile-and-a-half elevation intensifies this bone-penetrating chill. No wonder today is one of the Pueblo's feasts. From this point forward each day gradually brightens heralding spring's imminent warm return across immense sandstone mesas in western New Mexico.

Acoma Pueblo claims to be the oldest continually inhabited settlement in the U.S. established before the 10th century. Oral history suggests these Keresan speaking people migrated from the west and north around Chaco Canyon to this seventy acre pink and chalk white sandstone mesa jutting almost four hundred feet above chamisa covered valley floor. Nearly vertical cliff sides offered a superior defensive position enabling the Acoma to fend off raids by Apache and Navajo. The Pueblo was secure until 1598.

Don Juan de Oñate established the first permanent Spanish colony north of Santa Fe in that year. The Acoma people were very resistant to Oñate's attempt at outside rule. When traveling to Santa Fe in December of 1598, Juan de Zaldivar, a nephew of Oñate, sought shelter and food from Acoma for his party of two dozen soldiers. They were met by hundreds of warriors who slaughtered the troops except for several men who lived long enough to inform Governor Oñate about the massacre. Oñate's retribution was swift and brutal resulting in more than 600 dead. All male survivors over 25 years had one foot cut off and they joined women and children in a life of servitude.

San Estéban del Rey was constructed from 1629 until 1640 under the guidance of Friar Juan Ramírez. The central hall of the church is 120 feet long and 40 feet wide. Roof beams were harvested some thirty-plus miles away at 11,400 foot Mount Taylor known among Puebloans as *Kaweshtima*. One of the twin towers flanking the mission's entrance contains a cast-iron bell given to the Pueblo by the King of Spain in 1710. Ornate religious figures, paintings and carvings still fill the church that is used for Catholic masses and traditional Acoma ceremonies.

Across a russet-hued dirt floor laboriously carried four hundred feet to mesa top, the Buffalo and Deer Clans take center stage on the chair-less venue. Wearing headdresses festooned with cast-off antlers and intensely green pine boughs male members of the Deer Clan strut stiffly around the nave. Bending over to resemble their namesake, dancers' arms probe forward with vividly decorated three-foot canes mimicking slender deer legs. White tunics and pants are ornamented in lively colors blending down to pine boughs on the dancers' legs.

Members of the audience — mainly Acoma and friends with a sprinkling of outside visitors such as me — hug the church's earthen walls. Most are standing out of respect for the dancers and for elders swathed in blankets sitting motionless on cheap plastic or metal chairs. Wisps of frosty breath methodically curlicue toward viga beams overhead. Gloved hands are thrust deep within bulbous coats searching for a smidgen of warmth. The unheated church is like a gigantic freezer set on extreme low. Bystanders shuffle from one foot to the other in vain hopes of exciting enough circulation to keep from going numb.

The Deer Clan continues to weave slow concentric patterns emblazoned in their memories and handed down over the ages. Young boys try to emulate the precise steps, strut and deer-like motions of their fathers and grandfathers; learning the rhythms and movements that will one day grow into a graceful dance of celebration. Grandfathers are regal in their countenance, upholding the clan's honor. They are trailed by a long line of offspring who one day will lead this parade.

Despite the Deer Clan's stately promenade, it's the Buffalo Clan that sparkles this early afternoon. A combination of striking costume and lively tempo magnetically draw all eyes to their rapid shuffle – almost a gallop – from one wall of the church to the other, and then back again. An old grandmother who had nodded off with tan scarf wrapped tightly around her head suddenly blinks awake to pounding feet in syncopation with the drum's heartbeat. A crying three-year old in her mother's arms quiets and gazes with fascination as bison sprinkle across the church floor.

Wearing a headdress of pitch-black buffalo fur and weathered charcoal-gray horns flowing into a buffalo cape the dancers transform into the very animals they represent. Faces decorated with white and black paint are shrouded by rich buffalo fur. White tunics blend into black skirts etched in white and covering black leggings adorned with pine boughs. Heads held low and backs slightly arched like the Deer Clan, the performers rise to the swelling beat as the drum group levitates their hammering tempo.

Even the spectators transform as the sum of the ceremony's parts become more than a whole. Mission San Estéban del Rey – St. Stephen the King – converts into a breathing, pulsating, living organism; not just a church sheltering a few dancers and viewers.

THUMP, THUmp, thump, thump.

THUMP, THUmp, thump, thump.

The drummers take it up yet another notch and even the ten-foot thick adobe walls seem to be shaking. Dust begins to fall gently from corbels and vigas high above, dancing a gossamer rhythm in what little heat lies suspended above the high-stepping Buffalo Clan. Every molecule in my body is leaping with the galloping bison, dust particles, and young children along the wall shaking their heads to the drum's primordial pulse.

It's so beautiful, so primal, that I surreptitiously glance down to hide misty eyes. We're partaking in an extraordinary festival that has played out each year at this time over the centuries. Strangely it all seems so natural; almost as though it's my heritage that's being celebrated. Focusing on the mission's earthen floor, I notice the fellow next to me enthusiastically tapping out the beat with his foot. The sound is almost deafening as the bison gallop to the waiting wall.

Then...

THUMP, THUMP, THUMP, THUMP.

This raucous crescendo is followed by a very faint THUMP, THUmp, thump, thump; THUMP, THUmp, thump, thump; the drum group letting everyone know this spirited dance is over. Buffalo Clan members reorganize into a processional line and head out into a robin's-egg-blue sun-blasted sky. Gradually even the faint tempo slows and the celebrants' frenzy tones down while they morph back into bystanders, family, friends, and Pueblo.

Solemnly filing out of the church our sight is drawn to vast plateau lands beyond. The incredible visage is pristine wilderness cloaked like a snow-covered lake. There's virtually no imprint by humans save this little community on top of a lonesome mesa. It's exactly the same view that a millennium ago captivated Acoma Pueblo's original ancestors. Those ancient ones made an excellent choice when they decided to create Sky City on this breathtaking spot.

While the Deer and Buffalo Clans disperse towards their homes a lightly pounding beat continues until everyone is outside the church. If I strain to listen ever so carefully, faint pounding persists before tailing off in the distance.

A few more erratic beats and then nothing...

Silence fills our ears... but our bodies continue to hammer with the beat of ancient spirits – the heart beat of the universe.

Gradually outsiders like me return to a waiting bus before being driven a couple miles down a perilously steep road to the visitors' center and our waiting vehicles. It's almost heaven coming out of the freezing cold and as the bus departs a bit of us is left behind. Fortunately New Mexico's signature sun has melted most of the snow on the road. Only piles along the shoulders line this precipitous concrete ramp that yesterday would have been a perfect ski run.

At the visitors' center people scurry for their cars determined to be the first out of the parking lot come hell or high water. Already the spell of Acoma's ceremony appears to have been lost on these folk who are shifting back into their competitive urban modes. Worship inside that ancient mission seems to be evaporating. It's too bad they're in such a big rush because soft oranges and reds tint yellow mesas as the sun dips below the western horizon. Mt. Taylor is rosy pink, almost a giant strawberry with a dollop of pure white whipped cream on top.

An empty two-lane blacktop carries me back to Interstate 40 and a waiting Autobahn frenzy for sixty miles to Albuquerque. Lined with junipers and tough brown grasses pushing defiantly above five inches of snow, there's a rugged beauty along the two-lane that heightens as night approaches. Everything – mesas, grasses, chamisa, sandstone blocks, pastel green junipers, even the snow – reflects a soft pale yellow hue that is positively embracing.

All of this ends at Interstate 40 where Dancing Eagle Casino's garishly ugly neon lights beckon road-weary warriors to take a break, enjoy a pseudo home-cooked meal and come away a million dollar winner. It is difficult to imagine a bigger contrast than that between the glitzy casino and Sky City's ancient rites celebrating the interconnection of Earth, Universe, Creator and humans. That's the magic of the Southwest where ancestral ways collide head-on with the present.

***

Geographically the heart of the Southwest is defined by common borders shared among Nevada, Utah, Arizona, Colorado, and New Mexico. Many travelers experience this unique point as the highlight of their day; a chance to capture a moment in photos for everyone back home to see. After their dog has enjoyed a bit of exercise and refreshing treats have been extricated from a cooler everyone piles back in the car headed toward major cities such as Las Vegas, Denver, Salt Lake, Phoenix or Albuquerque.

As they wend their way to the Grand Canyon, Rocky Mountains or any other of the West's alluring natural attractions, tourists will pass by unnoticeable towns with unpronounceable names – Dennehotso, Tec Nos Pos, Moapa, Towaoc, Manuelito, or Naschiti – linked to an Indian legacy. Exasperated with the vast emptiness and lack of greenery they know at home, travelers aren't likely to enjoy Indian reservations gliding by as they struggle with getting from here to there before nightfall.

Visitors driving across rural areas of the Southwest probably leave disillusioned. Dilapidated homes with dusty gravel driveways add a depressing note to the scenery. Buildings seem to be losing an unrelenting battle with the elements. Sun-blistered siding and faded paint blend together in a milk chocolate pastiche. Shingles, siding and fences have been torn lose by the wind. Many homes serve as repositories for broken-down trucks and cars – especially pick-ups.

The human impression is in stark contrast to an overwhelmingly big sky, immense distances, arid lands, and monumental geological features. Few visitors passing through will appreciate the pervasive Indian heritage of the Southwest and suspect that there is more out there than deteriorating homes lining roadsides.

Take time to piece the Southwest states together and then trace a line clock-wise in a rough circular motion from Denver to Albuquerque. From there trace a path to Tucson and Phoenix before heading up to Las Vegas and then Salt Lake. Finish this crude diagram by heading back to Denver. Look carefully within this squishy circle sketched on interlocking maps. Inside is a vast land mass – home for many Southwestern Indian tribes. Notice the names of geological features and towns within the circle. Not surprisingly many of these prominent places link their names with Native American roots.

Now zoom to the edge of this crude circle. Despite hundreds of miles separating the major cities, all share a universal core: a mish mash of high desert plains, tortured canyons, baking deserts, world-class mountains, and endless mesas. Although any given metropolis' immediate terrain varies substantially from the others, they all are touched deeply by Indian country. Few other huge regions in the U.S. are so thoroughly linked or influenced in this manner.

The crux of the interconnection is this: those who live within or visit the Southwest are inevitably influenced by the Indian heritage of this land. It doesn't matter if someone resides in St. George, Utah; Searchlight, Nevada; Durango, Colorado; or, Tucson, Arizona. The effect is still the same. *Ancestral shadows claim this land and exert powerful pressures that contemporaries seldom realize.*

Some would argue that the Southwest's distinctive presence is attributable to other significant factors such as the land's grand scale. Soaring snow-capped peaks, yawning canyons, endless deserts and interminable miles of mesas and arroyos surround cities and towns. Although these spectacular features brought me, and many others, to the region in the first place, their influence tends not to be as indelibly powerful as the spiritual presence of the ancients.

Most years I make a pilgrimage to Great Sand Dunes National Monument in the San Luis Valley of south-central Colorado. In this particular section of the Rocky Mountains the Continental Divide's jagged-edge rises to 14,000 feet with spires like Blanca Peak (14,345), Crestone Peak (14,294), Crestone Needle (14, 197), Humboldt Peak (14,064) and, by comparison, diminutive Mount Adams (13, 931). Six thousand feet lower spread at the base of 13, 297-foot Mount Herald, the Great Sand Dunes repose like a colossal quilt.

Approaching from north, south or west, the view is spectacular and humbling due to a scale that is almost incomprehensible. Towering ramparts of the Sangre de Cristo Range loom heavily over a sage-covered valley floor. In the distance is a great sand pile hugging the base of these formidable mountains. From fifteen miles away it looks like some oversize kid playing with a dump truck of heroic proportions left wavy swells of smooth tan sand heaped against the mountains.

Every mile that clicks off on the odometer intensifies the scale of this land. It is so big, so grand, that I almost can't comprehend what I'm seeing. The sensation is akin to witnessing the Grand Canyon in person for the first time. Human accomplishments are absolutely dwarfed in comparison.

The Sangre de Cristos' majesty is phenomenal with their naked rocky steeples and avalanche chutes embedded with snow and ice. They have stiff competition from the San Luis Valley's breadth and the gargantuan dune mound waiting at the monument. The valley is so broad and expansive that I can almost detect the Earth's curvature. The closer I drive to the dunes the higher they rise – to almost 800 feet above the 8,000-foot valley floor.

It's a mind-boggling scale of incomprehensible proportions that draws me to this particular spot in the region. I *crave* the grandeur like a drug addict seeking his next fix. I need to be reassured that there is something more ineffable than human smudges on this Earth.

A couple of days are all it takes. When sated with the Great Sand Dunes immensity, I return home touched to my very soul and appreciative of the land's grand scale. It remains a pleasant memory for a week-or-two. *However, as days go by and the year wanes, the Great Sand Dunes' impact gradually diminishes.* I have to replenish the experience – this powerful feeling – next year.

Inevitable ebb of the Great Sand Dunes' weight is in sharp contrast to the impact of ancestral shadows. Back at home the memories of those who lived before are ever-present. Highway exits shout names of prehistoric tribal communities. Pueblo-style houses loom on city streets. Native jewelry dangles off ears, wrists and fingers. Everywhere I turn are reminders of ancient cultures that knew this land centuries before we contemporaries overwhelmed it.

Others might argue that the most distinctive quality of the Southwest is its inherent wildness. Residents in new suburban communities of Tucson, Las Vegas or Phoenix complain about invasions of rattlesnakes, scorpions, tarantulas and other nasty desert dwellers. Coyotes methodically harvest small dogs and cats — pets turned into the tricksters' poop. Runners and bikers have to be cautious about becoming puma prey. And, if the wild critters don't get you, then the weather will with devastating flash floods, erratic lightening strikes, desiccating dryness and oven-hot temperatures.

Wildness is a distinguishing characteristic of the Southwest. Frigid peaks flow to cruel sweltering desert. Water is always scarce. Two-mile high elevations take away my breath leaving me gasping for oxygen. When summer returns to the snow-filled mountains, they are raked by monsoon thunderstorms unleashing torrents of lightning and rain. An undeniable primeval feeling cloaks the land matched by a diversity and abundance of wildlife.

Just as I christen each year with a visit to the Great Sand Dunes, when fall turns to winter I seek out a commemorative moment rife with wildness. Typically I'm looking for some spot where aspens turn luminescent yellow and sultry orange-red or where a brief period of Indian summer flourishes burning the sun's warm embrace into my brain. Once I chose Rocky Mountain National Park well-known for undulating swells of yellowing aspens, bugling elk and frosty mornings beaten back by mellow mid-day sun.

Dusk is rapidly approaching after a day of trekking mountain trails. Washing off alpine basins a chill is distinctly in the still air. I'm exploring an expansive but meandering brown, half-mile wide grassy meadow through which the fledgling Colorado River flows. Across the valley steep hills rise into the Never Summer Wilderness, all rock and alpine tundra, while on the east side tree-covered slopes rise precipitously toward Ridge Road at 12,000 feet an extremely high byway.

Walking on a lumpy, rutted dirt road bisecting the valley's middle with the river's quiet murmuring, a hush as silent as the ages falls over Rocky Mountain National Park. A red-tail hawk soars down-valley. It's a spectacularly peaceful moment; and, then it changes in the most remarkable way.

Snorting, barking, whining and bugling a flood of hundreds of elk flows like water down onto the valley's grassy plain. One minute I can only see trees rising up forested slopes and then the next, at precisely 7:00 p.m., elk are materializing everywhere out of the trees for a mile up and down this gentle valley. They simply spill like an avalanche out onto the valley floor taking nourishment before retreating to higher ground for the night.

Surrounded by so much life, my excitement pegs. Imagine being in the center of a humongous elk herd. Bulls posture and chase other bulls in preparation for the rut. Cows and calves pool together congregating along the meandering stream where lush vegetation remains. An audacious coyote sauntering down-canyon in search of morsels makes the mistake of coming too close to the calves. In unison the cows form a moving barricade and quickly usher the coyote away from their young. They mean business and the coyote gets the message very quickly.

Wimpy bugles from bull elk, a shrill shrieking sound, ring up and down the grand valley in gathering twilight edging into purple. There's nothing noble or majestic about these calls, but I wouldn't want to tackle a half-ton-plus of bull elk at close quarters and I am at extremely close quarters. It's as if I'm invisible to the elk – nonexistent – they just don't care that I can almost touch them.

The elk keep feeding like teenagers at an all-you-can-eat buffet and moving along the valley. Winter cold diminishes forage up high and so in a last opportunity to enjoy the fat of the land, elk flood down to low country. Shortly, real cold will keep them at low elevations when the iron fist of winter culls out the weak, old and infirm. Up and down the meadow this spectacle lasts until it's almost too dark to see.

Then; *they vanish*.

The following evening I return to exactly the same spot where the elk flood occurred. Seven o'clock arrives and I wait. Fifteen minutes go by, then thirty. Only a few elk show up. Elk follow rhythms, but they don't follow stupid rhythms. They're smart enough to alter grazing patterns to keep from being dead elk.

Disappointed, but determined to see more wildlife, I drive further up the valley. Round a curve I come upon six moose – three bulls, one calf and two cows – congregating at a river bend. Belching grunts fill the darkening stillness as they strip willow leaves off soon-to-be-dormant branches. My little quest for wildlife – and wildness – has been fulfilled.

I'm ready for winter.

Elk, moose, coyotes, and a red-tail hawk that floats overhead; this is only a smattering of wildlife to be found in the Southwest. They are emblematic of the region's wildness. Like my annual infusion of bona fide big sky and grandiose scenery at the Great Sand Dunes, these wildlife moments tend to gradually evaporate until I can hunt them next year. Their ephemeral nature doesn't reduce my thirst for them or lessen their meaning. But, unlike ancestral shadows I can't enjoy these experiences every day.

Wild lands and wildlife are unique characteristics flavoring life within the geographic circle of connected dots linking Denver, Albuquerque, Phoenix, Las Vegas and Salt Lake City. There is no question that the region is blessed by awe-inspiring landscape and phenomenal wildness. These factors individually and collectively shape people who live there; however they are not unique solely to the Southwest.

Other places lay claim to spectacular geological features such as Jackson Hole, Carmel, West Yellowstone, Big Bend, or Niagara Falls. Other cities in the United States are surrounded by larger wilderness areas such as Anchorage, Boise, Winnemucca, Whitefish or Red Lodge.

In my mind what sets the Southwest apart from what might appear to be comparable regions in this nation is the pervasive shadow of the old ones. Breath-taking landscape and rugged wildness only accentuate this wonderful reality. No matter where you go within that squishy circle scribed around the region's major metropolitan complexes, life is inexorably influenced by an ancient heritage.

Residents may not always be cognizant of the how these ancestral shadows affect their lives, but that doesn't negate their tangible spiritual presence. Ancestral Puebloans – Anasazi – and predecessors of other indigenous people who called the Southwest home are long gone. However, in so many incredible ways they continue to live on exerting powerful influences.

Consider the architecture of homes and commercial buildings in cities throughout the Southwest. Traditional and neo Pueblo style designs abound. Even the most inexpensive tract homes attempt to emulate the graceful organic adobe structure of Taos Pueblo or the masonry of Salado dwellings. Some contemporary homes are adorned with sandstone facades – real or faux – mimicking Chaco Canyon.

Ancestral shadows also linger throughout the Southwest etched onto volcanic rock faces and sandstone tapestries. Rock art, pictographs and petroglyphs are inscribed throughout the region in thousands of locations. Phoenix boasts of Deer Valley Rock Art Center where 1,500 petroglyphs are engraved on 600 boulders. Bluff, Utah is surrounded by rock art such as Sand Island's expansive rock art panel. Near Tucson at Saguaro National Park rock art dates from A.D. 300 to 1450 primarily from the Hohokam tribe. Images range from simple swirls, hand prints, and stars to complex human figures, animals and stylized depictions of deities. Some hold great cachet such as Kokopelli — the jolly humpback flutist associated with fertility and feasts. Other portrayals are indecipherable; their exact meaning extinguished with their makers.

Petrogylph National Monument outside Albuquerque is only one of the many repositories in the region containing etchings that stretch back 12,000 years. The 7,236 acre monument lies along a basaltic escarpment with an estimated 25,000 images from prehistoric times. Although the artists may be long gone their handiwork sparkles in the sun as wind blows across the volcanic outcropping. Meanwhile thousands of visitors flock to the site trying to understand messages associated with the figures; reaching back to visualize others who walked this land all those years ago.

Urban growth is swarming past the monument. Housing developments back to the base of the escarpment and loom over the rock art quietly reposing, looking out across the Rio Grande toward the Sandia Mountains. This startling disconformity epitomizes the imprint of ancestral shadows.

Even though surrounded by distractions of modernity, local residents must occasionally sense the spirits of those who trod this land so many years before. Do they detect their predecessors' shadows when driving to work on a new day as sun first reflects off the escarpment? Do they realize that a similar experience is taking place among residents in myriad metropolises and smaller towns throughout the region?

Rock art repositories at the Palatki's ruins outside Sedona, Arizona, may not be as expansive as Petroglyph National Monument, but they similarly exert their own powerful presence. They are there because of the ancients – primeval people who like today's contemporaries woke to a new day and a life to be lived.

Ancestral shadows mantle the Southwest from the homes people live in to the foods they eat. Fashionable clothes – Santa Fe style – hark back to designs from Ancestral Puebloans and other indigenous people in the region. Sacred rock art has been commercialized as jewelry in the form of stylized bears, humpbacked Kokopelli tricksters, and symbols of the sun. It is all part of the palpable presence of people whose spirits still linger in this land.

Some may choose to ignore the indelible influence the ancient ones have over them or may argue that such an impact doesn't exist. Sadly, they fail to benefit from a rich legacy surrounding them. Others embrace the obvious and search for opportunities to fully understand those who went before and how those primeval beings connect with their own modern lives.

A person doesn't necessarily have to live in the Southwest to develop an appreciation of how ancestral shadows affect life in the Twenty-first Century. However, such understanding is made much easier due to widespread physical manifestations left by departed predecessors in the region. These physical remains add a tangible dimension to the spiritual.

People living in Montpelier, Vermont; Fargo, North Dakota; Springfield Missouri; Dothan, Alabama; Minneapolis, Minnesota; or Sarasota, Florida can also enjoy the Southwest's rich legacy in a broader sense. They can explore how long-departed forerunners from their own communities, especially those who were indigenous, left indelible impacts – both physically and spiritually – that flavor contemporary life.

Over one thousand years ago Native people from somewhere in northwest New Mexico, southeast Nevada, eastern Arizona, and southern Utah and Colorado, established a settlement on a flying buttress of a mesa known as Sky City. Today their ancestors still dance to commemorate the joy of life. Like Buffalo Clan dancers, we all can share in the celebration of human legacy that cloaks our communities. It's simply a matter of venerating ancestral shadows found in our communities.

Look closely as you walk through your town. Wonder about when and how names became attached to roads, rivers, meadows and hills. Question how a path along a stream was started. Search out extremely old trees or virgin forest. Remember that other people enjoyed these same forests when they were just beginning to throw off a bit of shade. Think about the generations of people who lived each day through good times and bad. There's a connection between you and them whether you care to admit it or not.

Are ancient spirits hovering in the distance?

Do you hear a faint drum beat?

THUMP, THUmp, thump, thump.

THUMP, THUmp, thump, thump.....

Quicksilver river,
a sinuous snake coiling.
Fish jumps, laughing.

3

Fly-fishing with the Anasazi

Death is a split-second away; waiting furtively for an oblivious pilgrim.

One more step and I'm toast.

With a child's innocence I volunteered to walk four miles back to our Jeep for more white gas and a high-end sleeping bag. An optimistic tenderfoot in our group thought he could survive the Gila Wilderness' frigid nights curled in a fetal ball, but Adam was wrong. Pull on a plush fleece cap. Add chunky gloves while swaddling his precious body with a heavy down parka. Borrow extra clothes. Slip his feet and legs into an empty pack for added insulation. Try all of these tricks and Adam was still terrifyingly cold without a proper sleeping bag. History repeats itself. I tried the same stupid stunt on my first trip to the West Fork of the Gila River.

Yes, those are the two-faces of the Gila. Beguiling sunny springtime warmth fooled Adam into thinking that summer arrived early; that is, until the sun went down. As cold slid down-canyon, drilling through many layers of clothing, penetrating to the bone, he realized too late what season actually reigned. Frosty conditions are also partly to blame for having used so much fuel. We simply don't have enough for our group – should have brought the 32 oz. bottle, not the 22 oz. canister – that's my fault and the reason I'm a split-second away from disaster. However, I'm getting ahead of myself. Let's make death wait a bit longer.

***

This trip is really about fly-fishing and the intersection of two crafty masters who live and breathe the sport. Everyone else thought we embarked on a great wilderness journey to hidden reaches in a vast labyrinth of meandering canyons and dusty juniper- and pine-covered mesas. How foolish – the Gila is first and foremost a sanctuary of precious fish-laden waters wending their way through canyon country. Proof enough is the fact that the river is the trail. Except when crossing over on mesas, we walk in or along the Gila's many tentacles. This isn't a hiking story, it's a tale of backcountry fly-fishing.

In my life I've known two bona fide fishing addicts – two people who will give up almost everything else to fish for love of the sport. To them fly-fishing isn't a passion, addiction or obsession. It's much more. For Dick and Luther, fishing is their very essence; their personification. If given the choice to do anything they wanted, Luther and Dick would be out there somewhere fishing; reading the water and habitat; selecting the perfect lure, fly or nymph; figuring out how to complete a cast just perfectly; and, basking in riparian beauty while a sensuous, serpentine stream gurgles past their feet.

From what I have witnessed first-hand, fly-fishing is their religion – the embodiment of what they believe spiritually. It isn't about catching the largest fish, or showing off by going for quantity. It isn't about having notched on their fly rods the most charismatic and infamous rivers in the nation; around the world. And it certainly isn't about the alluring paraphernalia accompanying this sport. Neither are gear-heads who must possess the latest accoutrements and finest equipment in order to feel that they have a fighting chance. It isn't even about a particular variety of fish, although they do have their favorites.

It's simply about fishing.

Every fish caught, every stealthy stalk and little victory, has value. I've watched Dick revel over the glory of a lushly green meadow in the Pecos Wilderness. A foot-wide stream slowly meanders before making its fall from grace toward New Mexico's lowlands and eventually Texas. He spent an entire afternoon pursuing, and catching, diminutive five-inch brown trout. Aglow and astonished about how careful he had to be when approaching the grassy stream bank, Dick waxed about the fight those little fish bravely demonstrated. He blended with the serene sub-alpine meadow, its sparkling and dancing water fresh out of Stewart Lake, and the backdrop of Santa Fe Baldy towering two-and-a-half thousand feet above puncturing a cerulean sky at 12,622 feet.

Only wizened veterans spend time fly-fishing this tiny stream coursing through foot-and-a-half high grasses. Everyone else is up at the lake trying their luck. How could they ever guess that fish love the stream, not the lake? But, Dick figured it out immediately. His experienced eye told him to go where others wouldn't. And talk about patience. Once he catches sight of darting little black submarines, plan on camping out until he catches one, only to release it and go after another. It's not about the fish to him, it's about the fishing.

I've seen Luther demonstrate this same intensity and soul-pleasing joy along the headwaters of the Rio Grande. After a full day using nymphs to lure lunkers hiding from run-of-the-mill anglers, he met me back at his Jeep. Opening the door he sat down with an "oof" – bone-tired from exertion.

We remained motionless for a while as a growling thunder-storm veered off to the south; staring at the dark but aching-ly clear river beginning to pick up speed as it hurled toward a sweeping bend. Sunlight fighting through the thunderhead and projecting in gauzy golden shafts glinted on wave crests. Except for the thunder, it was absolutely perfectly silent.

Most people are uncomfortable with silence and try to fill this gap with conversation as if noise adds value. Not Luther. He just sat there consumed by love for this river and the hours he had spent in its midst balancing from one moss-covered boul-der to the next. Searching, always searching, for that undulat-ing shape; movement along the yellow-brown gravel. And then deciding; figuring where to place his line, how much length to unfurl, and how to compensate for darting breezes conspiring to make a cast go awry.

We said nothing for many minutes before I broke the ice.

"There's fish down there with your name on them. They're calling you."

Silence filled the vacuum of my words. Then Luther replied matter-of-factly, "I suppose you're right."

Hesitating a few more minutes while gazing on the lovely stream, he finally opened the Jeep's door and struggled to his feet drawing out his vest in the process. He picked up his old friends, a coveted rod and reel that have stood him in good stead all these years, and said quite sparingly, "I'll just try a hole or two and then we'll go."

A late spring trip to the Gila Wilderness finally brought these two masters together for what some people might view as wasted days and wasted nights. We will wander wild lands in a quest for fish? For soul-satisfying regeneration? For adventure? For what? Sometimes you don't need to have a specific objective — that's linear goal-oriented thinking that we live by daily in the city. Sometimes it's just enough to immerse yourself in the silence of wildness, the embrace of the land and the spirit of pitch-dark nights with billions of twinkling stars overhead shouting about something more enduring than humans.

**

Early on a sun-drenched morning we cram everything into our packs and look despairingly around the trailhead parking lot. I'm thinking we've dawdled too long. It's cool in the shade of this overgrown willow, but I can see what lies ahead. There's lots of sun-baked flat to cover before entering the West Fork's canyon two-plus miles distant. We should have gotten a move on it earlier and wasted less time enjoying a sumptuous breakfast. But then, that would have been exactly the goal-directed thinking we're escaping from.

The others — Dick, Luther, Richard, Bill, Allen and Adam — are stalling so I take the lead and hoist my pack. It's a gratuitous gesture because they will continue to fight the inevitable for another ten minutes. I could avoid standing there with a heavy pack pulling me toward the center of the Earth, but I might as well get used to what's coming. Taking the cue, several others lift their boulders with grunts. No matter how light a pack is, it always weighs too much. Now comes peer pressure for the laggards — eventually we're off.

The sudden transition from city to wilderness initially seems bizarre. Only a few hours ago we were immersed in a megalopolis. Now excuses for failing to look at life in a different perspective have evaporated. Yet, it will take hours and days before most of us begin to reconnect with the land. It doesn't happen immediately; sometimes it never transpires on a trip. But, at least we're here trying — there's value in making the effort.

I scan the asphalt parking lot one last time. This is literally the end of the road; the final conclusion of tortured routes from the east to Truth-or-Consequences, New Mexico and Interstate 25, or south to Deming and Interstate 10. There is no easy way to reach the Gila Cliff Dwellings. However our effort in getting here is compensated by the raw beauty of wildness. Late spring is also an excellent time to visit since days are mild to very warm and sometimes hot. Wait a few weeks and it will be miserable. Over at the nearby visitor center a cooler already holds bottled water for sale — it's extremely dry down here.

The Cliff Dwellings were occupied from approximately 1280 AD until the early 1300s. They were inhabited by a Mimbres branch of the Mogollon culture, indigenous people who occupied southwestern New Mexico and southeastern Arizona. Six caves form a splendid site for mud-and-stone structures. Vigas, or wooden beams, can still be found protruding through thick walls. These stalwart beams supported roofs of various rooms that housed an estimated population of 10-15 families at this site. Signature "T" shaped doorways with low ceilings gave access to quarters protected by the caves. Anthropologists believe inhabitants cultivated foods such as squash and beans while also gathering provisions by hunting and fishing. Ruins and evidence of their habitation can be found throughout the Gila watershed.

The Mimbres band should be congratulated on choosing an excellent location. The caves provide priceless shade from hot summer sun. During winter, sun penetrates south-facing edifices adding a measure of warmth. If it gets too hot in summer, high forested reaches of the Gila are merely miles away. Meanwhile the West Fork delivers a precious year-round water supply. Twisting, convoluted canyons offer safety from marauding bands of warriors. Game-rich country is found throughout the wilderness. All-in-all, the Gila must have been a comforting home back in the early 1300s.

Gazing toward the north I can't help but feel a tiny tingle crawl up my spine. There in the distance is a watercourse on which these people lived, traveled and knew intimately. Were the Mogollons really any different from me; from those in our group? They were my kind of people; those who knew how to live with and from the land. They probably saw the Earth as sacred and part of the Great Mystery. Imagination pushes the envelope even further. Didn't they also have their Luther's and Dick's; men who melded with a stream and in the process were praised for their ability to bring home fish for the table?

Although others in our group may not be consciously thinking about parallels with the Cliff Dwellings' inhabitants, it's apparent that we're about to tread on sacred ground. So it's very apropos that this adventurous quest begins and ends at one of the Mimbres band's focal sites. To what extent do the spiritual reverberations of these people prevail even to this day? A good probability exists that we will be profoundly influenced, even unknowingly, by the same primal forces that shaped their spiritual mindset and everyday activities. It's moments like this, as we begin to temporarily dwell where they have walked, lived, loved, endured and prayed, that we awake from our stupor and gradually put it all together.

Our responsibility is to walk with lightness of step showing respect for their land. The stream isn't here just for the recreational act of fishing, the canyons present just so that we can run off from society's oppressive hold. The Gila Wilderness isn't just some high desert and montane theme park. It's about something more that in the course of our ramblings will become recognizable with crystal transparency. Until we do reconnect, the lingering presence of the ancient ones will be virtually undetected, remaining subliminally conscious.

I chew on these thoughts and fall in behind the others while walking north on a narrow dusty path to adventure; leaping ahead to a distant past. Out here we're stripped of annoying obstacles blocking our relationship to the land. With packs on our backs we once again experience what it's like to live close to nature much like the Mimbres band did.

Shortly the trail enters lush riverside growth associated with a side channel of the West Fork. Water makes all the difference in country like this and in the morning's fading chill air it's gratifying to become reacquainted with the smell of life — decaying leaves, sharp fragrance of willow against this canyon's vacuum of dry air, and saturated, dank soil. This reverie only lasts moments until our path bisects the valley headed toward narrowing canyon walls. We're passing between widely scattered clumps of willow and pine across a broad cobblestone-infested riverbed.

With little shade the sun beats down unmercifully; fortunately it's not the middle of the day. After a mile we cross the Gila and rise up on an extremely dry bench.

The West Fork's flow is down considerably over previous trips we've made at this time of year. At thirty feet across and a foot-plus deep the Gila's volume mimics what might be expected in mid-to-late summer, not late spring. This doesn't bode well for fishing, but it's too late to do anything about that now. Racing across the river to avoid soaking our boots, we climb forty feet to the top of a bench once on the other side. We're greeted by a few scrawny ponderosa pines standing as sentinels among charred-black skeletons of former trees. A red-hot fire destroyed what formerly had been a mature pine forest providing shelter from the scorching sun.

Gradually the trail wanders across this bench for a mile toward the West Fork's narrowing canyon entrance. A rock out-cropping one-hundred-and-fifty-feet above the Gila offers a tantalizing hint of the Gila's beguiling charm. Below the light-green river twists and turns on a rusty-orange-gold bed of rock and sand. Dense trees and shrubs, a hundred shades of green, bracket the river on both sides. Chalky-white canyon walls rise steeply toward mesas covered in stunted juniper and occasional pine. Birds are flitting throughout the canopy while high over-head several turkey buzzards funnel upward on rising thermals.

For a moment I'm having trouble keeping track of time. Is it the Thirteenth Century or the Twenty-first? This pastoral view reminds us of why we came here in the first place; of the Gila's splendor, charm and peace. Did the ancient ones see this river, this canyon, as just a place to live, or were they also captivated by its grandeur?

At this point our trail drops down into the canyon proper and the progressively narrowing mouth forming a gateway to wilderness. We're walking on cobblestone and sand through burnt sections of river growth – consumed by the same fire that scorched the bench – until suddenly the devastation just stops. From here trees shelter sun and parallel the gurgling river that's running deep and swift compared to its lethargic flow lower in the broad valley. In a couple miles we find a perfect camp amid profuse ponderosa pines, willow, cottonwoods and sycamores.

This isn't the first time we've camped at this pleasant little sweep of slightly orange-white cliff that morphs into subtle mauve when shadows grow long. The West Fork makes a gracefully sweeping ninety-degree turn here. It's truly magical. But, what make this site even more fascinating are remnants of the ancient ones. On the cliff some fifty feet up a slippery ravine of rock are ruins – stone and mud walls with vigas.

We will literally be sleeping with the Mimbres band tonight. This is a dwelling, outpost or perhaps a granary constructed by these early people. With such a physically tangible reminder looming above, I've noticed that our revelries tend to be a little more subdued. Our jokes are inclined to be a little less ribald than other backcountry camps. We're inexorably living under ancestral shadows and subconsciously respectful of their presence.

The first order of business is sloughing off packs – a moment we always wait for with child-like anticipation. It feels so good to have that stone off our backs and to be able to walk around buoyant without the weight. The next task is erecting tents and within minutes we've set up our little village. As tents rise Dick and Luther begin to swap notes on fly-fishing strategy. Since entering the canyon they've been keeping watch on the West

Fork and stopping occasionally to turn rocks over at river's edge to read about bug-life.

After a quick lunch, everyone just seems to scatter. I'm filtering water beneath the ruins trying to build up a reserve of four gallons. It's not an unpleasant task hunkered down in dappled shade along a beautiful stream flowing against red-white-tan walls soaring overhead. I just love the riparian scent that shouts about life and the indelible strength of the Gila. Mostly I'm conscious about how the simple things in life suddenly have much greater importance.

It's roughly 70 pumps on the water filter per quart, and after about 350 pumps my mind drifts back to the Cliff Dwellings and to the ruins above. We've gone back in time to appreciate the finer things in life and to mimic habits of those from 800 years earlier. Our focus, like theirs, is on the basics. I'm collecting water. Bill and Adam are off gathering firewood. Dick and Luther are stalking sustenance. Collectively we've already taken care of setting up shelter, but Allen is making some fine touches by rearranging the campfire ring and surrounding logs. No wonder the Mogollon culture's spirit dominates this canyon; we're living the same rhythms they lived, completing the same daily activities they completed.

After pumping four gallons of water and refilling several quart bottles it's time to wander in the canyon. Before leaving camp I slide my wristwatch off and hide it in my pack – now I can begin to live attuned to the sun and the canyon's cadence.

Hours pass until early evening; then people begin to gather around the fire pit for dinner following their afternoon ramblings. It's happy hour because this has been such an absolutely mellow day. Hors d'oeuvres are being shared and libations quench our thirst. Allen lights the campfire officially signaling this shift to communal sharing. We're waiting for the fishermen to return with news of their progress.

First in is Luther with a satisfied and confident look on his face, but the report is not too inspiring – there are lots of little trout and a few bottom dwellers. He thinks he knows what flies to use and he's optimistic about the prospects upstream tomorrow. Within minutes Dick arrives with much the same report. He talks about hooking a real keeper of a brown trout, but it got away – familiar story. They confer about the types of flies that work best – technical jargon to the rest of us – and then drift over to share in the feast.

At the top of the campfire storyboard are fishing tales from today and past trips to the Gila, and then stories of other impressive waters, legendary catches. Soon the topic of discussion will drift to this past hunting season and Richard's anguish about being shut out on elk for another year.

Things gradually grow quiet as we peer into glowing red embers. It's been a long day and a lengthy transition from modernity to the basics eight centuries ago. This is perhaps the most precious time, the ultimate hour, on a backcountry adventure. In the closing moments of a communal fire people turn inward, savoring thoughts about the day, remembering others who are not along on the trip, and preparing for sleep. Without saying a word and reluctant to let go, we bathe in a tangible bond of friendship. Eventually the coals begin to wink out of existence as we turn to our respective down-filled cocoons.

Night closes in around our desert canyon camp. Without conversation, noises from outside the fire's glow are more audible. A slight breeze rustles the pines thirty feet overhead. I could swear that I hear a fish jump in the river, mocking Dick and Luther.

Cooling coals crackle and break; a juniper stick flares and sparks. It's the sound of the land at rest.

Unlike the Mimbres band we don't have to fear a marauding tribe so no one is on watch. But, life does come alive at night. We're not deep enough into the Gila to have a good chance of encountering bear or cougar, but we have seen wolf tracks no more than one-eighth of a mile up canyon. Nonetheless we've taken precautions by hanging our food.

An hour later before nodding off some large mammal... bear?...sheep?...wolf?...puma?... comes down the scree pile just east of camp, letting off a mini-avalanche of rocks.

Crunch! Bam!

Whump!

Swish!

The rock-fall cascades raucously before slowing to a stop. Then; silence reigns except for distant patterns of muffled snoring.

***

Contrary to popular lore, Luther believes that fishing is best after the day initially warms up. So, we're taking our time and having a special breakfast today – Eggs Discenza consisting of toasted English muffins, Canadian bacon, Walla Walla sweet onions, easy-over eggs, and a thin slab of cheese. As Richard cooks he points out that our fuel supply is rapidly diminishing. This is due to a simple mistake on my part – I thought that the 22 ounce fuel bottle was actually a 32 ounce bottle. Tonight's meal will use up a ton of fuel and tomorrow's breakfast will do the same.

The Mimbres band would just throw another log on the fire. We could too, except that our cooking pots and utensils are designed for highly focused, intensely-hot flames. Another consideration surfaces; Adam, one of our younger members, did not bring a sleeping bag. No wonder he was virtually running up the trail, his pack was light as a feather. Given low eighty-degree daytime temperatures reported at Silver City — the gateway to the Gila — Adam didn't see any need for a sleeping bag. He would just sleep in his clothes. Unfortunately he didn't count on the Gila's phenomenal temperature swing. Nights are often 50 degrees cooler, or more, than daytime temperatures. To make matters worse, a cold front is expected to sweep down to the Mexican border. Last night he didn't sleep a wink.

A fuel shortage is my fault, I planned the trip. Richard wants to walk four miles back to the car to get more fuel because there's no question that we'll run out. I'm obliged to accompany him and see the side benefit of bringing back an extra sleeping bag stashed away in the Jeep.

Luther and Dick are putting on their game faces. Yesterday was simply the prelude; today they get serious about catching some protein to supplement our meal. There's no strategy sharing anymore. This is war and may the best fisherman win. They decide to head upstream where each will adhere to the unwritten code of fly-fishing protocol. Left unsaid is the objective of bringing back many fish for our large contingent. Both of these masters have a reputation to protect which shows in their steely demeanor, the regal manner in which they carry their rods as they set off for battle. I can't think of two better matched opponents.

Richard and I retrace our steps from yesterday. It's a beautiful day with a few clouds and light breezes, harbinger of the descending cold front.

On reaching the Jeep, Richard and I have a long moment to indulge in an ice-cold soda and salt-lathered potato chips. It doesn't take very long in the backcountry to covet things that normally are taken for granted back in the city. The drink is especially satisfying because we'll be walking back in the heat of the day. Then I load my flaccid pack with sleeping bag, fuel and a few fresh carrots and tomatoes from our beat-up cooler.

Richard is fooling around with his scuffed-up duffle bag so I wander over to some meager shade under a cottonwood watching visitors coming and going at the interpretive center. Most have a harried look on their faces. They've raced over winding tortured roads for a few minutes pleasure at the Cliff Dwellings before racing back home. Only a few will make a connection with the land; experience what the Mogollon culture experienced in the course of a typical day.

When Richard is ready to go I take the lead on leaving the trailhead. He's rambling on about some nagging issue at work so my head is turned almost 90 degrees to hear him. Trekking pole flicking out in front as a rhythm is established, I listen intently to his concerns, oblivious of our surroundings. We were here only yesterday and the same lush growth borders our path with all of the attendant fragrances from the stagnant side-channel. I twist a bit further to better hear Richard's thoughts.

That's when death comes calling.

I can't quite make out Richard's conversation because a small cicada is buzzing off in the bushes somewhere. The obvious doesn't register, because it isn't obvious. It takes about a half second for my subconscious to put it together as I flick the trekking pole forward another stride. And then my brain gets the message and grabs hold of my body before commandeering my consciousness.

Cicadas aren't out at this time of year; otherwise we would have heard them before. No, this is an altogether dissimilar sound. Now that my subconscious is informing consciousness, my brain reacts by grabbing my right leg back in a flash. I stumble to a halt.

In eternally slow motion I scan the trail as Richard runs up my butt. It has to be something besides a cicada. And finally eyes, ears, brain and body put it together. There is a thick five foot rattler on the left side of the trail ready to strike. Fortunately it reacted to my trekking pole. Had that well-warmed leg of mine fully swung forward the rattler was poised to inflict punishment for invading its turf.

Richard and I go through that slow motion dance of backing off before we know where to look and why. It isn't a very graceful retreat but by stumbling backwards we get the job done.

My first thought, after checking to see whether I need to change my shorts, is the lack of fair-play. Snake encounters are something you worry about deep in the Gila Wilderness along streams or rocky benches flanking the canyon. This big bugger violates all standards of proper sportsmanship in hiking. You don't run into rattlers in the Gila at the trailhead; you encounter them in wilderness bush miles from the car. Our indignation is justified given this breach of wilderness etiquette.

The matter is made worse by the puny cicada-like rattle from a full-grown and threateningly healthy snake. On closer examination we see that it only has a tiny partial rattle. Somehow, somewhere, it lost the bulk of its rattle. Had it been playing with a full deck – a full healthy rattle for its size – there would have been no mistaking the sound. Our braking would have been much earlier, taking us well out of harm's way. Until this moment I have never been a trekking pole aficionado. Suddenly I've got religion, big time. Had it not been for the high tech pole confusing the snake with its cool metal tubing, I probably would have been nailed on the leg.

What happens next is entirely predictable as we've gone through the drill many times before. After an encounter this close, we hear, see and think snakes are everywhere. Talk about walking in a fully alert manner. I've completely snapped out of any warm and fuzzy feelings I may have been soaking in on this leisurely, and quite innocent, trip for more fuel and a sleeping bag.

The rest of the way back to camp goes uneventfully, but Richard and I literally walk on eggshells. A bite from a snake that large would have devastating repercussions out here far from medical assistance. Now we're fully attuned to what lies ahead on the trail, scanning the sides for any possible threat, and ready to take evasive action. It's a totally different way of walking akin to turning down a dark alley in a big city. Anticipate the worst and hopefully avoid grief.

On reaching camp, all are present except the fly-fishing masters. Word has it that they are still upstream a ways. As Allen and Bill returned from hiking several miles up-canyon, they saw Dick down along the stream. They rather casually mention running into two rattlesnakes in the course of their journey. The most menacing was a bitty one right at the edge of where our trail runs into the Gila River. This determined little bugger just would not give any ground. The other larger, more mature, rattlesnake had its say and then slowly retreated with dignity still intact.

While we swap snake stories Luther comes waltzing into camp, boots dripping from being immersed all day long. He caught several fish but only one was a verifiable keeper. According to his story, he hooked a hog close to camp that eventually slipped off the hook. Luther left the fish alone intending to catch it when he returned. First a bit of food and a drink and then he will go reel it in. With this pronouncement, in strides Dick. He too has seen far better days. In his creel are two Brookies, one substantial and one just at the limit. Unknowingly he has just raised the ante for Luther. The score is two-to-one.

What follows is a classic battle between masters. Luther swaggers down to the hole in which his trophy is swimming, patiently waiting. This fish will assuredly top Dick's bounty. And, it goes without saying that Luther owns this fish. He already hooked it once and almost had it ashore. All he has to do is use the same fly, in the same spot, and bring home the victory. Luther draws a proper amount of line off his reel to begin the graceful art of casting toward a certain catch.

The first cast is aesthetically beautiful, but a bit short.

He strips more line for the coup de grace and begins that sensuous flow back and forth.

The fly lands just perfectly....

We're sharing grub, watching the entertainment, as Luther makes his cast. Whether he catches the fish or not with this cast, or the next, or the one thereafter means nothing. It's all part of the larger experience of connecting with a palpable spirit of place and people who lived, loved and fished here almost a millennium ago. If Luther catches the fish we have a special treat, but that's our luxury compared to the Mogollon culture. Otherwise the more things have changed over those hundreds of intervening years, the more they have remained the same – these ripples from the past keep reverberating.

***

Next morning heading back toward the trailhead, we begin to mentally and emotionally leave this canyon and its signature river. We return more connected to the land than disconnected. It's impossible to leave behind the fact that we have been touched deeply in the course of this trip. It wasn't just a little Disneyland entertainment in a corner of southwestern New Mexico. It wasn't just trite appreciation of gorgeous scenery that visitors come to expect from the Land of Enchantment.

When we leave the West Fork we carry the spirit of the ancient ones having lived for a brief period in their ancestral home. Our mode of travel and level of accoutrements were somewhat on par with how they managed to exist all of those years. The snakes were no less threatening, the campfires no less enjoyable, and the fishing no less challenging. Our experience – their experience – shapes who we are and how we think, behave and react in a contemporary world waiting 250-some miles away.

To ambitious A-type personalities waiting in the city who only see value in material gain and modern, civilized comfort, our time was essentially nothing more than wasted days and wasted nights. Funny, but that's precisely what we're thinking about city folks' obsession with things – stuff – and small agendas.

Look deeply into that flickering campfire, into that swirling pool of clear light-green water below a red-sandstone overhand, or that stunning view of narrowing canyon from which flows the West Fork of the Gila.

Is that your reflection you see?

Are you alone, or are there shadows of the ancient ones standing behind you? Perhaps your perception is fuzzy because you are too rooted to modern society?

Gaze hypnotically and judge whether your eyes, their eyes, don't shout back about the phenomenal joy of connecting with a beautiful land. Those aren't wasted days and wasted nights; they're the beginning of a life lived fully.

Spiritual Energy

Ice and old fire,
ancient volcanoes long gone.
Bear scratches her back.

Sky islands thrust up
dancing with cerulean.
Talons slice earthward.

TERRYE BULLERS

4

Walking on Sacred Ground

oyote lay patiently waiting; his bristling gray-brown fur camouflaged perfectly within a sea of brown field stubble; or so he thought. Truth be told, thousands of snow geese with twice as many eyes figured out hours ago that the clever trickster was nearby. Coyote couldn't quite get the big picture, his brain addled by all those geese – dinner on webbed feet – swarming around him in a recently mowed field.

From my vantage the sight was something to snicker about. Imagine a football placed at the twenty-yard line – that's coyote.

Then conjure up hundreds, thousands, of brilliant white geese decked out in burnt-black-orange bills and webbed feet behind the goal line, along both sidelines and covering the rest of the field from the forty-yard line.

No goose was about to cross that intervening forty-yard goose-free zone surrounding Mr. Coyote. They knew exactly where he was and how far away to maintain an escape perimeter in case he made a frantic run for them. Meanwhile the November sun was rapidly fading to a soft rosy glow; dusk lurked around the corner.

"Just don't flinch," he told himself, "Dinner is coming home to Papa. This is magic time when these stupid geese return from foraging along the Rio Grande Valley. With luck some dumb klutz will mistake this part of the field for a landing zone and then he's mine, all mine."

Coyote suddenly twitched his head to the left causing a ripple of wing-flapping and honking among the flock recently returned from summering on the Arctic tundra.

"What's that," he thought to himself. "That goose over there just doesn't seem right, its left wing hanging a shade out of kilter...son-of-a-bitch... I bet it's hurt. Showtime."

Despite exercising world-class stealth, enough geese see muscles flex in Mr. Coyote's leg as he begins to rise. Thus commences a desperate dash for his dinner across razor-sharp corn stubble while a massive white cloud ascends.

One-thousand, nine-hundred and ninety-nine wings beat in unison as the geese lift like rising gray fog. Flapping wings sound as though a 737 is launching on take-off; warning cries rise like hundreds of car alarms going off at once. In brief seconds the encounter is over and feathers, shreds of corn stalk and leaves, dust and dun-brown cottonwood leaves float to earth.

Coyote is left standing all alone. Even the goose with her hurt wing manages to frantically grab enough air that she is able to glide to an adjoining pasture. Coyote is right – this solitary goose is plainly impaired. She suffered a wing-full of buckshot only twenty-five minutes ago on what should have been a casual glide back home.

"Well, what to do now?"

Mr. Coyote thinks about this question while sitting on his furry haunches with a dozen soiled feathers ringing his muzzle. He could sneak over the acequia and try to come at them on a flat-out run. However, he is growing tired of waiting and that dull ache in his belly solidified his resolve to eat dinner. It is getting colder each day and he needs to keep his energy level up. Come to think of it, he'd much prefer a nice plate of rabbit and he knows exactly where to try next. Perhaps that family of bunnies munching along the river bank is taking a few bites before disappearing down their tricky burrows. "I'll run over to the acequia and then swing back this way if nothing pans out."

Coyote trots off with his dignity not the least bit ruffled. All it takes is patience. As Mr. Coyote breaks out into a lope he cannot see a pair of dark forms sailing like rockets right behind him. Two well-seasoned bald eagles are racing twenty feet off the ground as though fired from canons. They are on a mission with radar locked in place, thanks to Coyote. From their fifty-foot high perch in an ancient leafless cottonwood a half-mile away they too caught a glimpse of the lame snow goose.

So begins her final forty-five seconds of life.

Three weeks ago Mrs. Goose migrated some 3,000 miles to her (and her hubby's) favorite southern retreat – the Bosque del Apache Wildlife Refuge near Socorro, New Mexico. During summer on the tundra they safely avoided a pestering fox family drawn to a neighboring set of goslings. Bloody carnage was not a pretty sight, but this sacrifice gave her slightly older and more mobile daughter a chance to use those new wings.

Flying south certainly wasn't an easy trip with kettles of hawks and other raptors migrating to warmer climes. Cell towers squashed several of her acquaintances while guy-lines on radio towers had decapitated poor old Mr. Blackfoot. He was such an odd duck – oh, insult of insults – with that black left foot in sharp contrast to his proper burnt-black-orange right foot; an early victim of global warming and soon-to-be rampant genetic mutation.

Similar to her three previous migrations, weather turned nasty in Colorado. But it was really no big deal given her fluffy down coat. It just meant a little extra rest and relaxation in a game refuge southwest of Alamosa. Then it was just a hop-skip-and-a-jump to home.

It was so good to see all of their friends again and to remember those that didn't make it safely through another migration. Much to Mr. Goose's delight, surrounding fields were rife with grain. During the day this couple only had to fly a short distance from the refuge to fertile fields. It looked to be another pleasant over-wintering for these snowbirds. That is until those sneaky hunters blasted their shotguns from outside the refuge's boundary just shy of a sheltering line of cottonwoods. Mrs. Goose took a direct hit on her wing.

Two bald eagles streak in unison like MIG fighters toward the goose. They're too low and too fast for a gaggle of Canada geese blithely foraging on the ground to lift off. This time they're lucky because the eagles are already locked in on a kill. The slightly larger eagle female breaks tandem, pulls ahead by twenty paces and descends five feet to barely clear a ditch bank by a tall weed's height.

Talons down.

Trim slightly to the right.

A crescendo of alarm cries trails in the distance from ducks, geese, ravens, Sandhill cranes, red-winged blackbirds, and other assorted avian residents who finally woke up to a near catastrophe.

Female eagle tucks tightly in the final closing thirty yards with her eyes riveted on the pathetic target. Our goose sees her coming and literally has an "Oh shit" look on her face; my Minox binoculars deliver the image with crystal clarity. Then the lead eagle sets her flaps and pulls up six feet away from Mrs. Goose, plopping to the ground while every other bird, including Mr. Goose, scatters for the hills. Male eagle lands ten feet back from his mate, tucks his wings, and waits to see what will happen next.

Female eagle and goose stare at each other for fifteen seconds. Mrs. Goose has fooled the eagles by standing perfectly still — they don't know what to make of it.

She takes a deep breath.

It's enough for eagle eyes to register and the female eagle springs into the air three feet high completing a perfect arc and landing squarely on Mrs. Goose. She's dead on impact and her royal majesty, the eagle, begins feeding on succulent goose flesh served piping hot. Blood spurts everywhere amid small clouds of fluffy red-smeared white feathers.

Mr. Eagle takes a few cowboys struts toward the gorging female. He wants his share, but he knows who rules the roost. She continues, ripping shreds of meat from a juicy breast. It's too much for him to stand any longer so he hops twice and then springs toward his mate with talons extended. There's a brief tussle but she relinquishes the prize. Besides she's had her fill. He ravages the broken and bloodied carcass.

Show over? Not quite.

From out of the bruise-colored east lumbers a frighteningly large black mass; gliding on an eight- (perhaps ten-?) foot wing-span. A golden eagle as large as a 747 is aiming for the male bald eagle whose head is sequestered inside the goose's body cavity. Flaps up and braking by rear thrust, the golden lands like a clumsy gymnastics star woozy from too much practice. It half runs as claws hit the ground then stops a yard from the bald eagle. Startled just like Mrs. Goose was, the bald eagle assumes defensive posture with wings spread two-thirds open. His mate follows suit.

The golden is massively enormous compared to the bald eagles, at least two-thirds again as large. Male bald eagle looks menacingly at the golden, wings flapping slightly as he backs off the goose a foot or so but the altercation is over before it began. Our behemoth golden eagle stiffly struts straight for the frazzled goose carcass; there's no dillydallying or zigzagging. She knows who is boss and it isn't the bald eagles even though they out-number her. With a foot as big as a dinner plate, talons flick out and eviscerate what's left of the rag-doll goose. Dinner time as dusk fades to purple-blue amid stone-silent fields.

***

Golden eagles and bald eagles are honored by many Indian tribes and widely incorporated in religious ceremonies. This is particularly true in the Southwest with its cultural wealth of American Indians. Powers attributed to eagles vary from tribe to tribe, but typically center around ferocity (linked with strong talons and claws, hooked beaks and power when diving at speeds reaching 200 miles per hour for bald eagles and 230 miles per hour for golden eagles), flying ability (e.g. the capability to soar to the heavens), keen sight, monogamy and regal appearance. Golden eagles which are frequently larger than bald eagles tend to be ascribed greater status.

In the Southwest eagles and high mountain peaks maintain obvious symbiotic and revered relationships. Eagles soar above these peaks which demarcate tribal lands and often important places of origin. In effect, eagles figuratively look over tribal members and their welfare. Lofty alpine summits are typically surrounded by extensive ponderosa pine and fir forests which provide prime nesting sites. Eagles also build huge nests on rocky cliffs widely prevalent throughout canyon country.

Substantial controversy surrounds American Indian practices of gathering eagles for ceremonial purposes. The Hopi Tribe is at the forefront. Some Hopi sacrifice golden eagles as part of their religious practices and consequently have taken eagles from nearby Wupatki National Monument near Flagstaff, Arizona. In contrast other Hopi tribal members — such as the Eagle Clan — honor eagles as the embodiment of their ancestors, and abhor ritual eagle killing.

Somewhat less controversial is the fact that many tribes covet eagle feathers for headdresses, robes, shields, and other ceremonial accouterments. The Fish and Wildlife Service's Eagle Repository located in Colorado collects and distributes dead eagles and their feathers. Although 1,500 are given out in any year, a three-year backlog of demand exists. Like many things these days, when there is an unmet demand entrepreneurial and sometimes illegal sources surface to fill these desires. In turn, this tends to perpetuate the endangered nature of eagles in the Southwest.

Despite the debate surrounding eagles and ritual practices by Indians, there are fewer arguments about the thrill of seeing this top-of-the-food-chain raptor in flight. To most Americans, eagles symbolize freedom and strength; a small minority fear that eagles will take livestock such as new born calves or lambs. Looking past these concerns there remains a dispassionate realization that eagles signify what's best in our country. Watching an eagle play with the wind through minute adjustments of wing and tail feathers when soaring over a dense forest or sage-covered plain is an inarguably stirring spiritual experience.

Eagles on the wing over Indian country offer an unparalleled opportunity to sense a vital connection between the Anasazi and contemporary indigenous people. Travelers in the Southwest should remember to continually look skyward for a symbolic link to the old ones.

***

Mt. Baldy in the White Mountains of eastern Arizona nurtures perfect eagle habitat as well as an emblematic counterpoint to the state's low deserts. Its 11,590-foot summit is restricted to Tribal members of the White Mountain Apache Reservation, although public access is permitted to 11,200 feet. Thick stands of ponderosa blend to aspen and fir surrounding lush meadows. If you blindfolded a person and took her to the Mt. Baldy Wilderness she would think that she had been driven to Colorado. It's lovely country supporting elk, deer, and bear as well as a rich diversity of plant life. Pleasant streams course through the wilderness, eagles often circle overhead.

Fall is a faultless time to wander the West Baldy Trail while reconnoitering the high country of Arizona and climbing Mt. Baldy – to have a smidgen of backcountry adventure before this remote wilderness slams shut with winter's embrace. The trail gradually gains elevation on Mt. Baldy's lower reaches followed by a serious ascent in forest and then scrambling through rocky reaches.

Lovely meadows cover the route offering tempting spots to loiter. Patches of recent snow linger in shadows under the trees down by the trailhead, snow that will eventually make a full ascent of the peak impossible on this trip. Stream, a sometimes meadow, forest and mountain fit together in such a serendipitous way that I'm dawdling when my actual intentions are to reach the high country. This is the challenge most people face when roaming the wilderness' lower miles.

Fall is edging into winter however morning's chilly bite fades as sun warms the day. Icicles are thickly abundant in grass bordering the West Fork of the Little Colorado, a gentle stream destined for the Grand Canyon. Large daggers of ice drip off small boulders edging myriad little waterfalls coursing through the meadows.

Instead of going full blast for the summit, I'm investigating a small stand of ancient aspen, dropping down to inspect a diminutive waterfall and its perfect cascade into a dark pool. Penetrating sun warms to the bone, but doesn't fry. At the back of my mind is the thought that this lovely scene will undergo a metamorphosis to a thousand shades of green months later.

Although impressed with Mt. Baldy's beauty, it isn't until reaching a campsite roughly three miles in that I begin to fully appreciate this wilderness. Expecting a pleasant backcountry experience in sub-alpine country on par with the finest anywhere, I didn't count on a how enticing the lower trail would be. I had mistakenly focused on bagging a peak, the destination; not being consumed by the journey.

Thus begins a running dialog I'm having with myself about the precise purpose of this early fall adventure. What does it say about me when I brush past meadows, stream and aspens bound-and-determined to bag a peak? If I linger and don't carve another notch on my peak-bagging pistol haven't I failed the test of wilderness adventuring? When the trip reduces to only a walk in the woods with a bulbous pack on my back hasn't adventure been depreciated? Fortunately, these questions are about to be answered for me.

On the northern edge of an open meadow, the West Fork of the Little Colorado flows in serpentine meanders, bounded by infinite forest on both sides, sunlight reflecting off swift waters. The Little Colorado converts into a golden snake winding throughout a luminescent green-brown meadow. Until sunlight hits it just right, stream, meadow, forest and mountain qualify as something of beauty; a scene worthy of the highest accolades. Now they elevate to something far grander and supremely extraordinary— the epitome of wildness. However, it's more than just beautiful.

In the eyes of the Apache it's also sacred ground.

A glistening, sparkling, dancing, undulating and bouncing ribbon of golden-yellow light winds its way in snake-like motion down the meadow. It's so beguiling that I stand transfixed almost unable to believe that the expected has become the miraculous. No wonder that the White Mountain Apache were drawn to this enticingly mysterious land. They preferred forest-robed summits, broad grassy meadows and secreted dancing streams to stark sandstone canyon country surrounding their alpine islands. It's easy to understand how eons ago Mt. Baldy became a sacred icon; a peak above which eagles wheeled and myths germinated.

Unlike so many other goal-oriented treks, this one is about to stall. As snow blankets the trail and a passing cloud quick-chills the air I've suddenly lost my appetite for going further. It's still a long climb to the turnaround point and I don't doubt that it will be one arduous slog over slippery drifts and rock-hard ice before it's done. Pausing to consider the matter it seems as though someone or something is urging me to cool it for once. Maybe I'm just tired; maybe ancestral spirits of the Apaches are inviting me to join them around the campfire. There will be other days for macho exploits and heroic mileage. It's the time of year to harvest and look back on a year of endeavors and blessings. Could there be a better – more sacred – spot for reflection?

At camp a melancholy afternoon floods with little sorties and forays. There is so much life to enjoy in the surrounding forest – a porcupine hugging a spruce, hundreds of what most bird-illiterate types like me call little gray birds (dark-eyed juncos and Oregon juncos wintering-over) hunting and pecking through the under story, Northern flickers and Downy woodpeckers. Life surges over the little basin and copse of trees I'm calling home for tonight. And, as the sun winks out leaving breathtakingly cold air in its vacuum, a crackling red-yellow campfire breaks the isolation. No doubt apparitions of Apache ancestors are also mesmerized by the flickering flames, their presence unspoken but palpable – who could feel lonely at such a moment?

A frigidly cold night follows but my sleeping bag is more than a match. Morning will find thick ice covering pools and eddies. Rich humus smells of earth are months distant waiting until sun slowly warms the land. Aspens will remain stark skeletons, bare of gently fluttering leaves until it is definitely safe to come out.

As most people conceive it, this wilderness isn't truly alive because it's already on the road to hibernation. They don't understand that in the shadows of fall sliding into winter West Baldy is a conduit to the spirit of Apache elders and the quintessence of wildness. Yes, bagging a peak isn't the only criterion of time well spent in wilderness; sometimes backcountry adventuring is made far richer simply by the experience of connecting with spirits in a wild land.

As I return to the trailhead bundled in great swaths of down atop layers of high tech underwear I spot a lone bird in flight stratospherically high to the northwest. It's too distant for me to determine whether it's a vulture or eagle or perhaps a condor from the Grand Canyon that has drifted off course. If eagle, who will claim this bird?

From its lofty vantage this avian deity might well be looking down upon Second Mesa and a Hopi village. The Apache inculcated eagles within their ceremonies and rituals. Surely they view the eagle as one of their spirits. However, I would like to selfishly think that the apparition is totally mine; a symbol of my spirit, free and funneling upward toward the heights of heaven.

***

Fall offers extraordinary opportunities to bond with ancestral spirits and their divine eagle emissaries in the mountains. But you must look hard and fast; see beyond the veneer of land headed toward deep slumber. On rare occasions you may be given incredibly precious insights. For a few seconds, or in some cases minutes, you are blessed by the very best that nature has to offer – thousands of white snow geese congregating before winter; an eagle circling overhead; a stream lined with ice glistening in frigid warmth of disappearing sunlight; or, an aspen cloaked in brilliant orange-red or pure yellow – and then the window closes. An astonishing experience leaves you yearning for more, much more.

As a result, it's easy to relate to Annie Dillard's[1] transcendent moment when she walked on sacred ground: "Then one day I was walking along Tinker Creek thinking of nothing at all and I saw the tree with the lights in it. I saw the backyard cedar where the mourning doves roost charged and transfigured, each cell buzzing with flame. I stood on the grass with the lights in it, grass that was wholly fire, utterly focused and utterly dreamed. It was less like seeing than like being for the first time seen, knocked breathless by a powerful glance." The undulating snake of the Little Colorado had transfigured for me like Dillard in an astonishing way that seemed to charge every water droplet with glimmering fire.

Dillard goes on to say in *Pilgrim at Tinker Creek*: "The flood of the fire abated, but I'm still spending the power. Gradually the lights went out in the cedar, the colors died, the cells unflamed and disappeared. I was still ringing. I had been my whole life a bell, and never knew it until at that moment I was lifted and struck." It only took me one second of walking on sacred ground with the transfigured Little Colorado to launch a life-long search for more of these blessedly splendid moments.

Dillard's melodious passage resonates with my thoughts and emotions on the West Fork Trail. But at that point I lacked words to explain the experience. Who knows why I was chosen to enjoy the transfiguration of the Little Colorado River? The simple fact remains that occasionally nature is manifest in truly unique and powerful ways. From that flash forward I was never the same and couldn't look at wildness with the same spectacles.

Now I anticipate and seek more, knowing the reality just beyond my grasp, knowing the glorious spirit along ancient paths.

A totally unassuming backcountry adventure on Mt. Baldy morphed into an unbelievable intersection with ancestral spirits. Like Dillard, I became transfixed as wilderness moved to an entirely elevated level almost beyond comprehension. My senses attenuated, not because of overt danger from a knife-edge ridge, an insidious storm or lurking wild boar. Sometimes the rush isn't due to impending physical danger, but rather a startling connection between me and wildness.

My Mt. Baldy moment had me ringing like Dillard's bell. I had been soundly struck and as the reverberations gradually dissipated beyond the confines of wilderness, a resonating rhythm began to rise within me. Wilderness suddenly possessed an entirely different dimension. To be certain, I still wanted those infusions of excitement when the rush of peril and risk to life let me know that I was unequivocally, vibrantly alive. However, now there was also room – space within me – for wholly unique spirit-laced experiences I had never believed possible. Ancestral overtones had touched me to the core.

Needing another fix, I turned westward toward the highest point in Arizona. Could lightning strike twice in the same fall?

***

Arizona's San Francisco Peaks offer a perfect prescription for autumn adventure since they climb relentlessly straight up from Flagstaff's 7,000 feet to 12,633 feet. The Peaks are one of four sacred mountains to the Navajos (and twelve other tribes). Soft sun is shining; a prelude to a warm fall day in Arizona's high country. From Arizona's Snowbowl Ski Area I pierce a maze of fences and grassy meadows at the base of the Scenic Skyride – the chair lift that takes visitors to 11,500 feet. The ride won't open for several hours. By that time I'll be headed to the highest peak.

Trail tread is damp, but not muddy – it seldom is on the west facing ski slope – and fragile vegetation is weeks past flowering as I follow along the ski run's laser straight cut through spruce forest heading up to the Skyride's terminus. It's sad to see green life disappear after a long summer, but that's the cycle of life. As dying plants fail to bounce back, there's no difficulty discerning the trail, only struggles to cope with an altitude change from 9,200 feet to the Peaks' stratospheric crown. On reaching the Skyride I will pick my way across a knife blade edge of rock and follow boot-beaten paths toward the highest summit.

Channeled between copses of trees – survivors that avoided girdling bites from loggers' saws – and struggling to gain a second wind, I jog my way up rocky hillocks. Physically challenged, I'm filled with a bit of apprehension – intuitive anxiety rising slightly – as I look up toward the towering peak hidden by lofty contours. I've climbed these mountains many times, but each ascent is special. You never know what waits at the top in terms of trail conditions or weather.

It's quiet in the chilling clinch of frosty air and I shiver when stopping to regain my breath. I've been in better shape that's for sure. There's not a lot of complexity to the chore ahead or so it seems, just one step upward at a time. Nonetheless, it's easy to forget that any time you walk ancient paths magic can occur. Each step upward breaks the tie to work and life lived for economic reasons; funny how this bond can be broken so easily. Only twenty-five minutes earlier I was pulling away from my garage. Now I'm beyond the edge of civilization verging on wilderness and about to enter territory Indians hold as sacred.

From their perspective, and mine, I'm symbolically climbing toward a spiritual pinnacle. At first glance rocky Mt. Humphreys looks just the same as it did yesterday, and the day before, from 5,000 feet lower in town. Nonetheless, as I go higher the more tangible is a nagging realization that this is a special peak among summits in Arizona. Mt. Humphreys is inexorably intertwined with religious overtones from regional cultures. This is not just another recreational playground.

Gasping for breath and slowing my pace to reach equilibrium, I glance to the right among shadowy spruces and am surprised to see just a smidgen of movement twenty feet up a tree. A furry lump moving like elementary school kids toward their first day of classes is a porcupine having breakfast. But, does the porcupine see me? It moves so slowly that it's difficult to tell whether it's just focused on the tree or on me. Porcupines move to distinct rhythms and this morning is no different than all others. While the San Francisco Peaks' forest warms it will finish a morsel or two before seeking a higher, safer resting spot away from the ski area, ensconced in the middle of trees safe from prying predator eyes.

Turning back to the task at hand it's like I've never hiked before – puffing and blowing vast frosty clouds, gasping for air, sweet air, in the high reaches of Arizona. How many people who have never visited Flagstaff before would be amazed by this sky island? It's not possible they think to expect such immense spruce forest standing above ponderosa pines and aspen glades lower down on Hart Prairie. Where's the cactus, scorpions, rattlesnakes and Gila monsters? This forest is as robust, as beautiful and vibrant, as any in high-precipitation east coast states.

Unbuttoning wool shirt to let perspiration evaporate I take a measure of the mountain. The top of the chair lift once seemed beyond reach, but it has progressively drawn nearer with each slow step. It's not pretty, but gradually I'm winning the battle as tree line is reached and volcanic rocks pave the way. My initial adrenaline surge is long gone and I've settled into the routine necessary to scale a major peak.

Views continue to open to the west and now south above ski run channels cutting through living high forest. What a vast and awesome sight prevails in thin air. Miles of ponderosa pine hills and mesas flow from aspen dotted prairies. To the north, pines merge with juniper and piñon before falling abruptly into the great chasm of the Grand Canyon. You really cannot see the Canyon very well at this point, but there's a definite sense of vacuum beyond the tree line, as though the world just stopped. Views will improve once on Mt. Humphreys, the highest peak.

Past the Scenic Skyride a path is boot-beaten into black-rusty red volcanic ash, stones, pumice and rocks. In prehistoric times, crude sandals fashioned the initial path across scree slopes. From here the trail switchbacks to a southern shoulder reaching for the first of the San Francisco Peaks, Mt. Agassiz. Then it proceeds north along an undulating ridge ever higher toward Mt. Humphreys.

Scrambling along on lava chock-a-blocks and icy snow, I'm transported a few weeks back to the first major fall storm. Although others have stomped through here, persistent melting has erased much of the path atop the snow leaving me free to choose my own way. Six-hundred feet above on the summit of this vast lava rock and snow wonderland a four-foot high rock windbreak lays waiting in the sun, a beacon offering respite from scouring winds – the breath of our Earth.

Frigid breezes occasionally whip through still, warming air. I peer up at the snowy route and calculate the prospects for how chilly it will be on this exposed ascent. Thirty minutes ago my trusty wind parka provided adequate protection from this on-slaught; but the wind's power is just too much, the cold too penetrating for shorts. I stop and add wind pants. Slightly light-headed, but determined not to be beaten back, I continue weav-ing a path toward the summit, confident that victory is merely minutes away if I don't do something stupid – like fall. Still, a nervous edge persists. To be alone on this peak under these con-ditions is tempting fate.

So cautiously intent on safely navigating the final reach of Mt. Humphreys' summit, the stupendous views are simply fuzzy background. And then; it's all over – no more moun-tain left to scale. But, it is cold, very cold. I retreat behind the windbreak, pull on hat and gloves, drink a bit of water, and enjoy a Snickers Bar. Still, I'm freezing. It then registers that I'm sitting on ash and pumice covered ice hidden in the windbreak's shadow, a giant ice cube melting from body heat. Great, my butt is all wet – just the sort of initial mistake that can cost you plenty under more perilous conditions.

Facing the four directions, views are absolutely unparalleled. I see hundreds of miles in all directions until finally the Earth's curve renders further sight impossible. East, the Mogollon Plateau forest stretches only a few miles until red and white rock canyon country prevails. Out there somewhere is Petrified Forest National Monument and the Meteor Crater. South, harsh sun terminates views in the depths of dense forest. West, a mottled mosaic of green forest, dry grass meadows, small rolling hills and canyon cleavages spread like a blanket. North, the mysteri-ous space of the Grand Canyon is easily discernible; calling. Gad, no wonder the ancient ones concluded this is sacred ground.

In remnants of stratovolcanic caldera falling from the summit's eastern slope, vegetation is pretty sparse. The caldera's wonderful bowl is filled with snow up high, gradually transforming to steep talus slopes sliding toward tentative fingers of spruce at elevations where life is possible year-round. Still, given winter's often-generous helpings of snow, it appears that trees have a very difficult time establishing themselves and maintaining a foothold. Powerful avalanches routinely rake these marble-infested slopes preventing the upper forest from advancing.

Hunkering down beneath this meager little windbreak smothered on its northern side with the last storm's remnants, I receive a Biggie-sized reward. *It's the silence of the spheres filling my ears and overwhelming me.* Swirling gusts bluster by, inviting me to stay and in the same moment trying to steal from me – rob the warmth I need to live. Their siren call is alluring. So this is how others inadvertently succumb to hypothermia and death.

I shut my ears and rise, not yet ready to depart on that ultimate adventure. It's all downhill from here after a first step.

***

The personification of fall – alluring sunny days, nipping bite in the air, and punky aromas from decaying vegetation – offers a splendid stage for wilderness adventuring. Fall brings rich moments for bagging peaks, the sort of physical challenge and personal victories that we can revisit in the depths of winter. These feats provide laudable fodder to brag about over a pizza and beer during halftime at a football game, or to impress others during happy hour on a lonesome Friday night.

Like so many others I went out to conquer Arizona's high country and to demonstrate that I could take whatever nature dished out, and then some. But, somehow it didn't end up quite

as expected. Physical tests materialized that I passed with flying colors, and that validated my honored membership in the
legion of fearless weekend warriors. But, in the process I came
back transformed from adventuring on hallowed ground. I had
run smack into an entirely different dimension that I never knew
laid waiting in those heartless mountains.

Just beyond Arizona's edge of civilization, among ethereal
shadows of the old ones, I discovered a new sort of adventure. It
was the opportunity to blend with the land – to become totally
connected with wildness – that made one-dimensional physical challenges seem second-rate and almost pedestrian by comparison. Sacred ground lies patiently waiting whether on Mt.
Baldy in eastern Arizona, or Mt. Humphreys along the fringe of
Flagstaff. In this respect the Earth spoke to me in dramatic ways
because I opened to its song. It's a voice that raises my consciousness if I listen carefully and enter wild areas intent on hearing its
message; a message made vibrant in fall.

Friends are always amazed when they receive gift subscrip-
tions to *Arizona Highways*. They don't understand the geological, biological, and climatologic diversity of the state, choosing
only to perceive baking desert laced with cactus, rattlesnakes,
scorpions and tumbleweeds. Arizona isn't a place they want to
visit; it's only a place they endure in driving somewhere else –
like Chevy Chase as Clark Griswold driving his family to Wally
World in the movie *National Lampoon's Vacation*.

Many folks who tour Arizona and the Four Corners are very
interested in seeing Indians. They come; they see; they encounter; but, they seldom perceive beyond the veneer. Most only take
away visual images of mud hovels and trashed-out yards on the
reservations. They stare indiscreetly on shriveled faces of the elders and plump faces of pre-diabetic young. Typically family and

friends are unable to look into the hearts of these indigenous people. Cultural blinders prevent them from understanding their struggle to bond the old with the new – of trying to live harmoniously.

Living in balance is a central compelling metaphysic in the lives of indigenous people of the Southwest. Over millennia Native forbearers began each day seeking harmony and pursuing this ideal until the sun winked out of existence. They tried to remain in balance because they understood fundamental primal forces at work. Not everyone can walk in this fashion every minute of the day. Many wander from this path and never give a second look back at what they leave behind.

Today non-Native people who reside in the Southwest, and those who visit, inevitably intersect with this underlying characteristic defining life. They realize that they too are *walking on sacred ground* – territory where the ancient ones maintained a fierce allegiance to harmony with the Earth. As non-Native culture overwhelms the Southwest, faithfulness to this tenant of balance is diluted and gradually subjugated. Nonetheless, vestiges remain. Search carefully because these overtones remain ready for discovery when walking ancient paths in these ancestral places.

Grand Canyon calls me -
limestone, sandstone, basalt, schist
geologic dreams...

TERRYE BULLERS

5

Fountain of Life

It was as a very pleasant drive along the North Rim of the Grand Canyon. Few other cars shared the road and my mind was miles elsewhere, specifically at the bottom of this astounding gorge. When suddenly....

"Duck for your life."

I silently shouted these words as an enormous purple shadow gobbled-up my car. One minute it was dazzling white-hot brilliance as only northern Arizona and southern Utah skies can be in the middle of summer, and the next it was as though an eclipse completely exhausted that unrelenting orb. Funny thing, the eclipse was only happening over my pathetically tiny car.

Meteor on collision course?

Century-old ponderosa on its way down?

Huge slab of fiery red sandstone sloughing off towering cliffs?

I ticked off the possibilities in rapid-fire succession waiting for sheet metal to crumple overhead with a sickening screech pinning me to my seat like Garfield on glass.

I was about to be dead meat even before setting foot outside to sample the North Rim's sprawling vista – the more awe-inspiring, less inhabited and comparatively commercial-free step-child to the South Rim. The North Rim is a whole different world compared to the three-ring circus happening directly south across this mind-boggling chasm. Over there twelve miles away are diesel-belching tourist busses, easy access to Interstates, overweight tourons in tasteless attire, and every manner of commercial come-on outside park boundaries. Over here one thousand feet higher are a plethora of nature and almost infinite solitude.

When the grotesque shadow ate my vehicle I was descending from the North Rim's massive forest toward Arizona's Vermilion Cliffs. Check out almost any road map and this undulating rock wall is highlighted as a noteworthy geological feature due north of Marble Canyon. Such simple deadpan labeling – the Vermilion Cliffs – hardly conveys their shocking grandeur and thirty-some mile escarpment comprised of blood-red sandstone. Depending on sunlight's angle and intensity, the cliffs often appear as rose, scarlet, pink or even orange. On this desiccating furnace-hot summer day, vermilion is a very fitting moniker.

Slick rock and canyon country flow north of the cliffs along with the Paria Plateau. This is land beloved by Ancestral Puebloans; their ruins are sprinkled like valuable diamonds across the Southwest. Rock art abounds as well as gradually crumbling mud and stone structures persevering in this arid land. Watch towers, granaries, small villages and more await those who venture deep in slot canyons with their hidden alcoves, amphitheaters and sandstone caves. No matter where I go in the Southwest this past is omnipresent – always magically appearing when least expected.

Although ancient artifacts are undeniably intriguing, they can't hold a candle to the immensity of this country's twisted-tortured configurations. The scale exceeds my ability to comprehend. Want to feel totally insignificant? Pull off on one of the North Rim's acrophobia-inducing overlooks. The cerulean sky and infinite spread of mesas, canyons, buttes, and cliffs let me know what it feels like to be an ant in a limitless backyard. Throw in a wonking mile-plus deep ditch to boot and the visage is literally prodigious.

No wonder the earliest record of human habitation dates back 12,000-some years in the Four Corners area. The Vermilion Cliff's 3,000 foot escarpment exerts a magnetic pull that's irresistible. Those earliest hunters and gatherers recorded their pleasures, discoveries, tragedies and worship about the cliffs and vast Paria Plateau in pictographs, petroglyphs, and other forms of rock art. These depictions serve as a constant reminder that I am only one in a long line of others to gasp at the enormity of vividly riveting cliffs stretching beyond the horizon.

"I've got to see what's passing overhead," says my curious conscious forcing me to slam on the brakes.

Acrid stench of hyper-heated brake dust and melting tires fills my nostrils as I screech to a halt on the side of this bottomless abyss.

Swinging the door wide-open and jumping out ready for battle – reminiscent of the worst Bruce Willis flick – I stumble a bit due to a blast of heat-from-hell. If my car had an air conditioner I would have been knocked on my butt. Fortunately I'm driving with windows down and already semi-acclimated. Freed from the metal tomb I'm prepared for action; determined to inflict a bit of damage before meeting my fate.

Waltzing a complete three-sixty, I clumsily seek equilibrium, vainly scanning overhead for the offending source of the ominous shadow. I'm wondering why Darth Vader's storm troopers are picking on me amid this desolation? Mind and body aren't synchronized; my butt's been riveted in the seat for too long. Eventually things snap together and I spin ninety degrees with head thrown back as far as it will go.

Directly above is the biggest damn turkey vulture I've ever seen. Or is it? The wingspread is just shy of a two-seater Cessna. Chortling a bit, I blow out a little whistle of appreciation. Why shouldn't vultures out here have proportions equal to this cosmic landscape? It all fits together so perfectly.

Other seemingly trivial coincidences the past few miles begin to add up. Only with phenomenal luck had I missed plowing into a herd of five mule deer, slender as can be, back around the bend. Minutes before, they crossed to browse on the northern side of the road. All morning long I've been dive-bombed by raucously squawking blue jays proclaiming dominion over the juniper/pin on forest. Before that I caught a glimpse of pronghorn antelope cleverly camouflaged against the backdrop of a coulee's thigh-high brown grasses.

Add to this several sightings of coyotes slinking around Jacob Lake's turn-off to the North Rim. Then there was a freak blind corner encounter that scared a somewhat rotund coyote off what appeared to be Kaibab squirrel road-kill. In other spots the road seemed to be paved with golden-mantled ground squirrels. It must have been a healthy winter that drove vegetation and animal reproduction wild, as the multitude of fat ravens scavenging tasty morsels can testify.

This munificence of life fits with the ancestors. Where there's game, there's life. Kneading this connection over in my mind another convincing thought begins to take hold. Perhaps the linkage is even deeper than I initially speculated. Many Indian tribes in the Four Corners such as the Havasupai, Hualapai, Zuni, and Hopi, believe that life originated out of the Grand Canyon.

To them the canyon is a holy fountain from which life sprang.

My lightheadedness from suddenly getting out of the car and spinning around slowly vanishes. The vulture's assault begins to vaporize. But, what if it had been one of the transplanted Californian condors? Perhaps my diminutive vehicle would have ended up an easy meal.

One last glance over this fountain of life nurtures a better understanding of the ancient ones who called this place home. The Grand Canyon is supremely bigger than other geological features. Due to its all-consuming vastness, the canyon exudes an inherent persona of mysticism and supernatural energy. It's perfectly clear why the elders decided the Grand Canyon *is* the portal from which life emanated.

Punchy from the drilling heat I flop back into my seat, slam the door shut and pick my way beneath soaring red cliffs and dancing apparitions of people from long ago. I leave determined to explore the inner reaches of this icon — this Grand Canyon — in search of what the old ones discovered centuries before.

***

One day at work I was pontificating to several acquaintances about the coming weekend: "At least once in your life you really should walk to the bottom and back in a day just to know that you're alive. And, this coming Saturday is my turn." Out of the corner of my eye I watch Jack hanging on every word while others murmur about their plans.

As our little group breaks up, Jack comes rushing over, "Would you mind if I come along? I've always dreamed of hiking to the bottom of the Grand Canyon."

From my perspective this will be a perfect addition otherwise it will be only me attempting a legendary pilgrimage; one of the world's ultimate day hiking challenges. There's safety in numbers even if they are only two.

"Fabulous. We'll leave at 6:00 a.m. in order to start down the trail just after 7:00 a.m. Make certain you bring plenty of water." Thus begins a magnificent mid-October adventure.

Jack and I drive the back road from Flagstaff to the South Rim under partially cloudy skies. Weaving through the world's largest ponderosa forest and glancing over to the aspen- and spruce-laced forest of Hart Prairie at 9,000 feet, it's hard to believe that soon we'll drop to the Colorado River at 2,350 feet. This morning's temperature is cold enough, in the low 30's, to have the heater going so we discuss what the prospects will be at the bottom of the gorge. One thing is certain; it will be an upside-down day where all the strain of hiking comes in clawing our way back out of the canyon.

Are we up to the challenge? Both young Jack and I quietly meditate on this question not wanting the other to know of unspoken trepidations. We're confident, even cocky, but the elevation gain (and loss) is gruesomely intimidating for a day trip. My car has the faint odor of adrenaline on the rise.

Over 12,000 feet high, the San Francisco Peaks cast long gloomy shadows covering forest on this lonesome back route toward the South Rim. To the west a half-hour from now, sun will be shining brightly on grasslands, piñons and junipers that stretch to higher elevations on the canyon's lip. Meanwhile the Vermilion Cliffs sparkle crimson red on the northern horizon where the North Rim broods over the canyon. Suddenly a hawk soars past headed toward vast grassy fields to the west. We aren't the only ones out before sunrise today.

On entering the park we drive carefully along a swath of trees and there's little hint of what lies ahead on the forest's edge. The end of the road comes almost without warning. The canyon simply materializes out of nowhere leaving you staring into the Earth's very bowels. Jack looks pretty apprehensive, but it's too late to turn back now. If given half-a-chance to gracefully retreat I bet we both would tuck tail and run. Then again; maybe not.

The gaping chasm falls away at our feet like a bad dream leaving no time to prepare mentally or emotionally. Cognitively our brains register its presence, depth, distance and tremendous scale, but it's so big that it takes minutes, hours, to fully under-stand the canyon's immensity. Even then the Grand Canyon is startling in its enormity leaving a lingering feeling that it may unexpectedly begin sucking us and the entire Coconino Plateau into its gaping mouth. Everyone should experience this knot in their stomach. Think of how differently we would walk through life if we visited the canyon once every year and tasted a bit of humility about our place in the scheme of things.

Despite morning's chill, we're wearing shorts to cope with heat expected later in the day. Parka shells will keep us warm from waist-up until the sun finds its way into northern-slope recesses. Since we're hiking down, it takes longer to generate warmth and the sun's low arc means that hours will pass before heating rays touch steep sides of the canyon. It's a battle between comfort and practicality because eventually we will turn around at the hottest part of the day. At that point we don't want to be lugging any unnecessary weight.

Picking our way down a dusty four-foot wide trail beaten in ivory limestone, cool air fills our lungs. Scarcely a sound is audible in the canyon's enormous vacuum. I can even hear Jack's gentle breathing ahead of me. There's no decision-making about which way to go as the trail descends along a series of switchbacks – simply follow the path and put one foot in front of the other.

We have chosen seven-mile long Kaibab Trail to descend instead of the more popular, and almost twice as long, Bright Angel Trail. The Kaibab is particularly well liked by mule trains ferrying riders to and from Phantom Ranch at the bottom of the gorge. On the Kaibab Trail they're able to avoid pressing throngs of ambitious tourists who are tempted to try a bit of the trail. Although hikers give way to mules, there's always the risk someone will do something stupid. If the mules are startled they may unceremoniously dump their loads and the unfolding scenario has potential for grave consequences. Riders and cargo can fall hundreds of feet in some steep locations.

Jack enthusiastically takes the lead going down, setting a very brisk pace that stokes our internal fires. He's out to show the old man how it's done. I don't crowd him, but remain about ten yards back. It's a pleasant jaunt following the dusty and rocky trail as it switchbacks terrifyingly down upon itself in the first several hundred feet.

Although focused on the trail, we have plenty of opportunities to take in the big picture, especially the view of the canyon as a whole, and the stupendous grandeur of the 1,000-foot higher north rim. It's breathtaking, but the single factor that overwhelms us is utter silence. Sound just seems to evaporate. Occasionally at a turn in the trail you glimpse the Colorado River almost a mile below carving an even deeper abyss. A faint roar can often be heard depending on wind and the canyon's washboard architecture of ravines, arroyos and ridges.

Almost perfect silence magnifies our boot falls making them seem more audible and significant in this vast temple. Infrequent birdcalls are heard or a sudden swoosh as one darts overhead bound for who knows where. These sounds break the sense of lifelessness within the canyon. It's so dry and so big that life seems to be absorbed within the very rock walls like water to a sponge. Imagine how summer's heat magnifies this impression of a lifeless vacuum.

Jack jumps around a rather damp, putrid spot on the trail — moisture that at first is mysteriously out of place, a gift from the mules. Apparently they have adopted a habit that if one urinates, others retaliate. In time these sections of trail become a sort of signal to mark territory whether they really have the urge to pee or not. In some ways it's not unlike gas stations and rest stops occurring along lonely sections of the nation's interstate highways; people will stop just because other people are stopping to use facilities or to buy food and trinkets.

Kaibab Trail drops in thousand foot increments related to geological formations. At each increment there is leveling, more or less, on a plateau reflecting variations of rock strata. The trail starts with Kaibab Limestone forming the Coconino Plateau before descending through Paleozoic strata including the Toroweap Formation, Coconino Sandstone, a modest slice of Hermit Shale, the amalgamation of Supai Formation, Redwall Limestone, a thin band of Mauv Limestone, Bright Angel Shale and finally Tapeats Sandstone resting on early Precambrian Schist and

Gneiss. In the final 1,000 feet to river level, the "vee" shaped gorge is comprised of this almost gray-black rock.

Although estimates vary, you literally walk through time from 225 million year old Kaibab Limestone to 1 billion year old Precambrian schist and gneiss. These numbers are impressive, but they are a little difficult to put into perspective. In *Deep Play* Diane Ackerman[2] ruminates about our tendency to deify the grandeur of the canyon by labeling rock formations: Wotan's Throne, Vishnu Temple, Shiva Temple, Tower of Ra, and so forth. At the same time we try to impose our humanity on something more colossal than that which our minds can comprehend.

Ackerman observes: "With binoculars as various as they are, visitors search the canyon for trails, mules, signs of other people. The need to humanize the marvel is obsessive, obvious and universal. With glass lenses extending real eyes, canyon visitors become part of the evolution on show. If we cannot go backward in time, we can at least creep into it, above desert floors and red-rock mesas and ponderosa pine, then suddenly slip over the rim of dreams and down through the layers of geological time." Jack and I have crept to the rim and launched ourselves physically, mentally and metaphysically into the abyss, and in the course of walking down and back up we try to understand what it all means, these vastly ancient rock strata reflecting rhythms of the Earth.

While Jack busies himself with setting a brisk pace my mind is drifting to that North Rim. It wasn't all that long ago that I was driving past the Vermilion Cliffs with Indian ruins scattered about. By comparison Jack and I are almost walking within civilization given this well-worn path, frequent mule trains, and knowledge that Phantom Ranch waits below.

Hiking above the Tonto Plateau we run into a mule train on its way out from the bottom. Stepping aside a considerable distance we pause for a drink and snack. How uncomfortable the riders appear atop laboring mules. One good-natured lady, scores of pounds overweight, calls out a lusty and cheery hello.

Jack yells back, "How's it going?"

She blows hard and says, "This is really tough."

I smile and wonder what's going on in the mule's mind. If it could speak the reply would probably be something like, "Get your fat ass off my back and walk up."

On the other hand these folks are gaining intimacy with the canyon. They're investing physically in the trip and I would not want to be that sore between my legs after the winding, rocking, bobbing rides down and back.

With mid-morning waning, Jack and I level out on the Tonto Plateau, a noticeable broad ledge just above the final descent into the innermost canyon. By now the temperature is very pleasant, not too hot. Hunger gnaws at our stomachs and we are eager to reach the river and our destination for lunch. The trail hits "The Tipoff," a point of descent into the canyon's final bowels. Knowing that we're close to the river our pace picks up since young Jack is starving. The Colorado River can be seen and heard very clearly at this point, beckoning us to get it over with.

In the canyon's shadow we reach rock bottom and a skinny black steel suspension bridge crossing a massive olive green river below. What a fantastic feeling to know that we've just descended a mile of elevation as the trail spans the fabled Colorado River. We peer over the waist high rail and are drawn into the mysterious depths of a colossal river sliding along, determined to find a way out to the sea.

On the other side of the bridge, Jack doubles back toward a barren chalky tan-white beach of fine sand. Like kids at the ocean we immediately take off boots and socks to soak hot feet. What sweet relief. Sandwiches in hand and replenishing our sorry dehydrated bodies with refreshing water, we rest knowing turn-around has been reached early in the day — it's still only 11:00 am after we finish eating. There's plenty of time left to crawl up or be carried out.

The Colorado River is awesomely powerful, gliding along in a wave- and rapids-free portion of the canyon, having just exited from Granite Gorge and several major league rapids. The bright olive green color is surprising. You cannot see the bottom of eddies, side pools or the middle of the river. More than anything, we're spellbound by deep swirls within the river. This is mass against mass — river versus rock. A powerful war of attrition is being waged at this very moment; a war of proportions almost beyond comprehension as the river seeks to grind a straighter and wider path through steel-hard canyon walls.

There's enough time to visit Phantom Ranch. Following a sandy path to the north we pass stark and depressing tent sites offering little privacy or shade. It's not where I would want to camp given the activity around Phantom Ranch and the inter-section of the Bright Angel and Kaibab Trails. Compared to the campground, bunkhouses and mess hall of Phantom Ranch reek with sun-bleached charm in a pleasant setting along Bright Angel Creek. Many a weary traveler has probably rejoiced when reaching this Mecca of civilization in the canyon.

Under beautiful cottonwoods just beginning to turn fall yellow at their edges Jack and I spin around to begin the trek out. Here's when the adrenaline begins to rise and a palpable dryness coats our tongues like a morning hangover. It's intimidating knowing that we now retrace our steps more than a mile higher to our vehicle. Looking to the South Rim and Yavapai Point, it's a long, long way up there as the canyon rises in thousand foot steps toward a very distant thin ribbon of greenery. A bit of panic sets in – will we make it back?

After crossing another suspension bridge I tell Jack that I'm willing to lead going out since he led coming down. We cannot rush this task. Victory will be hard won, one step at a time. Rushing it accomplishes nothing except to wear ourselves out before we've even gotten started. Young Jack doesn't protest, but for the first thousand feet out of the canyon's deepest rock he's right on my boot heels, breathing down my neck. It's hot enough without a blow-dryer focused on my back. However, out of sheer stubbornness I'm not going to stop in order to let him go by until we reach the Tonto Plateau – he can wait. Thirty-some minutes later when we scramble to the plateau I swing aside saying, "Go ahead Jack. I'll see you on top."

He rushes by me like a young colt released to pasture buoyant with freedom and determined to race to the top – youth and its impetuousness. I go back to my time honored "bring'em back alive pace." One foot falls in front of the other without rush or fuss. The pace is just short of breathing hard, just fast enough to achieve something on order of two and a half miles an hour in view of distance and elevation to be gained. And, young Jack? He's a little speck about three hundred yards ahead. Ten minutes later he's about two hundred yards ahead. Just shy of thirty minutes after rushing for the top, I step carefully around him.

Although Jack has the advantage of young legs and boundless energy on his side, he lacks wisdom of experience for this situation. No matter how fit and trim you are, no matter how many marathons you have run, you need to pace yourself on this trail.

Jack has simply fizzled out and needs to slow down in order for his body to catch up with his ambitions. We mutually fall into a slower, consistent, cadence and gradually grind out the miles.

In perpetually plodding upward, there's plenty of time for introspection. It's difficult not to keep thinking about the enormity of time illustrated by the one thousand foot high steps we're taking. When you're locked into an average 70-80 year life time frame 500 million years much less a billion are a bit difficult to comprehend. Yet the relatively youthful canyon did not materialize all at once. It was a succession of days such as this where the Colorado River continued to chip away at its bed. It was freezing rain that split a rock in two; a flash flood that scoured a side canyon; a fire started by lightning that made the earth vulnerable in the next rainstorm; and, many cumulative events over millions of years creating the gorge we navigate today.

Rhythms resonate when you walk the course of the Grand Canyon. They are engrained in the magnificent geology. Events we have seen today – a breeze blowing sand from a limestone ridge at the canyon's lip; a shoe-sized rock dislodged by a clumsy mule; sun burning a patch of grass; Clear Creek digging imperceptibly into a ravine – are the rhythms of a living, breathing ecosystem. It's upon these rhythms that the canyon is formed – an overlay of rhythm upon rhythm upon rhythm over the millennia.

After two hours of almost continuous hiking we slow for a refreshing water break. Sweat slathered bodies itch with minute bits of sandy grit. Cooled by evaporation, both of us are tired, not ready to give in, but ready to be finished. We have been successful in carefully measuring out precious water – the elixir of life. With a bit more than one mile to go, we still have half a quart – but it seems pretty meager. Although the temperature borders between warm and too warm, we're in no danger of over-heating. Victory has been won.

A new form of entertainment waits on the trail in the form of tourists clad in sandals or dress shoes; holding a can of soda as they saunter down what must be to them an easy trail. How amusing. Wait until they turn around. Then their pleasant little stroll will intensify beyond their wildest dreams. By the time they crawl out with parched throats they will never make that mistake again – take the intimidating canyon for granted. The pleasant warmth of a fall day morphs into the hell of summer as they realize there is only one way out and they desperately want, need, a glass of water.

In good time Jack and I make our final steps and walk out onto the asphalt parking lot. There is no melodious marching band, no prancing cheerleaders to proclaim a great feat. Indeed, thousands, probably millions, of people have walked down to the bottom of the Grand Canyon and back in one day. Many have set a blistering pace that makes our time seem pretty pathetic. These facts don't matter.

What does matter is the lasting knowledge that when we could do it, we did. What matters is learning about hugely important rhythms of the Earth in a way that we can interpret. We might not be able to really understand what a billion years is, but we now know what one day in the endless rhythm of weeks, months, years, centuries, and millennia means to this magnificent natural wonder.

***

A strenuous day hike to the bottom of the Grand Canyon provides an amazing amount of insight about life's brevity on this Earth. For Jack and me the connection became quite tangible when navigating all of those thousand-foot layers of rock. They represent a metaphor for the millennia – a visual confirmation of how old the Earth is.

Although the old ones didn't have the benefit of modern geological science to accurately comprehend the historical breadth of the canyon, they must have contemplated the connection between a river far below and the passage of time. In this respect a wizened wrinkled shaman may have intuitively guessed that life originated somewhere in conjunction with this distant river's methodical passage. It would not take too much to infer that life originated from the depths below.

Humans continue to wrestle with an explanation for life's origin. Perhaps the Zuni, Havasupai, Hualapai, Hopi and other tribes are correct in believing that life sprang from the Grand Canyon; perhaps not. Nonetheless, they certainly are on target in observing the canyon as a fountain of life. Verdant forests and plains reach to the Grand Canyon's edge. Upon those wild lands are a bounty of animal life such as elk, deer, bear and puma. In the air a dizzying array of birds – large and small – call this place home. Mountain streams high on peaks above run flush with fish.

A very long day in the canyon whetted my appetite to better understand the breadth of this geological phenomenon and its connection to the ancient ones. A few months later Havasu Falls presented another perfect portal to observe the canyon and its relationship with ancestral spirits of the Southwest.

***

Several inches of air separate spinning tires from rough rutted road. Flying over a small hilltop, gravity pulls my car back toward hard pack mixed with marbles for traction on the other side. Brief weightlessness is quickly forgotten and none too soon for that matter. This road jukes down to the left, but standing in a shallow depression at roadside is a bulbous brown and white cow with half-grown calf. As the car gains traction only one thought dominates my mind.

Which way will they go, these precious Indian cattle?

Sometimes luck prevails when you least expect it. Bovines scatter to the wind, running away from our car instead of into it. We start breathing again as tires slip and grab on the winding road – disaster avoided.

Esther, Jim and I are in a rush to get through this dry repetitively beige grass and rocky country of the Coconino Plateau leading to Hualapai Hilltop. Destined for Havasu Canyon on the Havasupai Indian Reservation in early March, we know that a sparkling turquoise river waits with marvelous waterfalls to excite our imaginations. It won't take much to get a rise out of us – it has been a long, bitter winter in Northern Arizona. I've shoveled ten feet of snow off my driveway.

We've forgotten what fresh green vegetation looks like, locked away in a freezer of winter. Warmth sounds luxurious; emerald trees and vibrant shiny leaves of grass decadent. Hiking guidebooks declare that these treasures await us in a narrow canyon below the Havasupai town of Supai. The problem is getting to the trailhead and then to Supai. Like so many adventures, you have to earn this mother lode the hard way – a seven plus mile trail to campsite heaven.

Our start is completely inauspicious due to monochromatic dust, dirt and rock at a football field-sized parking lot – pretty ugly even by an optimist's standards. I think back to all of those spectacular photographs of Monument Valley, Grand Canyon, and slick rock country. Where are the brilliant color contrasts, inviting glens and hollows, mysterious hoodoos and crystalline air? Hualapai Hilltop seems so flat and uninviting. Perhaps it's simply our inability to appreciate the grand scale.

One reassuring fact is evident. The weather here is much nicer than Flagstaff. It's not warm, but the low fifties is definitely not bad, not bad at all given arctic winter on the Mogollon Rim. And there's a bonus of knowing our trail will drop several hundred feet to a canyon wash, and then fall even further by the time we reach Supai — relatively little strenuous climbing until we come out. Best of all is a shift from snowshoeing and cross country skiing to backpacking. It seems weird walking on firm ground after months of shuffling across snow-covered forest floors.

I almost need a crane to lift bulging backpacks out of the trunk. We've come from winter and prepared as though we're backpacking into winter. Although there's no snow on the ground, winter's chill is only temporarily beaten into submission each day. As the sun goes down frosty gusts steal back down canyon draws and arroyos flooding high desert plateau and Grand Canyon basin with a glacial blanket of air.

This will only be a one night journey so some concessions are made in packing. We've tried to keep food to a minimum, but our packs carry two quarts of water that have to last until reaching springs past Supai. Huge green and red backpacks swing from thighs to shoulders. Before they're cinched into place we remove jackets and add them to the enormous piles riding our backs. Our optimism about warmer spring weather shows, I just hope we're not deluding ourselves.

While Esther and Jim fiddle with their packs I take in the big picture from Hualapai Hilltop's trailhead. It's an upside-down trail that's a bit disconcerting at the start. We're hiking down into a wash that narrows to just one more canyon in a sea of ravines – small, large or gigantic – running toward the Mother – the Colorado River. Jim and Esther pull alongside saying nothing. No words need be spoken. In the back of our minds is knowledge that we will pay when hiking out – and up – in retracing our steps. The most strenuous part of this walk will be exiting a chalky rock-carved staircase cleverly designed for giants and challenging those who walk with heavy packs on back.

Our first tentative footsteps down the rough path are like an elixir. It's downright balmy with hazy pale-yellow sun warming the hillside. All of a sudden winter begins to seem like a distant memory and the prospects for spring are alluring. Little breezes blow past, but they lack the bite of winter's teeth. Nonetheless, there are no discernible odors of spring in the air. It's almost scentless, tasteless, but still far better than the lifeless freezer back in Flagstaff.

I fall in behind Esther and Jim as they try to pace themselves according to the bizarre rise and pitch of steps cum trail. Going in will be easy compared to climbing back up this slope. Minutes later the trail's strange gradient becomes a fact of hiking tucked away in my mind. I'm focusing on the joy of walking free from bundles of clothing; warmed to the core by gentle sun. It's as though we have set sail on a grand voyage by stealing two days from winter.

Dropping several hundred feet of cliff- and hill-side into a sandy wash passes quickly and our attitudes improve with each step. In part we're distracted by the enormous view of canyon country stretching mile after mile. It's hard to place things into perspective given the breadth and depth of the land, a little like looking through binoculars the wrong way. Additionally, it's much warmer down in the arroyo. Less light is reflected from across vast canyon bowls and off high mesa walls. We're entering a womb of warm comfort, cheating winter's frigid blanket.

This journey *down* is symbolic of the Havasupai and other Southwestern tribes who ascribe to origin beliefs centered on the Grand Canyon. Only in this case the Havasuapi claim that *they* are the long-established ancestors; the first among first. So in many respects we are heading to the very fountain of life – the first people, the inner depths of the Grand Canyon and a source of origin beliefs.

Decomposed rock, sand and gravel form our footpath weaving around boulders and occasional sage, Apache plume, and four-wing salt bush. There's no question about how frequently the Tribe and visitors have used this ancient trail to access a very special place hunkered down in Grand Canyon's bosom. That's because trash seems to be everywhere – plastic drink bottles, dirty diapers, wrappers of one sort or another, and newspapers. This is more than just random mistakes. People have simply been careless about maintaining such a lovely canyon.

Walking is easy except for frequent piles and pools of horse droppings. As still air in the arroyo warms, a bitter fragrance of ammonia assaults our noses. This isn't quite the bouquet I was looking for as an early start to spring.

Despite the proliferation of litter our odyssey continues to blossom. I can't remember how long it's been since I felt truly baked to the bone. I even contemplate stripping down to short-sleeve shirt before slipping into a warmth-induced trance. There's little on my mind except picking up one foot and setting it down in proper order. In many respects I'm walking under ancestral shadows. The Havasupai used to spend summer months in this canyon tending crops. In winter they migrated higher on the plateau for warmth-giving fuel. Modern technology lets them relinquish these time-honored migration patterns and enables them to enjoy Havasu Canyon year-round.

After several miles of stress-free hiking a hint of change comes in on our right. The arroyo, now mini canyon, opens to allow a surprisingly swift and clear creek two broad leaps across, flowing determinedly to the north. Best of all, squat cottonwoods shimmer with bright tender growth proclaiming a new season. It's like being reborn. Spring's tangible evidence flutters overhead wiping away months of below zero wind-chill, ten feet of snow, and winter's darkness. The sight of luminescent new growth is enough to make up for the long trip to Hualapai Hilltop's remote trailhead.

This spring moment passes quickly since we need to make tracks for our campsite. Following the stream we're shunted back down a narrow canyon highway. Visible changes appear in another half-mile. This canyon is gaining breadth; ahead is a transition to a vast open bowl – the fields and homes of Supai are within reach.

A welcoming party comes out to greet us – various snarling and barking dogs with mangy hides accentuating their menacing appearance and aggressiveness. A crazy quilt of fencing – rectangle wire and wooden slats – keeps people out of yards, dogs half-in and forms a channel leading to the Tribe's official registration complex. We stop just long enough to pay entrance and camping fees. With permits issued we continue north toward the famous falls and campground.

What a contrast the mini-town presents after all of those backcountry moments of gigantic landscape with vast canyons and never-ending sky – wildness one moment; concentrated humanity the next. There is no rhyme or reason to the pastiche of homes lining the narrow lane we're traveling. Down an alley a jeep roars – going where? How did it get down here and how do they keep it fueled? Supai ancestors must find this very amusing.

The town is no more than a half-mile long and as houses end abruptly, we catch back up with the stream, now wider, full, and deep. Children are playing in the water with their horses giving them a bath. It's a bucolic scene until one of the horses decides to deposit a load of manure in mid-stream. Jim and I share a furtive glance – we'll be living downstream.

The diminutive river broadens, flowing towards a bridge and drop-off just ahead. Our trail descends along a canyon wall to the base of a falls and suddenly everything is glorious and beautiful beyond compare. Havasu Falls, Navajo Falls, Mooney Falls and Beaver Falls are the signature attractions of Havasu Canyon. Alluring turquoise water gushing into delicately terraced travertine pools personifies this place.

It's beyond delightful.

Entrancing greenish-blue water filling this canyon offers a dramatically sharp contrast with surrounding cliffs painted in washed-out vanilla-red-yellows. Only ten-yards away from the river all is barren. But, where there's water, there's life. Consequently it's easy to speculate how 12,000 years ago one of the first inhabitants concluded that this sacred canyon harbors the source of all life.

Cottonwoods wallow in blinding sun, gently fanning humid air with zephyrs driven by numerous waterfalls. It is a positively supernatural spot brimming with holy waters and riotous green growth bordering a precipitous fall into the very bowels of the Grand Canyon. A distinctive spirit dwells within this canyon – flooding every nook and cranny. We feel it permeating the very pores of our skin. Havasupai elders hold court here nurtured by a magical mosaic of hallowed water, ever-present light, vegetation gone wild, and towering sandstone monoliths.

On the way down from the trailhead Jim and Esther talked enthusiastically about swimming in Havasu Canyon's turquoise waters. But, now that we're here it seems almost sacrilegious to think about violating the sanctity of this place in such a manner. Jim says his trepidations are more than knowing that horses, houses and people wait upstream, befouling the water. He can't quite put his finger on it; but he doesn't have to explain. This isn't a spot for carnal pleasures; it isn't right to defile the special atmosphere that lies like a blanket over this canyon, especially when ancestral shadows grow long while this day wanes.

As we set up camp for the night I realize that we've pushed the envelope on seasons to the limit. We've left winter, embraced spring and will never be the same. Back at home we'll still see snowfall, frigid temperatures and cutting wind in the weeks ahead. However for us winter's grip has been irrevocably broken. It will remain that way until a distant time when aspens shift into brilliant batons of yellow and orange signaling winter's return.

My tent seems to explode into an instant domicile. Facing north toward the Colorado River I kneel down to gently pull my goose down sleeping bag from its rip-stop nylon restraints. As it sucks up air my mind rises above this peculiar intersection of turquoise waters from Havasu Canyon melding with the Colorado River's raging muddy maelstrom tenaciously eating away into Mother Earth.

On the north shore of the Colorado River is the beginning of massive geological formations that rise 6,000 feet and more to the Vermilion Cliffs. It's a stupendous leap physically and spiritually from here to up there

Remembering many months ago the almost inconceivable largesse of life – antelope, deer, squirrels, vultures, chipmunks, and blue jays – on the North Rim, it's clear that the Grand Canyon has nurtured nature and humans over the eons. In so many ways the abundance of wild critters mimics the vastness of this land gone geologically cosmic. What better home for the Anasazi?

Spontaneous devotionals over I get ready to stand up; but, one more compelling thought crowds my mind.

This massive canyon is indeed a poignant source – *the* fountain – of life.

I need a mountain
bathed in sparkling solitude,
spiritual mojo.

TERRYE BULLERS

6
Lingering Scents of Tobacco, Sweetgrass and Sage

After a very snowy week everyone is chomping at the bit to get out and enjoy some exercise. Sandia Mountain Wilderness looming over Albuquerque has just received a foot of fluffy fresh snow. The mountain is dazzling on this early February morning with blue-white diamonds reflecting high on its saw-tooth crest as old Sol slowly climbs into the sky flashing rays of life-giving warmth. Despite the recent storm's intensity, weather forecasters indicate a mild day in the high forty-degree range. Surviving an arctic winter that only North Dakotans would relish, this seems perfect for a long walk up to 9,500-foot South Peak.

Beginning at 6,200 feet, lower reaches of Embudito Trail have their fair share of fluffy white powder, but this will be nothing compared to the backside – eastern conifer forest and thin air crest where snow piles higher, deeper. Sandia Peak Ski Area will be bustling with cool dude snowboarders raiding the runs of retentive down-hillers who despise competition. All probably do share one thing in common – they're jubilant because today shows not the slightest cloud. It's a fine reward for suffering a week of gray, gloom, dampness and gale-like winds. Best yet, since most will be heading to the slopes, I have the trail to myself by starting early.

Pulling out heavy duty Limmer boots – fine craftsmanship if only a bit overdone for the Land of Enchantment – I prepare for a first-rate physical test. These Limmers weigh a ton, but in snowy conditions offer a perfect platform for stomping through drifts and gaining purchase on slippery icy slopes. Deep in my pack is a trusty blue-black Michelin-Man down jacket with bulbous hood – how many times has its life-giving warmth saved my sorry rear-end? It will be an extra measure of safety if things turn unexpectedly bad. Other than these concessions, there's no reason to view this walk as different from thousands of others I've taken up Embudito Canyon.

Breaking trail through five inches of dry powder with the huge black boots crunching and squeaking every step, their rhythmic mourn warms my heart. This is as good a sign as it gets that the snow is dry; I'll have to worry less about becoming soaked as the day wears on. Despite a chilly start, with triathlon-like exertion I'm soon removing worn leather gloves, heavy duty black wool cap emblazoned with red and yellow mountain images, solid blue breathable shell, and fluffy down vest.

In Sandia Mountain's scraggly fir forest, birds flit about scavenging a meal and defending territories. Their antics confirm that spring is just around the corner. Amid piñon-forested corridors softened by the wealth of snow and soon-to-be water, I weave between seasons. In little vales sheltered from sun it's winter; on exposed sunny slopes drinking in pleasant warmth, it's spring. No wonder the birds are confused, uncertain about which way to go – hibernate or procreate?

I'm always amazed at how quickly civilization is left behind when gaining altitude and penetrating to the heart of wilderness on Albuquerque's outskirts. The city rapidly retreats and with it a persistent background hum that gradually fades within wilderness boundaries. Only the occasional roar of a muscle car or motorcycle reaches the forest. Turning into Embudito's canyon, a tree-shrouded ridgeline, boulders and snow-covered mountain mahogany muffle even these passing transgressions. The sense of pure solitude becomes complete, pervasive.

It's still too early in the morning for other hikers to be out so the trail is covered in an unbroken blanket of snow. Dry fluffy powder cakes my insteps and is left discarded as icy clumps like so many bread crumbs to the proverbial witch's house. On a ridge only twenty-five feet above me, sun sparkles on piñons; melted flakes form plump droplets glistening at the tip if each needle. Every tree is outlined in brilliant silver with the morning sun – a sparkling display of gems.

Entering a glade of blue spruce trees, chill well below freezing slaps me in the face and starts adrenaline flowing. It's definitely still winter back in the forest under story and will remain so for many weeks hence. A niggling little thought starts to grow: how cold is it going to be up at the peak?

The rapidly rising sun burns like a blow-torch on crowns of snow-covered trees – soon it's raining everywhere. I pull on a parka shell leaving it unzipped to compensate for my build-up of heat and perspiration. But, in no time at all, my parka becomes completely soaked through. There's some consolation knowing that tomorrow might be a different day – back to freezing temperatures and weather that could make a winter ascent of South Peak an entirely different proposition.

For the next three miles it's nothing more complex than an uphill slog. Climbing is especially tough due to an icy base beneath twelve inches of snow and any step is a venture into the unknown. Concentrating to prevent punching through waist-deep, my mind empties in the simple act of walking through deepening snow. Grateful for long-needed exercise, I have nothing to complain about despite slippery footing and the effort of seeking solid footing. Physical exertion becomes a soul-pleasing tonic driving away niggling little concerns about what conditions exist further ahead.

As I gain altitude, few birds are soaring through the hushed white-green forest; they're all down much lower competing for mates. Without feathered friends for company, it finally hits home that I am truly alone – in perfect solitude. Nothing more than the sound of falling snow intrudes on the wood's deep calm; plopping and sloughing to the ground. A rhythm that continues to pick up as sun claims the treetops.

Nearing a high shoulder of the mountain after gaining almost three-thousand feet in elevation I finally wake-up to how far I've traveled; much farther and higher than I've ever dreamed imaginable – within reach of the summit. A window of opportunity opens. Why not go for a winter ascent of 9,500-foot high South Peak? All of the conditions seem to be just right – moderating temperature, minimal wind, brightening sun, and time remaining in the day.

On Sandia Mountain's shoulder I stop momentarily to drink and reconsider while looking out on ridgelines that look like a small gathering of albino Galapagos tortoises. There's a lot of snow-covered wilderness between me and safety. Don't want to do anything stupid given the conditions especially because the temperature is near zero at this altitude. Soft zephyrs with razor harsh wind-chill cut through my layering, but continuing upward will turn up my furnace a notch or two. A little discomfort has to be weighed against an opportunity to summit South Peak in winter, a chance that doesn't come along every day.

I take another step toward the beckoning summit.

What had been glorious, effortless, walking is now a chore and my muscles are becoming depleted. The sun is losing a bit of its vigor as it begins its initial descent, softening the warmth and light. As if to make up for this challenge, views over a snowy land open up to the west.

At my feet is all of Albuquerque and three-quarters of a million people going about their business. Little figures of cars and trucks are scurrying about on snow-lined streets; a soft rumble wells up from the frenzy below. To the west sixty-some miles away at 11,400 feet, Mt. Taylor stands out in sharp relief punctuating a sapphire blue sky. Slight breezes swirl around the peak and my lonely spot high above a city of people living at the edge of wilderness. Tuning in to Sandia Mountain's mood, it's apparent that I've hiked high enough to be in the death zone of extreme conditions.

Climbing with purpose for twenty minutes, having lost physical and mental edge, realization hits that I should have stopped at the pass. The day is beginning to fade away. How stupid can you get? I didn't bring enough clothing for single-digit-to-below-zero temperatures. On the other hand the snow-shrouded peak is so close, so within reach. There is no choice – I've got to go on.

Each step with these monstrous boots is an effort, but in my mind I'm committed. Breezes kick up another notch or two raising the ante. Now I'm becoming chilled and exhausted – perfect ingredients for hypothermia. This is precisely how high altitude climbers get into trouble. They set a turnaround time and either stick with it, or face death as a result of their decision.

I try to turn off fear racing across my mind like a bothersome advertising banner on a favorite website. Two more pitches and I will be there with no higher summit to climb.

Stumbling to the top, frozen to the core, I'm relieved that it's over. Contemplation of a beautiful day and inspirational thoughts were left far below in the forest. This trip shifted into an objective laden mission. Puffing and blowing, my mind racing with the challenge, I'm trying to gather my wits. Looking down 4,000 feet to the Rio Grande River and Albuquerque spread like a robe at Sandia Mountain's throne, I realize just how far away five miles of trail can be from urban life.

Dehydrated from strenuous effort in hyper-dry mountain air, I take on water and add a Snickers Bar for good measure while throwing on the great navy-blue down parka. Shivering, I pull on gloves and cap. The temperature must be below zero and falling.

As soon as I have every last bit of clothing on, I inexplicably experience the grandness of wilderness; go from mundane thoughts of food, water, clothing and next steps for survival to an entirely higher level of thinking about my predicament and what was accomplished today.

For a few brief moments I'm bathed in the magic of the Sandia Mountains. It isn't simply the penetrating warmth of sun on body.

It's more; much more.

I feel like I am literally part of the mountain. It's a moment that Henry David Thoreau captured eloquently in *The Maine Woods,*[3] "Talk of mysteries. Think of our life in nature – daily to be shown matter, to come in contact with it – rocks, trees, wind on our cheeks! The solid earth! The actual world! The common sense! Contact! Contact! Who are we? Where are we?"

Sandia Mountain's spiritual mojo has lifted me from a physical plane of existence. All that's asked is for me to stand there with mind empty of its normal clutter, receptive to sparks flying off picturesque basins, shadowing firs and fresh breezes as sun lights the chill air on fire.

Light-headed from the altitude and cold beyond comprehension, I'm literally all alone with no help in sight. For the first time in my life I honestly do not think I have enough energy, *any* energy, to start downhill – too tired to even walk home. It's both panic and elation. Within sight of hundreds of thousands of souls living their dramas in the shadow of a magical mountain, it's gratifying to know that I alone labored to the top of this peak to see what Sandia Mountain has to say. Nonetheless, within sight of hundreds of thousands of people, I am about to eat it big time. Adrenaline is going full blast and with what may have been its last spike, the thought firmly registers that I must move it or die.

The Limmers are rooted in place, too heavy to lift, or so I think. My heart is pounding, pulse booming in my ears. On survival mode, I stumble two steps…

That's all the momentum that's needed; I'm on my way down. Walking to the north I'm flooded with the ethereal sight of wild mountains and forest high above the maddening throngs, safely at rest in another season. It's almost too beautiful for words as sunlight starts to evaporate. An hour from now a classic watermelon red sunset will cloak the Sandias.

The rest is easy once I get going. One foot in front of the other; slide along at appropriate spots without falling; don't stop for any reason. I just keep walking with no breaks until I reach the car. It isn't downhill all of the way and the few uphill sections are pure torture. However, I'm charged, infused with supernatural energy from Sandia Mountain. A few remaining uphill battles are trivial obstacles that can't diminish this day's revelry.

That night looking back up on the mountain I savor the victories, defeats and ultimate gift of knowing something grander out in the Sandia Wilderness. My posolé is dreadfully hot, just right considering frigid moments I endured at what seems like a distant time – only three hours before. I came to know the magical measure of a mountain on this winter ascent, but best of all, the mountain and I fused as one, if only for a brief moment.

***

Lot's of people have enjoyable epiphanies in the wild Southwest. That's all part and parcel of this mysterious land. Its spiritual energy is infectious. From Anasazi petroglyphs and kivas to New Age gurus sanctity reigns touching many in unanticipated moments and in unpredictable ways.

Later this year in November when snow blankets Ski Santa Fe above Santa Fe, New Mexico an impetuous forty-two-year-old-going-on-seventeen red head will ride to the top of a ski lift with her awesome banana yellow snowboard in tow. Her freckled face will wince with the frigid air's rush pass her trailing braids flapping out from under a black skull cap. She's off the lift and poised to take on the first run today; ready to slice gnarly turns and looking forward to that section mid-way down the run when she can catch air and begin a choreography of free style that will put her children to shame.

Before she begins to carve her line she stands momentarily mesmerized.

"When has it ever been this perfect?"

A foot of unusually fresh powder has fallen coating the legendary base for which Rocky Mountain ski areas are known. The rest of the mountain is completely silent here in mid-week.

So this is what she's been missing by only going on the weekends with her kids. None of her family is here to witness her soon-to-be extraordinary run, but somehow that doesn't matter. For this fleeting, but eternal, moment, a slight pause before radical maneuvers, she becomes part of the mountain. Ski lifts, hokey alpine music at the resort's base, early birds stealing the first runs, and all of the other human distractions are pushed aside for a few seconds while she undergoes a transfiguration.

"Gad," she thinks to herself. "Am I really becoming an old fossil?"

Frightened at the prospect, but simultaneously giving in to the moment, our middle-age snowboarder has a brief encounter of the spiritual kind. It's real; it's penetrating and commanding her full attention. She will never, ever, quite be the same, touched to her core by the wild Earth.

She gazes out on a frosty world not focused, not seeing, yet being with it all. And, for a nanosecond a seed grows in her mind that this is what it's all about, not just ripping tight turns as a prelude to her exquisite dance. A sudden shiver flows down her body. Beauty of this winter day has become more important than the sick action of snowboarding. As if to deny the inevitable, she cranks her iPod on high to drown out these alarming thoughts and pushes off, bound for a new adventure down an old familiar slope. But, our snowboarder will never be the same having lost some innocence, and gained insights of indelible significance.

***

Much to her horror, the snowboarder and I are kindred souls. For my part, I spent a few minutes atop a winter-blasted peak with an empty mind, open to all the wilderness had to offer. In return as an old Hasidic saying suggests, sparks of their souls from rocks, fir, snow banks, and the rest of the wilderness pastiche clung to me and became a holy fire within me. For her part, she paused long enough to gaze out on a winter tableau of startling beauty, her mind momentarily free from imprisoning thoughts about the pending run and blaring tunes on the iPod. In return, sparks of their souls from gathering snow drifts, hoarfrost- encrusted trees, scintillating diamonds of ice crystals lazily floating along with a gust of wind, and sunbeams bouncing off nearby peaks clung to her, becoming a sacred fire.

These unique moments are shared by many who venture outdoors in the Southwest. It's not an activity, but exposure to and immersion in wildness that enables us to see our world with an altogether different sort of view. No matter how callous the person, and regardless of age, gender or cultural background, the more contact you have with nature the more you are predisposed to experiencing these special encounters.

Even the most with-it teenage skateboarder eventually happens on an afternoon when the softness of summer breeze, interplay of light and shadow off concrete, tortured configuration of steel stair rails, background noise, and warmth of sun combine in an ultimate way to take his breath away. It isn't being "in the zone" of skateboarding perfection; of simply doing something you really love to do, and performing almost beyond your capability. It's, as Thoreau implied, contact with the Earth. And, even our totally-with-it skateboarder, someone who is beyond cool and who disdains any allusion to spiritual thinking; even our skateboarder is touched for a few seconds with the beauty of the wild Earth.

So, no matter what the outdoor activity; rock climbing, mountain biking, jogging, walking, road biking, canoeing, rafting, windsailing, hunting, fishing, skiing, snowshoeing, backpacking, horseback riding, and so forth; eventually a moment comes when you rise above physical activity to a different level of consciousness about the Earth. Many shrug off these moments and with renewed concentration go back to their distractions. Others soundly register the experience and begin to deliberately seek more of them.

Phil Caputo experienced this transformation once on a hike in the Black Range of New Mexico. He concluded that, "Maybe you don't believe in a Creator; so put it like this: Through that window we can see the grandeur in all creation, from atoms to galaxies; we can catch at least a transforming glimpse of something bigger than ourselves, something ineffable to remind us that consumption isn't the point of being human."[4]

That moment of perfection our young skateboarder pulled off sliding along a steel rail in the glow of an ideal afternoon wasn't the product of his skilled orchestration, but rather the result of something bigger than him. Imagine; what a heretical thought – that his cool persona was overshadowed. Nonetheless, he experienced the moment and now knows differently even if he won't openly admit it

In the final analysis we are more alike than dissimilar in our outdoor pursuits and potential to enjoy these special moments. The specific activity we relish doesn't matter as much as our intention to search for these experiences and our attentiveness to the unveiling of those unique incidents. As much as our middle-aged snowboarder and teenaged skateboarder may want to deny the fact that they dwelled momentarily in a bit of transformation, reality speaks loudly to the contrary.

***

Like many others, I haven't grown to a level where every trail hiked, river rafted, or night camped in the Southwest leads to a sacred revelation. I'm always alert to a special moment, but mostly I'm attending to the simple act of walking, or hiking, or staying on a raft while trying to free my mind from details of the activity and oppressive noise I carry around in my head about life and work. Nonetheless, there is seldom a hike, river rafted, walk, bike ride or snowshoe trip which simply results in physical activity completed. At the very least I observe a new vivid yellow wildflower blossoming, sparkling sun reflecting off mountain mahogany leaves in a special way, lithe deer bouncing through a copse of aspen, or bruise colored clouds coalescing in a breathtaking formation.

It *is* important to acknowledge this mysterious life lived in an incomprehensibly beautiful universe. Our young skateboarding and middle-aged snowboarding friends (and many of their contemporaries) would probably be astounded by the notion that we should approach these special moments with reverence; that we should even go so far as to give thanks for these rich gifts.

"Hey, it was just a charming afternoon on top of Ski Santa Fe; don't read too much into it." But, I do read too much into it and I suspect that many, perhaps you, do too.

I carry various aides that are Southwest-centric to assist in walking a little more gracefully on Earth and to express gratitude for wildness and life therein. There is no one best way to express appreciation. It only matters that I do; that I dedicate a few minutes in reflection – at the top of a ski run, skateboarding down a steel rail in perfect bliss, or pausing on South Peak – to remember that there is something far bigger than me and that consumption isn't the epitome of being human.

***

Many of the little objects and brief ceremonies I have adopted have their roots in animistic beliefs traced back to Ancestral Puebloans – that nature has a soul and that a supernatural spirit animates the universe. Please understand that I'm not advocating animism. The items and rituals are simply being used to express thanksgiving for life and this wonderful world we live in. This is entirely consistent with the fact that the vast majority of religions acknowledge the sacredness of life while sanctioning rites to celebrate it.

I'm almost always carrying a treasured turquoise bear fetish by honored Zuni Pueblo carver Georgianne Quandelacy. Her work as a legacy carver is on display in Washington, D.C. Fetishes are animals carved in stone. The Zuni, an indigenous tribe of New Mexico, believe that if fetishes are properly blessed they possess the carved animal's spirit. Fetishes are meant to help people with the problems they experience in daily life.

Georgianne Quandelacy carved my bear out of a piece of turquoise that is almost one inch square by three-eighths of an inch wide. It has a red "heartline" arrow running from its mouth and incisions representing legs and feet. Bears are viewed as omnipotent in most American Indian cultures. They are treated with honor and respect because they so closely resemble people not only physically, but also in the foods they eat. In Zuni culture bears are so powerful that nobody except a member of a curing society is permitted to touch them.

Symbolically this fetish connotes power and strength. Its continued presence in my pocket rekindles knowledge that there is honor in strength and that my actions toward others and this Earth should always reflect the greatest integrity. When I am under attack from whatever source I automatically reach for the fetish seeking strength and wisdom. Bear facilitates my connection with the Earth and Great Spirit.

I incorporate this bear in purification ceremonies involving tobacco, sage, cedar, sweetgrass and corn meal. Because it is a powerful talisman, I am very careful about its location. If by chance the fetish is accidentally left on my dresser its absence is palpable and the rest of the day I'm a bit uneasy. Bear is a calming presence when all else around me goes crazy.

A dear friend gave me my first turquoise bear fetish many years ago. I carried this emblem drawing on it for sustenance. One afternoon after a long hike I came home and pulled everything out of my pockets in order to change clothes. The last thing I pulled out was this bear. It slipped from my grasp and shattered to pieces on our kitchen's tile floor. I stood there dumbfounded. Here was a terrible loss; however, I didn't quite understand the bigger picture. I just didn't get it. This was an omen of the worst kind.

That night a beloved brother, a steadfast friend, died. The wretched phone call about his death came the next morning following the now departed bear spirit. Coincidence? I don't think so.

Reaching into my daypack a plastic pouch of American Spirit® brand organic shredded tobacco pops out. Some American Indians believe that tobacco was the first gift to indigenous people from the Creator. Therefore remarkable spiritual significance is attributed to this plant. Used predominately for ceremonial purposes, tobacco is treated as sacred medicine. By smoking tobacco in pipes or making an offering of tobacco a connection is made to the Great Spirit.

For me tobacco presents a fitting offering of gratitude. By sharing a pinch of tobacco, I am indicating thankfulness for my life and all of the blessings bestowed on me. Tobacco offerings also acknowledge appreciation for our Earth and all of creation.

Reaching further down into the pack my fingers grasp a plastic bag containing a butane lighter and sage bundle. Many cultures associate sage with wisdom and consequently sage is widely incorporated in ceremonial, culinary and medicinal applications. Like tobacco, sage is a gift imbued with the ability to purify or to drive away evil. Purification accompanies the burning of sage and the smoke's aromatic scent is quite memorable.

Before meditating or praying it is appropriate to cleanse or purify myself by burning sage, also known as smudging. This helps clear away evil contamination that might interfere with the connection I am seeking to achieve. I seem to walk through a world that is ripe with evil presence. By smudging I cleanse myself of both intentional and unintentional contamination. Smudging also displays respect. Symbolically it is little different than showering or bathing before you visit someone. In this sense smudging is an overt act of reverence.

Sometimes the plastic bag also (or alternatively) contains a braided strand of sweetgrass or pouch of cedar. Sweetgrass is a long reed that can be woven together to form a slender bundle. Indians use sweetgrass to purify, to send prayers, and to call in good spirits. Cedar bark, leaves and berries are also integrated in many ceremonies like sage and sweetgrass.

On extraordinarily special occasions I can reach down into the daypack and pull out a brilliant red linen cloth containing an eagle feather. The feather belongs to a Native brother. It's not mine in the sense that dominant Western culture thinks of things as possessions. I'm only caring for the feather in view of his express instructions to use it in ceremonial purposes and to pass it on to others at the right time. Eagles are very powerful winged-ones, or beings, in American Indian beliefs. The feather is used to fan sage, sweetgrass and cedar smoke during purification and to uplift prayers.

On other unique occasions a leather pouch of corn pollen, ground turquoise, abalone shell and a small fetish can be found in the bottom of my daypack. This ceremonial blend is used for blessings, thanksgiving, purification and protection. The fetish is nourished by the mixture thus increasing its power and sacred quality.

Many of the best things in life cost nothing or very little. In many respects this is certainly true if your goal is to create a medicine bundle. The contents of a medicine bundle include precious items related to a person's spiritual life. In some cases, such as animistic believers who attribute spiritual qualities to inanimate objects, medicine bundles may contain items that are considered holy. Thus, small pieces of special rocks, seeds, botanicals, feathers, bones, hair, cones, teeth or claws, and fur may find their way into medicine bundles.

My medicine bundle incorporates a specific mixture of botanicals: bearberry, spearmint, red willow bark, organic tobacco, and sage. These ingredients are bought in bulk, ground as necessary and mixed together in my own special concoction. Each constituent element holds some personal meaning unique to me. The Internet is a fruitful source for accessing reliable suppliers of natural plant products. Remember most botanicals are hand collected, so don't be surprised by attendant high prices.

Organic tobacco is readily available at merchants who retail cigarette products. Throughout Indian country American Spirit® brand pouch tobacco is widely obtainable. However, don't fall into the trap of romantically thinking about American Spirit as a small Native American enterprise. The firm was established in 1982 by Santa Fe Natural Tobacco Company. In 2002 it was sold to Reynolds America and now functions as an independent subsidiary of that corporate giant.

American Spirit markets four pouch tobaccos that might be incorporated within a medicine bundle: Original Blend (blue package); U.S. Grown (royal blue package); Organic Blend (maroon package); and, Pow-Wow Blend (purple package). The company claims that their tobacco products are 100% free of additives. Thus, customers can acquire from American Spirit not only organically grown tobacco (at a higher price) or the less expensive, but untainted, Original and Organic Blends. These distinctions may have particular importance to those who wish to incorporate only the purest tobacco in their spiritual ceremonies.

Beyond natural plant products, the Web is also a very convenient means for accessing other emblems, totems and objects to be incorporated within medicine bundles. Carved stone fetishes, bone whistles, quartz, cedar, sweetgrass, and similar products can also be found on the Internet.

Once the desired items have been acquired they can be carried in handmade leather pouches or festive handkerchiefs. Place the objects squarely in the middle of a handkerchief. Pull two corners together and tie them; then pull together the remaining two corners and tie them. Your medicine bundle is set to go.

Some prefer to carry all of these ceremonial items in an ornamental medicine bundle out of respect for their sacredness. I should too. But because they are used almost daily and travel in a daypack or backpack in which they are vulnerable to jostling and getting wet I rationalize that these ceremonial items can be carried in ordinary plastic bags. However, for really special occasions these objects are placed together in a medicine bundle fashioned out of a red bandana.

***

Given these ceremonial items, how do I use them? Let's take a quick hike. Each spring a little miracle unfolds on the west face of the Sandia Mountains as runoff percolates through cold blue spruce, immense ponderosa pines and scattered junipers. It's too early for Fendler bushes to share their luxuriance of flower and scent, but not too soon for lush green grass to grow optimistically on south-facing slopes and in rocky ravines receiving ample sunlight. The bounty of previous winter flows in periodic, or seasonal, streams.

Departing Pino Trail through a grove of cinnamon-barked ponderosa pine reeking of vanilla, across a velvety hushed carpet of needles bouncing like a waterbed, I'm seeking a bit of serenity in a glen that seldom sees human visitors. With fading soft afternoon light, night's chill descends upon a grotto ensconced in shade from branches of fir, pine and mountain mahogany. Sun radiates down upon a modest stream flowing through this ravine.

The unforgettably gentle and soothing sound of mountain water rises above raucous calls of jays. Caressing a slick white-gray granite boulder, this stream will steal your heart if you're not careful.

Having climbed almost 1,500 feet over 3 miles perspiration is dribbling off my forehead. The very first thing I do is catch my breath and take on a healthy dose of water. The last hundred yards toward this ponderosa bowl I've been acutely aware of my surroundings. Is anyone else near this basin? Can I head off-trail without anyone getting nosey and following me to this secret spot? How intensely is the sun shining and how cold is the temperature under the towering trees? Do I have to be careful about fire? Is there too much wind to consider lighting a sage bundle?

Answers to these questions come quickly for most trails. The idea is to find a spot for reflection, meditation or prayer – there's no ceremonial kiva waiting trailside. I wind down through the needle-strewn bowl following the path of least resistance – the path of flowing water. Almost tip-toeing to keep from being heard, I've gone to ground in hope of reaching this secret little alcove undetected. It's not that I'm doing anything wrong; in fact I'm doing everything right. Sometimes you don't want to share intensely personal things with strangers. Or, you simply want to luxuriate in being alone so that you can free your mind from the overwhelming presence of others. It's all about creating the right mood, spell or milieu that is impossible to form in another's presence.

Almost crawling beneath some of the over-hanging braches I suddenly reach the stream. This crystal clear rivulet of snowmelt is bouncing over small boulders and singing a merry tune. Directly north of the stream is a relatively barren decomposed granite hillside. It receives a full measure of sun and its lack of foliage is in sharp contrast to the hillside directly south. The line of disconformity couldn't be sharper. On one side are fir and big ponderosa pine — trees that need water and relief from the heat; on the other side are piñon pine, juniper and mountain mahogany — foliage that can take an added wallop of heat.

Bear fetish, tobacco packet, sage bundle and lighter are extricated from the pack. Standing, facing east, bear is placed at my feet. Using a butane cigar lighter (a superior flame to a normal cigarette lighter) the sage bundle is lit while blowing on it to ensure healthy, dense smoke. A hand cups around the bundle if it's too windy. Holding the smoldering bundle up to the east, thanks are expressed for the day.

Personal preferences and petitions vary, but sending prayers to the four directions (holding the burning sage high to the sky) might follow these suggestions:

> To the Spirit that Moves in all Things (East)
> To the Creator (South)
> To the Great Spirit (West)
> To the Mysterious One (North)
> Mitakuye Oyasin or All My Relations (East)
>
> To the Spring Light (East)
> To the Summer Rain (South)
> To the Fall Wind (West)
> To the Winter Snows (North)
> Mitakuye Oyasin or All My Relations (East)
>
> To the Winged Ones (East)
> To the Swimming and Crawling Ones (South)
> To the Four Leggeds and Two Leggeds (West)

To the Standing Ones (i.e., trees and bushes) (North)
Mitakuye Oyasin or All My Relations (East)

The ritual may stop after only one turn in honoring the sacred four directions or it may continue through three or more rounds. Some honor six sacred directions – east, south, west and north as well as up to the sky and down to the Earth.

Having expressed thanksgiving in four directions, smoke from smoldering sage is wafted over and around my head, around my heart and midsection, and finally around my legs and feet in seeking purification. Blowing on the sage to reenergize, it's laid next to bear and away from any combustible material.

From the tobacco pouch a heaping pinch of tobacco is held up to the east. Then, a smattering of tobacco is offered to the remaining directions giving thanks concerning blessings, invoking prayers for those who need healing and protection, or petitioning for guidance, strength, patience, energy, or any other desired quality as the case may be. I end up facing east and meditating until done.

That's it in a nutshell. It's an illustrative example of my ritual and the way I express thanksgiving while connecting with the Creator and Earth. But, I always try to make certain I'm not going through a ritual just to go through a ritual. If I sense that going through the motions is about to occur, or occurring, then I immediately stop and wait for the next day, the next connection.

***

Each person must make important decisions about the ceremonies they use when celebrating their life on Earth. Ritual(s) they practice and items incorporated in their celebrations are very personal. To me what's vitally important is that in the course of our lives we dedicate moments in reflection and thanksgiving for life itself, our planet, the universe and the Creator.

For our middle-age snowboarder, honoring the Earth may simply mean that on every trip to the mountains she intentionally stops during the heart of one run in a screening stand of fir. She might only spend a few moments in silence, or bow her head and express prayers. She could pull out a pouch of tobacco and sprinkle some to the wind offering this gift back to the Earth. She could light a sage bundle and seek purification. What matters is that in her own fashion and celebration of her choosing she uplifts what it means to be human and to connect with nature; or in Thoreau's words, to have contact.

For our teenage skateboarder, celebrating the Earth may mean that he seeks a quiet moment on the edge of frenetic action to contemplate a growing awareness about life and how he fits in. He continues to fulfill his passion for skateboarding but he also begins cultivating an appreciation for the beauty of how others orchestrate their bodies, defy gravity, assemble inspiring movements, and go about the give-and-take with other young people at passionate play. Maybe, just maybe, the next time it all comes together and when he is "in the zone" that seed will grow a bit bigger and he will reflect on this gloriousness of life in uncommon moments.

For me, those sublime moments on top of snow-covered South Peak when I was exhausted and freezing to death would have been made better by a simple act of reverence. I was too caught up with me, my semi-heroic achievement and getting back to safety to think about spending a few seconds in expressing gratitude. Even in the face of overwhelming beauty and Sandia Peak's spirit of place, I focused on me. How much better that moment on top of the world would have been if I simply had stopped to say a word of thanks for the magic of the Sandias.

Each river rafted, mile of road biked, trail hiked, campsite enjoyed, lane walked or other outdoor activity pursued in the Southwest offers a possibility for spiritual reflection and thanksgiving. Some with an extra helping of braggadocio may summarily dismiss the thought that we should offer thanksgivings to the Creator or honor the Earth. Sadly, they are already essentially dead. Others may want to take issue with my ceremony and the items used in celebration. They are missing the fundamentally bigger idea. Still others may object vehemently because such ritual is not consistent with rituals of their faith or religion. They have yet to expand their minds and to open their hearts to the obvious.

Everyone has the capacity within them to recognize and express appreciation for life and the world in which so much other life exists. Are we too wrapped up with our fancy latté's, electronic gadgets, gas guzzling cars, insipid media, and lives lived shallowly to acknowledge the obvious? As Phil Caputo suggests, through the window of our Earth – creation – we catch a glimpse of something bigger than consumption. We need to turn frequently to that window to catch a glimpse of what's really important in the course of living our lives.

Pervasive
Wildness

A guttural croak
echoes across the canyon.

Raven greets the dawn.

TERRYE BULLERS

7

Kindred Spirits

High teens, maybe a blazing 20 degrees under the feeble sun; heavy frost blankets the ground like sweet vanilla icing on a chocolate cake. It's as though all semblance of color was sucked out of these parched-dry grasses and forlorn bushes. Even an occasional cement gray juniper adding dimension to otherwise stark hills has shaded to translucent white, huddling until delicate sunny rays penetrate surrounding vertical coulees and draws flowing down the mountainside.

Quiet smothers this brittle air while three regal ladies, probably two sisters with a yearling, gallop at a high lope up a sage-infested ridge. They didn't expect anyone coming down the mountain at this early hour. Deeply startled, their ears convey the focused terror of vulnerable prey at sensitive alert – stiffly erect, bent slightly forward and swiveling occasionally to detect what else they missed when their muzzles were buried in a fortuitous clump of fresh grass. Most of the few feeble patches of browse in these hills were stripped clean by the trio several weeks ago; they're hungry to say the least.

Their bouncing prance is so graceful and paradoxically so powerful. I'm insanely jealous of their ability to glide at full throttle up a devilishly vertical incline that would have me screaming for air, bent in half, hands on hips, face between my legs and ready to dial 911 if I bothered to carry a phone. Imagine covering 10+ feet at a hop and never giving a second thought to it. How huge do lungs have to be in order to accomplish that remarkable feat?

Once these deer reach the same contour on which I'm standing, they back off a pace or two. They hate having any sort of life form above them, particularly humans. As their pace becomes a bit more measured rather than frantic and they rise above me, beauty of this moment sweeps down. Coats as thick as a high-end Patagonia retro pile jacket bristle in the cold. Beneath generous insulation taut bodies ripple with muscle. Two show promising perpetuation of the species by their swollen bellies – there'll be fawns come spring.

Half-light of early dawn radiates as a golden-mustard backdrop illuminating their features and effortless scramble toward safety. All thoughts empty from my mind like a railroad car dropping a load of burnt-yellow feed corn. How many zillion deer have I seen over the years? On this trail? The number must be astronomical, but the experience is somehow never diminished. Each and every encounter sparkles with fascination and, at this winter season, admiration that they can survive under these less than hospitable arctic conditions with so little nurturing.

On second thought; survival isn't quite what commandeers my respect.

It isn't their tenacity to thrive despite unimaginable circumstances that snaps me to attention. Everything that my vision embraces can claim a similar dedication to surviving on this mountain. That's not what's so special here.

It's an intersection with kindred spirits that has me marveling at this exceptionally powerful moment.

Confident of their superior position now 100 feet above me; intuitively reading my intentions; each doe gradually grinds to a halt and looks my way. What are they thinking?

"Where the hell did this guy come from?"

"I was just beginning to enjoy that clump of grass until this stupid bastard came along."

"Wow!! Was it ever cold down in that ravine."

"Why's he staring at us?"

"Is there never any end to these two-leggeds? They're proliferating like rabbits and hogging all of the choice grazing sites."

Perhaps I'm anthropomorphizing a bit too much...or, am I?

Who know what runs through the minds of animals? As far as I'm concerned it doesn't really matter whether I or anyone else can read their precise thoughts. Unequivocally I know this: *their presence uplifts my life and fills my heart with joy.*

The Southwest's bounty of wildlife is truly a gracious gift and its vast wilderness areas provide sustenance for all types of critters. Near-wilderness areas at the edge of cities and towns often teem with life. That's all part of the equation for this region. Those who live here long enough sometimes break beyond the stranglehold of civilization to see this life – these kindred spirits – as more than convenient targets in the sights of powerful rifles.

Abundant wildlife is a distinctive characteristic of the Southwest and, to me, the personification of wildness. But, it isn't just the signature presence of animals in this region that embodies wildness; it's the everyday opportunity to be reminded that wilderness is inexorably tied to the heritage of human life in these parts.

It is precisely wilderness and wildlife that sustained ancient civilizations in the Southwest. Nomadic tribes counted on the land and creatures it nourished for their sustenance. Where life flourished, the Anasazi also prospered. When wildlife evaporated Native American populations relied more heavily on agriculture – until drought sapped even these food sources.

Kindred spirits, such as these deer, inexorably bind me to those who went before – humans *and* animals. Did predecessors of these does enable an Anasazi family to make it through a rough winter? Or, was this morning's theater on the grace of four-leggeds played out centuries earlier for a tribal member out gathering firewood? I choose to believe that the indigenous ones who preceded me not only valued deer as a food source, but also as a fundamental manifestation of inherent beauty surrounding them.

***

These three ladies strike a connection in my mind with last week's venture to the Bosque del Apache National Wildlife Refuge in New Mexico. I was desperately searching for a single remaining whooping crane (Grus americana) among thousands of Sandhill cranes (Grus canadensis) littered like spilled gray pebbles on a tan shag carpet of pasture. Creeping along the refuge's gravel road my attention was focused on the field, not on navigating this crude road. I looked up just in time to see five svelte deer shuffle out of head-high willows moving east toward greener pastures.

Whatever prompted me to look up at that very moment remains a mystery. But, I'm thankful nonetheless. My car slid to a halt with gravel squirting out beneath the tires leaving me to enjoy the regal beauty of deer that were supremely confident about their place in the scheme of things – a herd that wasn't about to be rushed. They picked their way across the road and vanished in dense tamarisk. Here one minute; gone the next.

Rather than continue driving I shut off the motor and climbed out. Quiet buffeted my ears with a discernible backdrop of muted bird calls. Sun caressed my cheeks while a brisk breeze shot icy arrows at me. Scanning the field with binoculars I was looking for a diminutive patch of white floating in a sea of dirty gray. This particular field was approximately one-quarter mile wide by one-half mile long. It was filled with thousands of cranes squawking and croaking – a constant din that fed my soul.

Odds of spotting a whooper had diminished over the years. The Bosque del Apache once sustained a handful of birds. Yet, each year the number dropped. Now in early winter, only one whooper had been sighted according to a roadside tally at the refuge's entrance gate. Imagine trying to find that needle in a haystack. Already 8,000 Sandhills had been counted and twice as many would eventually end up at the refuge before the season ended.

One bird in 8,000. Was that too much to ask for?

One of the rarest birds in North America.

An icon of wildness.

The Bosque del Apache was created in the late 1930's. An ingenious design allows the refuge to draw water from the Rio Grande via a system of canals or acequias. Corn and alfalfa are grown during spring and summer. In winter the fields are flooded to create ideal bird habitat; enough crops are left for forage.

Results have been spectacular. In the first year 17 Sandhill cranes were enticed to the refuge. Sixty years later more than 18,000 Sandhill cranes called the Bosque home for the winter. However, the cranes aren't alone. Hundreds of Canada geese have found winter shelter in New Mexico as well as some 15,000 snow geese and over 38,000 ducks. And, where there are ducks, raptors congregate including bald and golden eagles, kestrels, peregrine falcons, goshawks, northern harriers and ubiquitous redtail hawks. Meanwhile, pheasants, quail and doves thrive in the fields.

And then there are the whoopers.

In 1975 biologists attempted to reintroduce whooping cranes in the Bosque by substituting whooper eggs for Sandhill eggs within nests located in Idaho. More than a dozen whooping cranes hatched and followed Sandhill parents south to the Bosque to over-winter. Things looked promising and it appeared as though biologists would be able to gradually increase the number of whooping cranes from a low point of 21 in 1941.

Unfortunately the Sandhill cranes were unable to teach their fledglings the intricate courting rituals associated with whoopers. There was no way to perpetuate the species. In one case a cross between a Sandhill crane and whooping crane was observed in the refuge – others have alternatively suggested that it was an albino Sandhill. But, that was it. Progressively the whooping cranes succumbed to hazards all birds face leaving the refuge resulting in a decreasing number each year. Although the Bosque population dried up, other efforts to grow whooper populations have been more successful with almost 400 birds estimated to exist in the wild.

One of the survivors was out there somewhere in an ocean of feathers. It only takes *one* to sparkle and light up your life.

Snow white, whooping cranes stand 5 feet tall and weigh some 14-17 pounds with males larger than females. They have a wingspan of nearly 8 feet. Large size isn't their sole distinguishing characteristic — a brilliant crimson crown and jet-black wingtips stand out against the white plumage.

Half an hour of concentrated scanning turned up nothing.

I moved to the next field that was rife with snow geese. A few hundred Sandhills are hanging out in a northwest corner as far from the road as possible.

Binoculars at hand I focus on this renegade band of misfits who choose to live at the edge. I sweep left-to-right and back-to-front with the field glasses.

No luck.

A goshawk rockets pass — anxious geese-alarm-cries float over the field.

One last glance before leaving turns the trick. Two Sandhills slowly move away from each other as if the sea was parting and there behind them is a formerly hidden whooper. Its stately strut is immediately recognizable. Size a dead give-away. More than this, the bird's crown flashes in dazzling red. I lock onto one of the rarest birds in North America for the remainder of an hour.

Just a bird; just a moment of unparalleled wildness.

An epitome of rarity.

This single, solitary bird is special to say the least.

But it isn't this surviving whooping crane that makes the moment. It is recognition that so many others — cranes, ducks,

geese, raptors, songbirds – are right before my eyes. And surrounding them is a web of other life – deer, coyotes, bear, snakes
and the rest of the mosaic that is the Bosque.

For a brief, but poignant, moment we share life and each
other's company.

***

Birds.

Birds by the thousands.

Birds of every shape, size, color, wingspan, beak, habitat
preference, song and call. Each one is completely different, yet
in many respects they all are the same.

Birds.

They personify the Southwest's wildness and symbolize a
heritage; an intimate relationship between humans and animals.
The ancient ones enjoyed a fulfilling connection with wildlife
that acknowledged the mystery of life. They too were fascinated
by the diverse types of birds; their sizes, shapes and colors.

Like many I've been romanced to this region by charismatic
mammals – bears, wolves, elk, moose and bison in the far northern reaches. However, despite their copious presence and imprint on Southwest life, birds are ultimately the ones who touch
us every day.

Birds.

Drive through the intermingling high plains and Chihuahuan
desert northeast of Roswell, New Mexico where the Bitter Lake
National Wildlife Refuge reposes alongside the Pecos River and
you better be watching the road. Snooze a little because of mo-
notony from chamisa filled flats and brushy river bottomlands
– that's a perfect recipe for not only running off the road, but

also missing out on a flock of spellbinding chukars (Alectoris chukar).

Chukars are part of the partridge species brought to North America as game birds; the Anasazi would have coveted their taste. Chukars thrive in desert canyon/plateau country such as that of eastern New Mexico where puddles of the Pecos branch off this meandering river. It's easy to mistake chukar for quail, but look for bold black barred flanks and a cream colored throat offset by a black outline and signature red beak. Like quail, you'll see chukhars in small groups sweeping over the desert brush as they devour insects and seeds.

Their plumage would have astounded the ancient ones.

Birds.

We lived in the North Valley of Albuquerque, a bucolic section of the city along the muddy Rio Grande River. Small ranches, outlandishly tasteful as well as tasteless trophy homes, modest suburban enclaves and hovels nestle cheek by ruddy jowl along shady lanes of luminescent cottonwoods and elms. Acequias, or earthen water canals, radiate from the mother river spreading life to verdant green alfalfa fields, red and golden delicious apple trees, and ubiquitous chilé crops. Horses and horse flies abound lending a distinct farmland character to surrounding bohemian neighborhoods.

Fowl are plentiful whether boisterous roosters calling in pre-dawn hours, raucous blue jays darting through the canopy, hummingbirds trolling for trumpet vines, gawky Sandhill cranes, iridescent mallards and rotund Canadian geese commandeering fields during winter, or ever-present crows and ravens ruling the treetops. They're attracted by the Rio Grande's bosque, a mixture of cottonwood trees and native vegetation such as four-wing salt bush, chamisa and Apache plume. Birds also shelter in tamarisk and Russian olive trees that are striving to dominate the indigenous ecosystem.

Virtually every morning when leaving home we ran smack into an enormous flock of Guinea fowl (Numida meleagris) on a nearby street. My wife would hum a short trumpeting prelude and ceremoniously announce, "There's the faculty." I worked at the local university and she was doing her best to cheer me up before I spent another day trying to toil with them.

Our days were a little richer, a little lighter, for seeing Guinea fowl on the loose, for their inability to be intimidated by cars as they saunter across the street, and for their awful ungainly ugliness; faces only Guinea hens could love.

They chose to roost together in a towering ponderosa pine tree in front of a house whose yard was constantly littered with copious droppings. Our community flock of guinea fowl spent each night high in the tree defecating on those lower in the pecking order; a similarity to faculty that did not go unnoticed. They perched throughout the pine's branches feeling a measure of safety in a ruthless world, aloof in their ponderosa tower

Descending in morning they first soaked up sunny warmth on the black asphalt street preening and fluffing to overcome night's chill. Then they migrated across the road to a neighboring house with its expansive lawn. There the guinea fowl hunted and pecked for little tidbits; morsels before heading out for serious foraging. An orange tabby crouched smack dab in the middle of the lawn hoping for an opportunity to catch one off guard, but the Guineas never paid it any mind. They had it surrounded thirty-to-one and the cat knew from hideous experience what would happen if it tried to get nasty.

All appeared to be well and good in the life of the North Valley's Guinea fowl. There's apparently lots of food to eat as their population continued to grow slowly and the flock divided. The most threatening predators were stealthy coyotes, brazen cats, aggressive dogs and unconscionable cars, but these hazards were safely managed by the large number of observant eyes. Truly horrendous weather seldom descended on the tranquil habitat. With sufficient water in the acequias, life was good.

But, there was just one little rub, and here is where the parable of the Guinea fowl has remarkable congruence with university faculty. For whatever reason, Guinea fowl cannot leave each other alone. If one is pecking in the grass for a tasty morsel, then two others will immediately rush over to steal its treat, leaving that poor individual battered and bruised.

If another Guinea fowl has the misfortune of innocently glancing in another's direction; this glance will detonate an explosive retaliation completely out-of-proportion with the offense. It is attacked belligerently by the offended counterpart. Punishment usually consists of being chased for several yards before falling victim to a bout of vicious pecking.

In short, Guinea fowl just can't get along. They are never satisfied. They want what the others have. They bully and intimidate to get their way. They fight and connive until they win a pyrrhic victory. And, on obtaining whatever it is that they want, Guinea fowl are grossly dissatisfied.

I learned a lot about university faculty simply by watching what many would conclude is just a bunch of birds. I credit Guinea fowl with any modicum of success I might have achieved in my job.

Birds.

Head over to Chase Hardware in the quaint village of Los Ranchos de Albuquerque to pick up a bit of Elmer's glue and what happens? A quarter-mile from the house I screech to a halt while a half-a-dozen mallards (Anas platyrhynchos) waddle across the road. Folks in this neighborhood are generally alert for the promenade as the ducks go from acequia to field across the blacktop. But every once in a while you come upon a little carnage where a driver thought one thing and a determined duck thought another.

Resident coyotes clean up the street at night, grateful that they don't have to work very hard for a convenient meal.

Waddling their fat little bodies that average 2.5 pounds toward some unknown bliss on the other side, they step tentatively off the roadside and almost flop on their heads before regaining equilibrium. Then, it's the decision of a lifetime, or so you'd think given how much they deliberate on whether to continue or not. They rock back-and-forth from beak to tail; looking like they'll tumble over any second. Orange legs and webbed feet post-hole the ducks toward their Nirvana.

Most of the mallard hens know what they want and where they want to go. The drakes follow obediently until a car approaches. Then they're not so certain. In other cases, half of the troop will migrate to the other side leaving the remaining half picking their way through shrubbery. Then someone lets out an alarm cry.

Wwwwhhhaaacckkkkk.

Wwwhhaaaaaaaaaaaaccckkkk.

Wwwhhaacckkkkkk.

Mostly they stop dead still; gawking this way and that.

Dark eyes strain to see the aggravating factor. Heads swivel with orange-yellow bills carving semi-circles in the air.

"What's going on?"

"Do I continue?"

If the cry keeps up and they can't make up their minds it only takes one flapping upward in escape to set off the entire bunch. A flurry of wings and they all launch skyward, away from what they'll never know. Pandemonium ensues while each seeks a clear trajectory. There's safety in the air.

Half a dozen feathers gradually float to earth after the flock has risen above the trees, squawking and honking their disapproval — indignant over being disrupted from their peaceful lives.

Drive another quarter mile and I may run into a baker's dozen of Canada geese (Branta Canadensis), the flock strung out in file heading toward a side street and ultimately the river. Last year was a great year for geese as this clutch with ten young of the year attests.

Canada geese don't take a lot of guff. If you're a dog or person on foot, watch out. These birds have heft, weighing anywhere from 4-10 pounds depending on which of the 11 subspecies is present. With a wingspan of 4-5 feet, it's an intimidating sight when those wings open in a display of aggression. They'd sooner challenge your presence then give ground. However, like the mallards they have difficulty making up their minds about whether to fight or flee.

When protecting goslings, Canada geese will vehemently stand their ground and even take the offensive by coming at you with neck stretched and mouth hissing. In dire circumstances, they'll make a run at you while doing all of the above and wildly flapping their wings. After having gotten bitten on the butt during one of these displays, our dog is very careful. She still thinks she can bluff chase them, but it doesn't take much for her to tuck tail and run if the tables turn.

Count on an aggressive and riotously noisy display of first-rate honking coming from this second largest species of water-fowl. Black necks stretch and undulate while black beaks with white cheeks poke menacingly, grabbing for a vulnerable pound of flesh.

And watch where you step. By comparison, pigeons have been maligned for their proclivity to defecate everywhere. After a flock of geese goes over your lawn looking for a morsel or two they will have conveniently left a nice organic fertilizer. Problem is they don't discriminate between concrete sidewalks or patios and the grass. I'm forever cleaning geese crap off my soles.

Despite these dysfunctional characteristics I love to watch geese – whether Canada or snow geese. They are bold companions who rule the roost. It's great fun to see their tails protruding straight-up in the air as they tip forward trying to glean feed off the bottom of a pond. Their bold and vigorous honking is a melancholy reminder of a change in seasons as they fly in vee-formations. And who isn't charmed by a brood of goslings becoming acquainted to swimming, feet paddling like mad to keep up with parents?

One person's pleasure is another's pain. That admonition is especially true concerning the ever-adaptive Canada goose.

Many cities and towns have discovered the appearance of a new subspecies – metro geese. Increasingly common are Canada geese that don't migrate; they reside full-time in urban and sub-urban settings. Some citizens relish this change in migratory patterns. It enables access to geese year-round. Other residents are flummoxed by pesky geese that rule the roost all year, sometimes chasing off other migratory birds.

Much of the problem is created by humans. We cultivate large grassy areas that shout like Madison Avenue's best advertising agencies about hospitable habitat. Our homes, commercial areas and streets as well as golf courses are covered in grass. This offers perfect forage for geese and affords them a very secure environment since they typically have unblocked 360 degree views. It's difficult for natural predators like foxes or coyotes, feral dogs or domesticated hounds to attack geese since they are surrounded by vast open areas in parks and other grass-covered landscapes. Hundreds of eyes keeping watch make for a very safe crib.

Add to this favorable habitat, farms surrounding cities, and the enticement is complete. Geese can forage in suburban and rural areas during the day and then commute back to the safety of the city at dusk. Throw in a large number of ponds or reservoirs with a river or two and geese have a faultless safe haven. Dependency is compounded by the generous, but misguided, attempts of people to supplement their diets with grain and bread. What more could a goose ask for – a free meal-ticket, places to bathe and preen, and secure surroundings for rest?

Geese are highly sociable animals so when they find a good thing, it's not uncommon for them to spread the delightful news. That's when too much of a good thing becomes abused. This is precisely the same problem that occurs in the wild. For example, snow geese (Chen caerulescens) have proliferated so substantially, in part due to lower mortality when over-wintering down south, that they exceed the capacity of arctic tundra to support feeding. Arctic vegetation can't recover quickly enough due to the short growing season. In turn this stresses all animals that are dependent on this vegetation.

Geese may have ownership of our cities and towns, but mountain bluebirds (Sialia currucoides) and western bluebirds (Sialia Mexicana) rule the high country. There is no more stunning experience than being swarmed by vivid blue bodies darting like colorful stones being flung from a slingshot as they madly rush from a craggy old Rocky Mountain juniper to a pine.

One ounce of power-packed life — that's the average weight of a 6-7 inch long mountain or western bluebird.

One ounce!

Bluebirds are members of the thrush family — the same family as robins. Like robins their diet is primarily animal in nature — miscellaneous bees, ants, wasps, flies, grasshoppers, beetles and crickets — supplemented by vegetable material — elderberries, sumac seeds, hackberries, and ubiquitous juniper or cedar berries

Coloring differentiates mountain and western bluebirds. Males of the mountain species are completely sky-blue shading from pale beneath to darker on top, although they may have a tinge of rufous coloring in their breast and throat, especially in winter. Females are duller, predominantly gray-blue with a brownish tinge on their breasts, much like western bluebirds, but lighter. Mountain bluebird bills are slim and black. Western bluebirds are stockier both in their bills and shorter wings. Male western bluebirds are deeper blue with very reddish chests, chestnut in color and flowing back on their scapulars (shoulder feathers).

Mountain bluebirds are generally found at higher elevations in the Four Corners. They nest in natural cavities and crevices, lining these sites with grass, twigs, hair, feathers, seeds and needles. They lay 5-6 eggs and incubate them over a two week period. Three weeks later the young are ready to be fledged.

Mountain bluebirds begin to migrate to the south well before western bluebirds begin migration. Both are destined for the southern United States as well as deep into central Mexico. Like other bird species there always are exceptions to the rule. Some northern mountain bluebirds have been observed in Alaska.

All bluebirds are stunning fliers and charming splotches of color. Look for them wending their way north in spring through the Four Corners.

Birds.

If you want to see them, often you have to make the effort to look for them. Such is the case for many of the raptors such as eagles or ospreys. But the search pays off. Peregrine falcons slicing above the Sandia Mountains still take the concept of flying to new levels whenever I see them.

Birds.

Say that word to most people and they think, "So what?" Wax eloquent about birds and many people tend to pigeon-hole you as a birder — some nerdy geek that goes around with a bad greasy hair-do, oversized binoculars, archaic clothing, buckteeth and a plastic pocket-protector housing a small writing tablet and pen.

Birds.

The more I ignored them the more they knocked on the doorway to my mind. For much of my life my affections were set on the big mammals. I wanted to run with buffalo, smash through bushes like bears and snort like elk. Howling wolves haunted my dreams as I schemed how to watch a pack take down a feeble old moose. I didn't have time to think about ounces of bone, diminutive bills, flesh and feathers. Give me the top of the food chain, not something that I can see almost every day.

In time I mellowed. *I began to see the variety of our avian friends as a barometer of wildness.* The higher the variety of birds, the wilder a place became. There were adjustments to be made in this formula — higher elevations are less hospitable and attract less birdlife. But, it was the rarity of those birds that vetted the land's wildness.

***

Birds.

The ancient ones revered them.

Eagles, owls, hawks, bluebirds, ducks, cranes, woodpeckers, hummingbirds, ducks, ravens, crows and other avian guests offered brightly colored feathers to adorn robes, blankets, clothing and ceremonial wares among the Anasazi. Artifacts from throughout the Four Corners attest to the use of feathers for decorating clothing or jewelry. Not surprising, archeological evidence also suggests that it was common practice to keep captive birds. Creating a reliable source of feathers seems to explain the primary motivation for bird captivity. However there appears to be some evidence that birds, such as turkeys, were domesticated both for feathers and food.

Contemporary Pueblo residents continue to gather bird feathers for ceremonial purposes. In an article published during 1999 in *Conservation Biology*, Robert V. Taylor and Stephen Albert of the University of New Mexico reported from interviews of 98 Zunis engaged in non-game bird hunting that most of this activity related to cultural purposes.[5] In fact five bird species explained 77% of all birds taken including bluebirds, woodpeckers, flickers, jays and kestrels with the two most heavily hunted species accounting for more than 10,000 birds collected.

Seven hundred years ago people throughout the Four Corners had access to parrots and other colorful avian captives brought up from Mexico and possibly Central America. Scarlet macaw feathers appeared to have played a prominent ceremonial role.

Prayer feathers (bundles and fans) fashioned from macaws continue to be made by indigenous people in the Southwest and Mexico.

Craig Childs is a self-trained naturalist who has studied the Anasazi and explored Native American ruins throughout the Southwest. In his book *House of Rain* Childs ponders the role of birds in Chacoan society.[6] He cites researcher Kathy Roler Durand's work investigating bird use in the post-Chaco period. Childs notes that bird use was very prevalent at Chaco where feathers are believed to have adorned priests' robes and other ceremonial (e.g., burial clothing) items. As Chaco declined it is believed that traffic in birds began to subside. Roler Durand's research supports the exact opposite conclusion. She notes that bird use after Chaco's decline *skyrocketed*.

Birds could be the key indicator variable, or flag, to changes in ritual practices among Anasazi in the Southwest. The precise nature of these practices is open to speculation. However, remains from Salmon Ruins in New Mexico revealed a turkey and macaw buried together. Both of these birds were associated with human sacrifice in Mesoamerica which may have implications for religious rites in the Southwest. Controversy regarding what religious ceremonies transpired at Chaco and other prominent Southwestern communities may likely never be solved. At the very least all signs suggest that birds held a special place among the Anasazi.

***

Birds.

They fill wildness with life.

Walking alongside the Pine River in Colorado dazzling light of a late summer's day suddenly transforms swift flowing water into an infinite blanket of sparkling reflections. A river so pure and crystalline, the liquid seems to be totally transparent. Round cobblestones pave meandering portions of this streambed in a perfectly blended mixture – orange, white, gold, brown and gray. It's as though I have never truly seen a river. Crystal clear Pine River calls invitingly to sample its refreshing waters, waters that can surely slake any thirst. Gazing upon a stream with lights, a silent forest plays humble companion to the scene.

Huge fir trees shade surrounding sun dappled vegetation and spongy emerald forest floor. A compelling crisp scent of raw forest draws me further into a setting where light overwhelms all else. How pristinely faultless it appears after years of seeing other beautiful streams, brooks, creeks, rivers and waterfalls. I have encountered hundreds and thousands of similar water-filled scenes, but never has a river with such light startled me out of complacency.

Despite the epitome of this moment, somehow it isn't enough. How ordinary it all appears when clouds block the sun, shade commandeers river, diamonds fail to reflect off sparkling waters, and firs press in with claustrophobic intensity. For a moment melancholy washes over me *until a diminutive little dark-eyed junco flits down to a branch.*

A charcoal-black hood gives away its identity immediately. This cap blends into a highly defined brown back and flanks that are almost the color of an ancient ponderosa pine's russet bark. The small, fragile bird, no more than half an ounce, swivels from side-to-side and then fixes a stare directly at me.

We make eye contact and it waits patiently, not looking away. Fifteen seconds pass....then it tilts its head back and tremolos with a few sharp humming melodies, "zeet, zeet, zeet."

A smile grabs my lips as the junco bobs and weaves a bit more. Then another chorus of "zeet, zeet, zeet" fills the otherwise perfectly still grove as the Pine River continues its relentless flow.

Without the dark-eyed junco, this forest and stream were less than they could be; even at a moment of seeming flawlessness. *A little ball of protoplasm, a mere half ounce of life*, fills this forest with an elusive perfection as two kindred spirits revel in each other's presence.

Birds.

For me they personify wildness in all of its glory.

I'll always feel an intimate connection with large mammals like bison, moose, wolves, elk, bears, puma, and others found in the Southwest. But, birds have expanded my horizons. They embody wildness as much, if not more, than the large critters.

Birds.

Kindred spirits.

Paria walking -
Salir si puede:
Get out if you can!

My mind's eye watches
bone-splitting torrent below.
Owl blinks sleepily.

TERRYE BULLERS

8

Cadence of the Canyonlands

A billowing gauzy dust plume almost a half-mile long trails behind my car as it bounces left, right, up, down and sideways
on a horrendous dirt road to Chaco National Monument. The
way to the ruins is supposedly easy to follow, but from the get-go
a wrong turn is taken and the "main" dirt road left behind. After
anxious moments wandering past squat Hogans and rough sandy
washes strewn with grapefruit-size boulders, occasional dead lizards and aromatic sage; an intersection with a slightly broader, but
equally wash-boarded, route appears. Going on the theory that a
somewhat larger (in size) road is better, I'm back on track toward
ancient Indian ruins in New Mexico's northwest corner.

The Southwestern mosaic includes high mesa, plateau and canyon country. Vast jagged mountain ranges jutting two-miles plus into indigo blue skies add punctuation points. Legendary rivers – such as the Colorado, Virgin, San Juan, and Green – flow off snow-covered peaks and grind down through high desert. Ancient people – Paleo-Indians – settled in tortured canyon mazes that offered security and sustenance. Remains of their civilization are spread widely across the Southwest and spring is a magical time to visit this land. Temperatures are just warming into the fifties and sixties; a perfect interlude until high mountains are freed from their snowy embrace.

Plowing along a thirty-foot wide rutted dirt road at fifty-five miles per hour with scarcely any road signs, much less convenient services, explains why Chaco Canyon remains an extraordinary place to visit. Most people are unwilling to take the risk of going off pavement for sixteen miles, especially when massive thunderstorms, torrential rain and hail render this dirt road a slick, impassible gumbo mess.

A signature big sky flows toward Colorado's San Juan Mountains – distant snow-capped pinnacles defining the northern boundary of sight. All other views eventually merge into endless high desert plateau. Traveling through parched land with coyote-high gray sage, brown grasses just beginning to show a hint of green and an occasional ragged juniper, this plateau seems to be almost infinite. Cut off from the safety of a paved highway, this is truly wild country. The panorama stretches for mile after mile, broken only by an infrequent dip into an eroded arroyo or by distant mountains whose white pinnacles and scale seem surreal, unfathomable given the land's largeness.

A lingering anxiety persists – what happens if the car breaks down? Only occasionally does a billowing cloud of vanilla dust with twinkling metal in the middle whiz by going the opposite direction. Help is many hours distant and with the land's vastness there is a lot of time to ponder this thought as well as what it must be like to live here with the ancestral people.

Contemplate the daily routine of living in widely scattered and dilapidated houses where nary a green plant thrives. Neighbors are miles apart. It's a pretty depressing tableau for those from humid environs until a few miles further where the landscape's grandeur becomes all-consuming. Then the resilience and resourcefulness of ancient people who lived here a thousand years ago becomes awe-inspiring. What kept them tied to this land with its harsh beauty?

Fascination in penetrating the Southwest's rough back roads intensifies as you drop into Chaco Wash; elegant layered red rock ruins come into view. What did a typical day look like a thousand years ago?

Strain to hear the laughter of children playing at the fringes of meager green fields. Listen carefully for rhythmic chanting and singing from ceremonial kiva Casa Rinconada. Walk silently with laborers trudging slowly, exhaustedly, back to Pueblo Bonito or Chetro Ketl after tending precious crops under New Mexico's unrelenting summer sun. Share in a mother's joy of new life brought into the world or sadness as a respected elder moves on to the spirit world. All of these visualizations are nothing more than mere speculation. The truth is we only can conjecture about the cycle of life lived on an arid desert plateau under an enormous expanse of indigo blue sky.

Guessing about what happened to the thriving Chacoan society, a population swelling to significant proportions around A.D. 1000-1140, is best left to anthropologists and archeologists. David Stuart presents no better interpretation than that in his book *Anasazi America*.[7] In Stuart's view Chaco Canyon served as the focal point of a complex society radiating like spokes from a wheel for hundreds of miles encompassing 50,000 square miles within the Four Corners region. It is commonly accepted that the Chaco culture traded as far north as Canada and south to the Gulf of Mexico and the Sea of Cortez. Religion played a very significant role in Chacoan society judging from artifacts and buildings left behind. Then, about A.D. 1090, things began to fall apart perhaps due to several intense droughts – growth couldn't be sustained. The infrastructure collapsed.

Embraced by the canyon's cool morning air and walking among what remains of Pueblo del Arroyo or Kin Kletso, it's natural to think of rhythms – daily rhythms of seasons lived during Chaco's heyday, rhythms of life on a high desert plateau that saw many cycles of drought and moisture, and rhythms of a remarkable planet in a distinctive solar system. In 1979 a rich discovery verified how Chacoans may have kept track of rhythms surrounding their lives. A stone edifice was found on Fajada Butte marking the exact moment of the summer solstice. With uncanny precision, a sun dagger bisects a concentric spiral etched on stone. In this manner the ancient ones may have kept track of the seasons.

***

Life is governed by seasons and cycles that are easily over-looked when urban tempos supplant naturally occurring rhythms. Birds migrate thousands of miles each year; hibernating plant life is resurrected each spring; mountains rise; and, wind, rain, snow and ice tear them down. A challenge for many of us is to build a deeper connection with natural rhythms – like the elders. Journeys for immersion in the outdoors, such as to

Chaco Canyon, refresh dormant memories about rhythms, how they govern life, and how people relate to wildness.

How many inveterate canyon country explorers have been drawn to desert places throughout their lives? To these folks the desert represents something grander, something sacred to be respected. The desert communicates a distinct spirit of intangibility larger than the anxious busyness of humans, just as early spring at Chaco Canyon speaks boldly about how humans have lived with and within nature.

It only takes a close look at the humbly impressive ruins of Chaco Canyon to whet our appetite for more rhythm-centric adventures in the backcountry of the Southwest.

***

Mid-May and the weather has been faultless for more than a week. At this time of year, intense summer heat is only an infrequent visitor to imperial mesas and mysterious canyons of northern Arizona and southern Utah. Mere miles away, infamous Antelope Canyon is beginning to wake up to a hammering yellow sun's sizzle. Soaring white anvil clouds with menacing blue-black bottoms – powerful summer thunderstorm clouds at their most majestic – are still a few weeks distant. This is a perfect opportunity for an exploration of Paria Canyon with its serpentine rock walls and narrow defiles that only Slim Jims dare navigate.

Our group recognizes the sinister danger of a stray bruise-colored thunderstorm. Visualizations haunt our minds of frothing, muddy flash floods whisking boulders, debarked logs, rotting cattle carcasses and assorted trash down upon us in an alley from which escape is impossible. Statistically mid-May is about as promising as it gets for secure passage in warm weather.

On reaching Page, Arizona, there's no doubt that the high desert landscape dominates everything else. Beautiful apparitions of dusty white and red stone monuments and eroding mesas sail distant seas across far desert floors. Temperatures are escalating into the low 80's — mere child's play compared with what will come in the dead of summer.

At an oasis in Page, we take on board gas and cool perspiring soft drinks in the warming, almost hot, day while munching on dribbling ice cream bars — our last luxury before wilderness. Beginning the final miles to Paria Canyon once past Glen Canyon Dam, white, yellow, vanilla, tan and red rock, with every shade of color in between, dominates mesas and canyons. Scant brush clings to rocks and crevices in country that knows little precipitation.

Paria Canyon's trailhead at 4,400 feet is located in a dusty, stark parking lot ground out of high desert. We load up and begin walking through scruffy low-lying vegetation of sage and occasional Apache plume, angling toward a depressingly muddy-brown river that is slowly meandering down a barren riverbed of sand and ground-up rock. The first time backpacking in months is always tough. Loaded to the gills with water, we trudge along wondering about the folly of being converted to pack animals. We're already perspiring like sinners at confession; water will be at a premium this trip.

It's rumored that plenty of water can be found in the Paria and that nourishing springs are located lower in the canyon from which sweet sustenance might be drawn. Nonetheless, I'm thankful for the pure water in my pack. There's four miles to our first camp and then another three before reaching Buckskin Gulch and access to springs. We have no intention of drinking from the Paria itself due to chemical (fertilizer) contamination seeping into the river from farming communities located miles in the distance.

Riverbed gradually funnels into deepening canyon and late in the afternoon we come slogging wearily into a last-chance camping spot before the narrows of Paria Canyon. On a very sandy slope twenty feet above the riverbed tents are erected. Sand is everywhere in an instant. Fine, red-white, gritty sand finds its way in every seam and through extra-fine gray mosquito netting. No need for a rain fly, the sky is brilliant blue with nary a cloud scudding across it. This is an especially good omen, as tomorrow will take us into the narrows – three miles of towering rock labyrinth with no escape.

***

By early morning my treasured water supply is beginning to run low. Last night we filled several gallon jugs with turbid brown water thinking that the muck will settle. However, after twelve hours there's still enough suspended silt to choke a horse if not quickly clog a water purifier. We resign ourselves to bringing back a substantial supply from springs further down canyon. From previous trips several in our group know where refreshing sources are in Buckskin Gulch.

Our plan is to hike to the Gulch, approximately three miles further down-river, and then explore the ever-narrowing slot canyon. A number of factors feed a trickle of adrenaline. First, there's a flash flood possibility – many people have lost their lives at nearby Antelope Canyon and other slot canyons during unexpected storms. Second, three members of our group have previously been halfway down the Paria when a flash flood stranded them high on talus slopes and rock benches above the river. Fortunately in each case they had already been camped for the night when water came roaring downstream. The aftermath was difficulty in reading longstanding water versus recent pooling. Longstanding water is typically associated with quicksand. Third, I'm rapidly losing confidence in assurances that there are plenty of springs from which to obtain fresh water.

Assembling clothing and food for a long day, I look over to the canyon's entrance and into a dark cavern that swallows our muddy stream – our trail. With canyon walls soaring two hundred feet, the entry conveys an ominous welcome. Air this morning is crisp in the shade, but rapidly warming in brilliant sun. While others slowly organize I walk down canyon a bit.

Sandstone walls tower progressively higher over the riverbed. Here and there at serpentine bends standing black pools of water cast ominous reflections of pebble-studded walls and baby blue sky above. To while away time I cast several large stones into pools that swallow the rocks whole and emit a resounding "ker-pluck" as though signifying bottomless pits. Quicksand? These seem to be likely spots. Edward Abbey loved Buckskin Gulch and Paria Canyon (or Pariah Canyon as he called it) for their beauty and quicksand danger; oxymoronic opposites.

Looking down the Paria's somewhat ominous throat I'm reminded that we'll be treading where the Anasazi trod. Archaeologists discovered ruins from the ancient ones dating to between 1100 and 1150 at the mouth of the Paria and on the surrounding plateau. Petroglyphs can also been seen in the river canyon. These Pueblo ancestors aren't the only ones who found the Paria intriguing. The Southern Paiutes ventured to and across the Colorado River in the course of hunting and trading. The Navajo came to the Paria later in the 16th Century.

What a rich legacy to follow. Did a little shiver course down their spines when Paria Canyon exhaled cool air as they breached the entrance? Will their spirits be walking with us to enjoy our fascination with swirling sandstone walls clamping upon us like a vise while a blue ribbon floats overhead? There aren't any hard-and-fast answers to these questions except for the palpable spiritual embrace we feel in their former home. It's difficult to capture with great accuracy, but their essence floats in the air, permeating our pores, the colorful rock and depthless sky.

Gradually our group ambles away from camp. Taking the lead, Bill and Terrye provide wise instructions as the once-wide canyon quickly narrows to thirty feet and less. The lessons seem simple enough. Standing water is a sure sign of quicksand. Stay in the middle of the river, particularly where water is flowing quickly because these conditions are adverse to quicksand. Be prepared for "sticky mud," a condition in which flowing water covers mud that sticks to your shoes – this may be a prelude to quicksand. Above all, try to read the river – the current, its direction and undercuts of hanging walls.

Sounds elementary to me, but right away we come upon a new conundrum. The canyon curves with current flowing hard against a wall forming a five foot deep pool. This means that you have to walk on a sloping riverbed with the high point in almost placid water – the harbinger of quicksand. We quicken our pace through the jelly-like riverbed. Visions of sinking to an eternal grave cross my mind and I think back to a documentary about a film crew in red rock country similar to the Paria.

Two crewmembers decide to clown for the camera. On the edge of a riverbed they mockingly grind their feet and legs down into the sandy bottom up almost to their knees. Acting as though they are stuck, the camera keeps rolling as they mime inability to extricate themselves. Funny stuff.

After their antics, the camera keeps rolling as they try to climb out. To their amazement they cannot pull their feet out. Meanwhile, a thunderstorm is growling just north of their canyon. In a panic, several crewmembers try to dig and pull them out. The pair remains stuck. It takes almost an hour of hard digging to free them from their concrete goulashes. The peril of a looming thunderstorm adds to the emotion-charged atmosphere. This funny pantomime becomes a life-and-death crisis. Disaster is averted at the last minute as menacing mud grudgingly gives up its exhausted prey.

After walking a mile I begin to get the drift of reading the river and press on down canyon. By now rosy red-hued sandstone walls are looming several hundred feet above the beautiful narrow defile. In darkness with a slim ribbon of blue above, it's natural to think of being trapped when a rollicking mass of boulders, splintered logs, pulverized branches, bloated carcasses and other detritus come roaring down upon an unlucky traveler.

Looking back up-stream as our group spreads out into clumps of sauntering hikers the sheer beauty of water-carved walls is incredible. Smooth sides tell a tale of powerful flows that sand walls to a fine polish. Locked between massive pillars, a thousand swirling shades of red and white rock speak warmly of pastels that can never be replicated except there in the depths of a remote wilderness canyon in northern Arizona and southern Utah.

In no time at all, a half-mile separates me from others as I follow the simple instructions: "Walk downstream three miles until the opening of Buckskin Gulch. You cannot miss it as Paria Canyon clearly opens up." I'm maintaining my normal hiking pace – about four miles an hour under these easy conditions – allowing plenty of time to appreciate the beauty of Paria Canyon.

Meanwhile, walls progressively narrow and I lose sight of others. Turbidity obscures the river's bed with its hot chocolate color making it extremely difficult to determine what foundation lies below the current.

Walking as lightly as possible and expecting quicksand, I reach a long stretch of river, perhaps fifty yards, where there's little choice but to sprint down a narrow water-filled alley. A large, denuded tree trunk hangs precariously in air twenty feet above the riverbed; crammed there by powerful forces difficult to imagine.

This seems to be my mental turning point. About two miles downriver since leaving camp, I'm gaining confidence and no longer concerned about progressively leaving others behind. Ready for a return to open spaces and warm sun upon skin, I keep on trucking; marveling at this multi-hued sandstone shrine and thin slice of distant sky, but a string floating overhead. At points skinny side arroyos and gentle troughs hanging high above our maze penetrate each wall, but none is wide enough to suggest Buckskin Gulch. "I will know it when I see it."

For a moment Paria Canyon widens briefly, but fallen rock monoliths suggest undercutting by the river, not the anticipated breadth and space of a significant branch canyon in this watershed. Within another ten minutes downstream the canyon opens up to sunlight and a beautiful cottonwood high on a talus slope. By now the canyon's surrounding walls seem diminished and less imposing. It gradually dawns on me that I can evade any flash-flood up on the rock-strewn talus slopes and narrow benches. Small junipers and dense desert brush on the slopes signal stability, land that will only be vulnerable in a most massive flood.

Glancing at my watch, I note that it has taken about fifty minutes to reach this point. Surely Buckskin Gulch is just ahead. Picking up the pace I weave through canyon terrain that is increasing penetrated by bright sunlight before alternating back into shadowy gloom. Paria's river is often hurriedly rushing down the center of a narrow gap, only to broaden to a wider wandering canyon bottom. A large opening in the canyon appears around a bend, but I cannot detect any incoming side stream or access out other than up fairly steep canyon walls. Several cottonwoods breezily wave their delicate luminescent immature leaves in a steady wind being exhaled by the canyon. This can't be Buckskin Gulch — it's too open.

Pushing on with growing interest in finding Buckskin Gulch and an opportunity to eat lunch, the canyon continues to widen. By now I'm an hour and a half from the beginning and this just doesn't seem right. With superbly easy terrain and rapid pace I should have already reached the Gulch. Have my friends miscalculated how far downstream the Gulch enters the main canyon? Am I traveling slower than I think? Have I missed an important turn?

At once the dilemma comes crashing into clarity. Here I am without a map, miles into a wilderness labyrinth, with no notion of where I am or where I may be headed. In short, these thoughts smack of someone who is lost.

Just before fear surges through my veins, I have a revelation. It's almost as though I view the situation from outside my body. Canyon walls are less imposing at this point compared to just a few miles upstream. Nonetheless, the canyon is pristine and unbelievably beautiful. In fact, its lack of awe-inspiring grandeur makes it that much more captivating.

I've taken the measure of this land, of chocolate silted stream, harsh overhead sun, drought-tolerant vegetation, and gorgeous multi-hued rock embracing utter wildness. Occasional lime green cottonwoods hide among the chaos of rock falls. Without a map I now know more clearly the immense spread of red rock country and tortuous maze of canyons here in the Four Corners area.

It's at this point that I'm struck dead center about my humble place in the grander scheme of canyon country. Most would see this little wide spot of Paria Canyon as ugly — no grove of stately trees providing dappled shade; filthy brown water laden with pollutants carrying more earth than liquid and no charismatic wildlife, or any wildlife for that matter. Harsh bright yellow sun reflects back from monotonous chalky sandstone. Dryness dehydrates your body into jerky under a boring blue sky where there is no view with any grandeur. This would be the perception of many people.

Inexplicably, despite rising realization that I'm lost, alone and on the brink of possible real trouble, my thoughts soar with swallows flying above the canyon. What incredible beauty this country possesses. And the scale of things is almost beyond belief. How fortunate to be able to penetrate just the margin of this mysterious and magical land. I can feel this immense desert country tugging at me to go on downstream. Think of the beauty that lies around each bend? Where will I find the fabled springs and seeps high on canyon walls? What type of fern gardens and rock art will surround them? How many ancient ones trod this very path in the course of a life without any guidebook?

This country doesn't just happen to be this way; certainly it is part of a grander design that we cannot fathom. Sensuous serpentine river channels with majestic soaring walls of red sandstone topped by chalky white caps are greater than just another erosion bed writ large and old in the course of Earth's history. There's a beauty that tugs persistently at your soul begging you to open your mind to the Earth as something more than an inert assembly of organic and inorganic material. Here is our life; a grand design beyond comprehension.

These thoughts percolate in my mind while absorbing a gift that I'll never relinquish. Standing there with a mild tepid breeze pressing gently on my face, I munch an overly sweet candy bar and sip some precious water – clear water that now seems alien in this environment. I vow to become more a part of the land than apart from the land. And as this noble thought begins to fade I return to the logical, rational world in which we dwell. Head fresh with purposeful thoughts about the certainty of being able to return back to camp, I stash my goods in a faded blue pack and turn to go.

From a little boulder perch on the side of the river I lengthen my stride to reach canyon wall and in one swift move bounce off the wall and back into the stream.

Quicksand!

With lightning reactions I recoil back to the wall and then the boulder. It's really here after all; a reality, not some theory. Composing myself and swept by a sense of aloneness in a vast wilderness, I contemplate this new experience.

Quicksand is bizarre. There's just enough substance in the sand and water mixture for me to jump back after testing the foothold. Yet, there's also this illusion of firmness and façade that this is just another part of the riverbed. Looking down on the patch I can now see how the surface is covered by about one-half inch of stagnant, but clear, water. Did this shining mirror sucker some of the ancient people into taking a wrong step like me?

It takes several interminable minutes to process this new challenge that Paria's river offers. As adrenaline evaporates, I remember so well the caress of a very gentle breeze. Penetrating warmth of sun bores into my shoulders and arms amid stillness and vast silence. The Paria silently works down canyon while tenacious desert vegetation stubbornly gears up for another intense summer. Time is almost standing still, but not in my mind. With incredible certainty I know that I have really blown it. I'm probably two miles down canyon from where the rest of the group is lounging.

Confident resolve takes command as I step back out into the middle of the Paria – firm riverbed. Walking purposefully and quickly ahead, I know what must be done. No longer anxious about running into quicksand, I'm cognizant of what to look for and how to read the river, mud and stagnant pools. Sure, I'm still somewhat fearful of getting stuck in quicksand with no one to aid me, but a new attitude has gradually taken hold – trust no more than one footfall at a time. Back off if anything feels suspicious. Remember the basic rules about standing water and the friendly hydraulics of a fast flowing stream. Still, when the dark canyon closes in, sandstone walls rise hundreds of feet above, the sky narrows to a ribbon of azure, and there's no trail except a river, it's impossible not to become hyper alert.

***

Sadly, on the very brisk walk back up canyon, my previous fascination with the scale of canyon country, wildness and interconnections among constituent pieces, gradually dissipates. The spiritual grip of Indian predecessors evaporates. I have a specific mission to fulfill and no time to reflect on bigger thoughts that brought me to this beautiful and wild place.

Progress is measured by time, figuring that one-mile will be covered every fifteen minutes. Consequently, a new surge of anxiety emerges at one-half hour on the return.

Where is Buckskin Gulch?

In part my problem is being able to see properly. Returning up canyon brings an entirely new perspective on the landscape. It's as though I've never been down the Paria in the first place. For about ten minutes a seed of doubt begins to flourish and with it the initial illusion of panic. Am I really lost after all? The twists and turns of Paria Canyon are now jumbled in my mind. But, honestly, how can you get lost when there's only one main river? Seems silly to be ignoring this fact, however, our minds are often powerful masters.

Replaying these thoughts over and over again, the canyon widens briefly, fluttering cottonwoods act as beacons to Buckskin Gulch, and now I can see where I erred. A jumbled confusion of fallen rock hides the entrance to Buckskin Gulch and obscures the inflow of its stream to the Paria. In a dark grotto behind fallen slabs my friends are casually taking their lunch. Their embrace is fast and furious.

"So, there you are."

"Where have you been?"

"We thought you had gotten lost."

"Want to come with us up the Gulch?"

I tell about my excellent little adventure to the amusement of all. The wiser, more experienced canyoneers simply nod gravely at revelations about experiencing quicksand. No one forgets that first encounter. And, the offer of a side trip up a very narrow fat man's misery has lost all of its appeal. They're anxious to get going and I leave them with the admonition to bring back lots of pure water. I never did see any seeps or springs on my jaunt, but then much of the time my vision was limited to a few steps ahead. They assure me that they will come back loaded with fine water to drink. With that I turn toward camp.

The way back is anticlimactic and passes very fast now that I know how to negotiate the terrain. There are more opportunities to appreciate the beautiful rock and play of the river upon its walls both at stream level and up on the high reaches at flood stage. Some pretty phenomenal floods powered their way down this canyon. It must be a spectacle to behold from the mesa top.

Back in camp I settle against an overhanging sandstone wall seeking what shade this country can provide with its scarcity of trees. The thermometer is climbing and I take stock of my water cache – one quart. It'll have to last until the others return with a fresh supply. I parcel it out over the course of the afternoon luxuriating in thoughts about wild canyon country.

***

With what some would consider nothing to do, nowhere to go and no one to talk to, I slowly return to the pinnacle of this special day. It's not the adventure of quicksand that captures my mind, but that rare moment when I looked at the land with a more encompassing lens, where I saw the grand design of wonderful canyon country and felt the proximity of Native spirits. I had seen the beauty of the whole, of something much larger than what passing tourists see from their cars – suicidal slot canyons, desolate mesa tops, and parched land.

I think about the writings of SueEllen Campbell in her book *Bringing the Mountain Home*.[8] She recounts a fantastically beautiful day in the Big Blue Wilderness of Colorado when elk and hawks play in the largesse of a sunny July day: "On days like this, beauty grabs you by the throat and shakes you breathless all day long. You can hope for this gift, but you can't demand it. Most days we're separated by sheets of glass from what's around us. But sometimes, when you're somehow ready, or just in the right place and moment, the glass shatters and falls at your feet in piles of rhinestones, and you see everything differently. For hours or for seconds, you're locked in the present, and you are absolutely where you are."

My walk in Paria Canyon shattered sheets of glass giving me fresh, transforming insights on the beauty of the Paria; land that many others would see as pretty ordinary in the scheme of things – a polluted muddy creek crawling down a bunch of forsaken dirty ravines.

Late that afternoon my compatriots return triumphant about their excursions up Buckskin Gulch. They continued until its passage was too narrow, challenging and gloomy.

Funny, here in a land of light, darkness inevitably found its own sanctuary.

Several of my friends mentioned that they felt this mysterious energy compelling them to turn around. I'm happy they're back. But, where's the water they promised? Turns out that they never were able to acquire much from an agonizingly slow seep and in the end they gave up.

When we finally hike out and reach our van, I know exactly what to do. In one long swig I down a precious liter of spring water before opening the second; locked in the present.

***

A walk down Paria Canyon or Chaco Canyon will indelibly touch anyone who invests time and effort to make the sojourn. Even the most callous adventurer will have a difficult time leaving Paria Canyon unaffected by swirling chocolate brown water against a cinnamon red sandstone wall or chilled humid air in a grotto whose walls can be touched by outstretched arms while an azure sky floats hundreds of feet above a sandy gravel wash. The Paria is a lifeline to a massive ecosystem of torturous canyons and breathtakingly beautiful mesas. It spawns unexpectedly verdant communities of fragile plant life closing around life-giving seeps on rocky walls.

Paria Canyon imparts special gifts, such as petroglyphs from earlier travelers, speaking forcefully about something grand embodied in backcountry adventure. It also reminds me of others who have been touched deeply by rivers.

Stanley Crawford lives on a small farm in northern New Mexico and has melded with a nearby river that replenishes his crops and his very life. In *The River in Winter* Crawford writes eloquently about how he has been influenced by a river that is more than just a river: "I carry the river around in that floating landscape of memories, images, and ideas that makes up one transitory human being, this 'myself.' As through the narrow mountain valley where I live, it runs through the center of my being...I am but an aspect of the river, one of its points of consciousness. Even when not in its presence, I feel the river running."[9] Imagine how it might benefit a person, benefit a society, and benefit our civilization, to carry in our collective consciousness a constant notion of a river.

Whether Chaco Canyon, Paria Canyon, or some other magical spot, our Earth speaks softly, but persistently, about the essence of wildness that we should inculcate within our very beings. My adventures in Chaco Canyon and Paria Canyon remain in my consciousness. I am but one aspect of Paria River, one aspect of Chaco Canyon. Even now I sense the thrill of their beauty, the tug of adventure, and knowledge that my being rises once again by only thinking about them.

Bridge over the Colorado River at Phantom Ranch, Grand Canyon

Mt. Humphreys looking north to the Grand Canyon

Grand Canyon from the South Rim

Early morning start down the Kaibab Trail, Grand Canyon

South Peak, Sandia Mountains, New Mexico

West Fork of the Little Colorado River

Middle Fork of the Gila River

Havasu Canyon, Supai Reservation

Indian ruins along the West Fork of the Gila River

*View down into Beaver Creek from the Continental Divide in Weminuche
Wildnerness, Colorado*

Renewal and Invigoration

Ancestral shadows
weave in and out of the canyon.
Trout's a silver dart.

TERRYE BULLERS

9

El Rito de los Frijoles

Wham! Suddenly it's so blazingly bright that she can hardly see.

For the first time today Father Sun's scintillating rays spill over a saw-tooth skyline and soaring mountain range – a land so distant that few in her tribe have ever been there. Centuries from now the peaks will be known as the Sangre de Cristos, but for right now elders call them the great snowy range.

And; is it ever cold. Only yesterday her village's shaman promised everyone that winter had turned for good. Now they can begin planting beans and squash – no more freezing mornings to get in the way. That's bad news for this ten year old native girl. She's the one in her family who has to do all the back-breaking, dirty work of hoeing weeds and watering tender plants. Meanwhile her older brother who last month endured frightening rites of passage will go hunting with her father.

How come he has all of the fun?

Pulling a soft rabbit fur cape around her shoulders for a tad bit more warmth she turns toward a glorious golden globe showering life-giving warmth over her village. It's not that she disrespects the Sun God by audaciously staring right at it; she's merely paying homage for this wonderful day. Eyes squinting, chill broken, she revels in a pestering thought that when her work is done she and three other pals plan to go swimming in the large river – the Rio Grande as it will be branded four centuries from now when Spanish conquerors claim this land for the Mother country. How refreshing and cleansing those swims can be, but first to the chores.

Humming a little tune she's made up to while away boring hours spent cultivating fertile fields, our young girl turns to go. An angelic smile is plastered across her face. In part she's happy because her favorite season of the year has come again – just like the old wrinkled shaman said it would. There'll be more time for enjoying life free from the smoky recesses of her mud and rock-hewn home.

This afternoon she and her friends will follow a lovely little stream – El Rito de los Frijoles as it will be named centuries later – to the big river. Her smile also reveals the hope that she may once again catch a glimpse of that cute black-haired young fellow living only ten minutes down-canyon. Two days ago she actually talked to him for what seemed like an hour. Yes, today is a good day to be alive.

***

Spring is a fickle and chaotic companion. A day in these Jemez Mountains may span the continuum from tentative pale sun, to spotty rain showers, then consuming bruised clouds, to snow falling on spruces, and back to promising yellow rays. Yet, despite these vagaries we love spring because it presents hope for full-on exploration and immersion deep in wilderness. Spring is a time to gnaw on the marrow of life.

Grand outdoor adventures wait with lengthening sunny days and warming, comforting temperatures. Wildlife is more visible, perfect counterpoint to an epidemic of vibrant blossoming that overwhelms trees, grasses, shrubs. Spring connotes new beginnings and a time to leave unrealized dreams behind; that raft trip not taken due to anemically low water, a planned three-day backpack into distant pristine alpine lakes squeezed out by work, or a peak not bagged because lightning-laced thunderstorms stubbornly refused to yield.

Rites of spring mean savoring warmer temperatures mixed with gentle breezes, longer languid days and accessibility to destinations made difficult by winter's command. Every mountain, desert, lake, canyon, river, basin or ocean possesses an ultimate spring moment, a point where winter has definitely been left behind and warmth rules until fall closes over the land. When that perfect spring moment unfolds, the entire world seems right.

In the Southwest, the epitome of spring can be found waiting in Bandelier National Monument. Set against the heavily forested eastern base of the Jemez Mountains and bracketed across the Rio Grande by the soaring Sangre de Cristos above Santa Fe, mid-April generally offers absolutely fabulous spring hiking. With high desert elevations ranging from 5,000 to 8,000 feet in the monument, spring weather can be very capricious. Yet, wait two weeks under the faulty assumption that spring simply needs a tiny bit of aging and your seasonal window of opportunity slams shut by summer's sapping heat. When you hit it just right, there is no finer adventure than that first really long hike in the wilds of Bandelier National Monument.

***

Springtime hikes up the Pajarito Plateau and down El Rito de los Frijoles capture the very essence of New Mexico's signature – a land of enchantment. Late April is a magnificently captivating time for roaming across warm fertile earth while enjoying optimistically effervescent vegetation, unruly birds with in-your-face attitudes protecting nesting territories, and winter's munificence in the form of a swirling, burbling stream – *El Rito de los Frijoles*.

Every journey along the Frijoles is thrilling particularly because of the chance to walk paths where the ancient ones have left their discernible mark. During springtime explorations Bandelier's weather shines at its best. Artifacts such as pottery shards, arrowheads, and crude tools mysteriously rise, breaking through topsoil from winter's daily freezing and thawing cycles. Like nearby patches of remnant beans or squash formerly tended by young girls verging on womanhood, they are tangible reminders that flourishing native communities called these parched mesas and rugged canyons home centuries ago. Visual images of early inhabitants seemingly shimmer around their ruins.

With blazing banana yellow sun just beginning to warm the Pajarito Plateau's 7,500-foot high desert mesa, my friend, Dick, and I leave Bandelier's Visitor Center. Cool almost frigid black shadows of the canyon's depths are the starting point for a twelve-mile round trip hike. Dick is training for his climb up Mt. Whitney later this summer. I'm training for a graduate degree in life lived well; this is a very important part of my study plan.

An historic visitor center offers a wealth of information about the monument. Adolf Bandelier, famed ethnologist from the late 1800s, and author Charles Lummis initially recorded Bandelier National Monument's legacy. They participated in and promoted research into native cultures associated with ancient ruins spread throughout the monument. Evidence collected from archeological studies indicates that the most intensive period of occupation occurred from 1200 A.D. to 1600 A.D. Subsequent studies in the late 1970's suggest that indigenous people inhabited this area along the Rio Grande from as far back as 1750 B.C.

These facts inevitably flavor any backcountry foray within the monument. Others claimed this mesmerizing place as home and in many respects it's like I'm trespassing – an uninvited guest. With this omnipresent primeval history in mind, I tend to mind my manners knowing that the old ones may be watching. It's a unique atmosphere enriching the exhilaration of traveling within the monument's 23,267 wilderness acres.

In mellow early morning hours it's far too easy to close my eyes, shut out every visible shred of contemporary life, and mentally transport myself back to 1300 A.D. or earlier. The same frigid springtime chill hangs in the air. Dank bouquet of riverine vegetation wafts downstream. Lusty aroma of a ponderosa pine's cinnamon bark warms in optimistic sunlight. A palpable dryness prevails, leaving a dusty tang in nose and on tongue. These reminders accentuate our quest today; it's not just another hike, what we're doing is deeply connected with a past whose ancestors still haunt this land.

Our trail begins under mottled cover of ponderosa pines, locust, box elder and cottonwood trees nurtured by a bubbling El

Rito de los Frijoles, or the Frijoles River; bean river. No wonder the ancient ones chose this beautiful canyon, carving homes in volcanic tuff walls and cave pocketed cliffs of this valley. All the essentials are here — water, sun, shade, protection, privacy, and magic. The allure is obvious, but exactly how did they find such a delightful spot? Only they know because the answer lies buried with them.

We have to climb four hundred feet above the valley floor toward mesa top and full exposure to energetic sun. Seven-forty-five a.m. and the mesa's sun-drenched bounty calls like a sea nymph singing beguiling songs to passing sailors. At this early hour temperatures in Frijoles Canyon are in the low 40 degree range. They will gradually moderate toward mid 80's this afternoon. As far as we're concerned that will be too hot for walking the mesa. We're planning on being in shady canyon recesses by then. For now boots pound clouds of beige dust on the ascent; muscles stretching and warming to the task with bodies and minds acclimating to the challenge waiting ahead.

Shrub infested canyon is left for a juniper, piñon and ponderosa strewn mesa. Unlike the valley that was a central focus of the Anasazi, vegetation on the open, vulnerable Pajarito Plateau is quite sparse testifying to meager moisture and harsh sunny exposure. Nonetheless it's great country in spring — light, airy, warm and promising now that winter is past. We wend our way through scattered stands of squat junipers while puffs of tuff splash up caking our boots, socks and calves. Off trail, the soil is fractured and uplifted like veins on the back of an old man's hands from winter's periodic freezing and thawing. We're on the lookout for prehistoric ruins and evidence of early inhabitants, hundreds of years old.

Six miles of trail due west on the mesa are straightforward. This path slowly climbs up the Pajarito Plateau until mesa and mountain collide. Then it drops into lovely Frijoles Canyon and a return to the visitor center. Until we reach the end of the mesa there will be lots of small discoveries requiring further investigation. We stop frequently at decomposing ruins, acre-sized plots of tossed-and-tumbled rocks. A chaos of tuff blocks and moss-covered stones etch remains of communal housing. Potshards of varied hues – black, vanilla, red – litter the ground. Freshly driven to the surface by persistent freezing and thawing, they're admired but left resting quietly.

With over 1,000 Anasazi sites throughout the monument, it's difficult not to turn a corner and inadvertently be staring straight into the face of someone's family home. The walls and shape of these prehistoric structures may not be perfectly recognizable, but there is no mistaking that Bandelier's mesa tops once nurtured vibrantly healthy communities. Shadows under junipers and ponderosa pines guarding fallen dwellings resonate with the spirit of those from long ago.

Progressing west on the mesa, Dick and I marvel at how long it's taking for the forest to recover from catastrophic forest fires. Twenty-plus years ago a massive fire consumed the pine forest covering this plateau. Then, several years ago a misguided "controlled burn" by the Forest Service leveled much of what remains. There's not much left, vast savannah plains on top of this plateau have widely scattered ponderosa pines and wheatgrass sprinkled roundabout, meager browse for several deer we see in the distance. Huge elk also frequent the monument, but it's been a long time since we've seen them wandering off the mountains to the plateau.

Miles roll by having hit upon a comfortable pace keeping us warm in the chilly morning air. It just feels good to stretch after being confined for much of a cold winter. Conversation jumps back and forth from one topic to another; there are lapses and moments of intensity. This first major outing is like learning to walk all over again. I have to synchronize mouth and feet. Over winter's breadth we hiked, skied, snow-shoed, walked, camped and pursued all manner of outdoor activities. But, spring is the time for lengthy and outrageously remote adventures. Dick and I are undergoing a metamorphosis.

Three miles have passed under our boots and we're straddling an intervening plateau between Cañon de los Frijoles and Lummis Canyon. The trail is weaving among jumbled blocks of ruins literally spread everywhere. It's like a giant hand scooped up dozens of jacks and threw them across the plateau. A stone's throw over Lummis Canyon on slightly higher ground scores more rest in the sun. It doesn't take much to envision how bustling this area was centuries ago – smoke from kitchen fires lingering over the mesa, children sent to draw water, adults setting off on one mission or another.

At five miles, weary of grassy plateau and looking forward to unbridled vegetation lining the Frijoles' banks, a final undulating half-mile brings the base of the Jemez Mountains. Our trail drops precipitously four-hundred feet through fir and ponderosa on the canyon's northern-facing slope reaching for the so-called Upper Crossing of the Frijoles. In minutes the world changes to claustrophobically closed canyon brimming with life and a totally different environment. From here we start downstream, ready for shade and coolness of a streamside walk.

The Upper Crossing, euphemism for a trail junction, inevitably invokes a sense of wonder. Massive ponderosa mingle with more modest spruce and aspen in this hush canyon while the Frijoles meanders back-and-forth with sun reflecting magically from its surface, a golden blinding ribbon of life. We are about to trod a path that the Ancestral Puebloans walked – they in their adventure of life, we in a moment of discovery. And, thus begins the most supernatural miles in a rite of spring.

The canyon closes to a quarter-of-a-mile across with rough rust-black volcanic walls to the north and verdant green covered walls to the south while the serpentine river of life burbles and gurgles at our sides. Each bend of the trail offers uncertainty – a startling vista, squirrel or snake scurrying from the path, vaporous column of shining yellow-white sun, copse of ancient fir trees, or volcanic hoodoos. We walk with anticipation, with a spring in our step, knowing that this is more than just a walk; it's become a post-winter ritual.

What's always remarkable to me is the surprising dichotomy between mesa and canyon. Without Frijoles Canyon's shade and river, this would be just another murderously hot ravine. But, it isn't – there is a special feel about this canyon, something sacred. The old ones must have sensed this uniqueness.

For us it did not go unnoticed that the number of ruins dropped off precipitously as we progressively climbed up the mesa. Surprisingly few ruins are evident on the west-most mesa and virtually none this far west along the Frijoles. Perhaps the canyon was considered holy ground and off-limits. Or, it may have been simply too cold to live this far up the canyon. Alternatively, the ancestors may have been seeking security in concentrated numbers lower down toward the Rio Grande. They're not here to answer, but debris from their dwellings shouts loudly about a purposeful design.

Maybe it's these unanswered questions that make Bandelier Monument's mysterious past so beguiling. I'm trying to think like they might have thought one thousand years ago; putting myself in their moccasins or sandals. Would I really have sacrificed the safety of numbers for the serenity of these western reaches? Wouldn't the logistics of daily living have demanded banding together? In the same vein I wonder about their connection to the land. Surely they had time and interest to simply take a walk in the woods – to enjoy a beautiful spring day before summer came slamming through. Or, did their time evaporate in eking out a living?

One thing is definite. There are many less desirable places to locate a home. I like to think that there are more similarities than differences between the ancient ones and me. They chose to live on the edge of forest at a high elevation where even today a year-round coolness dwells compared to heat of high desert further south. Sauntering along this path – undoubtedly a trail they beat into the earth – it is evident that the old ones and I had much in common. We both sought this beguiling forest-mesa-canyon country.

After dropping down into this canyon, we switch places so that I'm leading. Occasionally Dick and I exchange bits of conversation but mostly we're both living in the moment – absorbed in a delightful walk across a primal landscape. Eventually I stop and turn around to share a thought with Dick but he isn't anywhere in sight.

Where'd he go?

I grab several gulps of water and a few minutes later he comes shuffling around a bend. We're both tracking spring's progress down this canyon. Virgin growth on deciduous trees and shrubs – intense lime-green among mottled browns of ponderosa trunks – is in sharp counterpoint to white tuff over black lava.

A half-mile later, Dick inexplicably begins to slow down by a distinct order of magnitude. I try all manner of coaxing to keep him moving along – walking just a bit faster so that in order for him to converse he has to keep up the pace; not taking snacks or drinks when he wants to stop frequently for refreshment; pretending not to hear his exclamations about the magnificence of a particular glen (really meaning that he wants to stop to rest). In response he goes into his fishing mode, scanning the Frijoles for elusive, diminutive trout.

Two miles of bliss later, halfway down the Frijoles, Dick stops one more time to attend to something. I don't realize it until I glance back and he's disappeared. I've been casually walking along in no real rush, just enjoying the day and the scenery, not certain what the next alcove or forested bench will hold. It's then that our modest spring outing reaches an apex.

The path enters a narrowly steep canyon defile where weathered red hoodoos of tent rocks, topped by white hats, rise out of a supernatural landscape. Canyon walls close in to fifty feet across— walls of white pumice alternating with red and orange, laced with chunky rock fragments. Hundreds of feet higher, hard charcoal-black lava flows cap the soft skullcap of vanilla pumice. These flows are markedly porous with air holes and cleavages.

The Frijoles meanders according to hardness of rock in its path, its milky waters laden with white pumice. Dark green reeds, drinking straw straight, grow profusely under a canopy of black locust, ponderosa pine, shimmering aspen, occasional fragile maple and varieties of poplar and ever-present cottonwood. Tall emerald grasses hide the threat of rattlesnakes, yet resonate with the sounds of lizards and small mammals frightened from their hiding places.

Undercutting a huge red wall the Frijoles gurgles over gray rounded rock, pausing in pleasant liquid pools. The temperature must have cooled at least fifteen degrees over the exposed mesa, and perhaps more in this silent, dark alcove. Lost in a jungle of healthy river vegetation, it's impossible to see but a few hundred feet downstream. It's this beauty that keeps bringing us back to Bandelier. Surely this very recess must have knocked the breath out of the Anasazi as well.

Here is a spot that undoubtedly made them forget the aches and pains of a physically challenging existence. I'm certain that Bandelier's historic people threw off the heavy yoke of their lives at this quintessential shrine and murmured gratitude for its almost incomprehensible splendor.

I drop my pack and sit at the river's edge on a bank fresh with emerald grass, removing dusty boots and damp tuff encrusted socks, placing feet in the stream. How refreshing that feels – will I ever be able to get them back on? Leaning back I inexplicably sense a sort of detachment.

It's then that I'm blessed with the gift of ancestral shadows. I look beyond the thrilling beauty of this little glade along the Frijoles to the pattern of similar canyons dropping off the Jemez Mountains toward the Rio Grande. In this moment my mind moves beyond the easily recognizable magnificence of a mountain canyon to an understanding of something grander – of the Jemez watershed nurturing life for thousands of years past and years forward.

Humans have been pretty aggressive in the Jemez ecosystem. The most sacrilegious scar is Los Alamos National Laboratory, a repository for all things nuclear, the birthplace of the atomic bomb. What juxtaposition.

In a place of incredible spirit and beauty modern society established a monument to the destruction of Earth. It just doesn't reconcile – fit in – with the conspicuous character of the Sangre de Cristos, Rio Grande Valley and Jemez Mountains. There is something unique about this place that people feel intuitively. It is something grander – something far more important, universal and eternal than the dark technology being cultivated at the Laboratory.

The perfection of the Frijoles speaks softly, but persistently, about the larger scheme of things. Ancient people whose shadows descend over me at river's edge have vanished from these piñon covered mesas and tranquil valleys. What had they done, or not done, to merit that fate? What caused them to simply wink out of existence with almost no historical legacy for us to understand? Their apparitions hover just across the Frijoles unable to confide in me. Yet, they seem eager to share insights that might spell the difference in our society's future. How will our civilization measure up compared to the ancient ones? I cannot imagine that the scales will tip very favorably in our direction.

Buoyant with the realization that a grand design is discernible if we only look for it, but chilled by the premonition of how difficult it will be for us to simply explain away how we have treated the Earth, I sit back and rest. It's been quite a day; a day rich in personal challenges for Dick and me, one filled with a conspicuous connection to the old ones whose spirits claim this land. I now know that in spring unexpected insights from those who have gone before might surface at any time, especially when least expecting these old friends.

**

191

Robert Michael Pyle grew up by Ravenna Park in northeast Seattle. The park provided many opportunities for him to slip into wildness despite being surrounded by a growing metropolis He writes in *The Thunder Tree*: "When people connect with nature, it happens *somewhere*. Almost everyone who cares deeply about the outdoors can identify a particular place where contact occurred. This may have been a wilderness, a national park, or a stretch of unbounded countryside, but more often the place that makes a difference is unspectacular: a vacant lot, a scruffy patch of woods, a weedy field, a stream, a green ravine like Ravenna — or a ditch."[10]

We catch a glimpse of the spirit of the old ones *somewhere* in the same fashion as Robert Michael Pyle suggests for the connection with nature. In the case of the Four Corners region, their shadows are ever-present. Yet few contemporaries recognize how profoundly they are affected by those who have gone before. In many respects this failure to see, feel and hear comes from pride and belief about our infallibility as a modern civilization.

Torn by the comforts and security of life in which humans are central to understanding the world, people are often reluctant to cross that line toward a life filled with uncertainties, things that go bump in the night, and a natural order in which we play an important role, but not the only role. Nonetheless, it's a leap definitely worth taking. Bandelier National Monument provides a perfect medium for making this leap beyond the edge of civilization while inexorably mingling with the ancient ones. In such a context it is difficult *not* to sense the presence of those who have gone before many centuries ago.

Understanding the inherent grace of wild lands is easy to achieve when topping a 14,000 foot peak covered with rocky rubble while sub-peaks, vast forest, sapphire-blue lakes and meandering rivers kneel in respect; or, when gazing on a vast desert strewn with saguaro cactus in fading moments of a theatric thunderstorm while swirling curtains of rain, fresh aromas heightened by oxygenated purity, wash over the land. In truth, wilderness and connections we crave are everywhere – in the empty and neglected lot next door, a forgotten row of trees lining a parking lot, a weed-filled ditch draining a highway, or patch of forgotten garden hidden behind your garage.

For many an important aspect of a wilderness experience is personal challenge; to conquer a peak, run a rapid, survive an all-day march across grassy plains, or to ski through a blizzard reaching the safety of distant yurt. In the backcountry are opportunities to test our mettle – to determine whether we are the fabric of civilization or cut from wildness. However, Southwest wilderness experiences are more – much more – than merely walks in the woods. Backcountry excursions are laced with ancestral shadows from people who have trod these lands centuries before. Wilderness and familial heritage inevitably merge. In this sense reconnecting with the wild becomes synonymous with enjoying the spirit of the old ones.

There is no better time to experience this synchronicity than spring. Our jaunt down the Frijoles River opened our sight to the Earth reborn, wildness at the edge of civilization. The rites of spring fulfilled by this one trip, even an excellent little adventure at that, pale in comparison with immersion into an ancient way of life. Dick and I followed the same paths, walked through the same villages, marveled at the same artistic designs painted on earthen pots, and loved the same life-filled spring morning as those ancient ones thousands of years earlier.

Like Robert Michael Pyle we encountered wilderness somewhere – Bandelier National Monument. However, this wasn't just any run-of-the-mill backwoods. That's because few sublime wilderness experiences in the Southwest are devoid of ancestral connections. Overlaying these moments are shadows of the ancient ones. They bring an entirely more vibrant understanding of the land and its history. In this respect a vividly tangible ancestral presence provides greater insight about our lives and the value of wilderness.

**

My bright blue rip-stop tent collapses with a barely audible sigh as I rush to pack and head into sunlight one-quarter mile up slope.

In mid-April, one year after Dick and I shared our Bandelier journey, spring's fickleness is all too apparent here in Alamo Canyon where high mesa abuts mountain ridge. An extremely crisp morning in camp is following a surprisingly cold night at 6,800 feet a low ridgeline away from El Rito de los Frijoles. Alamo Canyon is shaded from the cozy warmth of dawn's first light. I could wait an eternity until things warm up, however the logical move is to pack and climb out of this glacial trough.

Early evening had been mellow; pleasant as an achingly lovely day shaded into night. Sun's warmth retained by surrounding rock provided an illusion that summer would linger on the Pajarito Plateau. Spring's embrace was irrevocably lost to winter's icy grip at 3:00 a.m. In the night a swarm of bandits had dropped down off surrounding peaks. These frigid breezes quickly lowered Alamo Canyon's temperature some forty-plus degrees.

Instinct takes over with a rush to desperately zip-up my sleeping bag, forming a cocoon and waiting the requisite fifteen minutes for designer goose down to loft. At moments like this the few extra dollars spent for top-of-the-line gear seem like a pittance. It always pays to purchase the best equipment even if it means sacrificing other little niceties back in town. Awakened from a deeply comforting cradle of sleep, I'll never fully return to the land of peaceful dreams as any light sleeper knows. Too bad; rest is exactly why I ventured alone to Alamo Canyon's dark enclave. Until morning's glow lightens this hollow, I'm content to eavesdrop on sounds of the night and a tiny gurgling mountain stream by my tent.

As dawn's first light chases night away I rise to begin time-honored rituals of a backcountry breakfast. My archaic but trusty Svea stove sputters to life with an optimistic yellow-red flame followed by its signature blue blowtorch roar. In minutes water is at a rolling boil in anticipation of hydrating oatmeal and hot chocolate – real food will wait until I'm home. In-between gulps and bites I hasten to stuff the over-inflated sleeping bag in its sack while sneaking in furtive efforts to lower the tent. I'm working at a fever pitch knowing that real warmth beckons tantalizingly on the plateau above this hollow.

Pack on back, I begin the sacrament of tightening this strap and loosening that strap. Cinch the belt, lengthen stride. Shuck the pack back to the left side for balance. These are the mundane, but significant, activities of a new day in wilderness. At the edge of the canyon's shade, just before emerging into the promising sun of a new day I pause and look east toward an ocean of mesas and the impressive snow-capped Sangre de Cristos beyond. Among the shadows two deer are feeding peacefully.

Which way will it be this morning? So many choices and they all are alluring in their own special way. I could cross the mesa and head southeast some three and one-half miles toward the Shrine of the Stone Lions – two effigies of mountain lions, side-by-side carved in the tuff and ceremoniously surrounded by a ring of boulders. Visitors have donated deer antlers and pottery shards as memorials to the lions. This shrine rests a quarter mile from the huge Pueblo of the Stone Lions. From the shrine it's another four miles back to the visitor center.

Alternatively I'm thinking about how nice it is to walk south down Capulin Canyon on the way to Painted Cave. That's quite a hike – seven miles to the rock art and then almost as much back to the car. How old are the paintings of red hands and crosses in the cave? Clearly several of these depictions came after the arrival of Spanish missionaries; reportedly many are the handiwork of shepherds. Large tuff blocks and cave-house ruins lie scattered below Painted Cave. Petroglyphs abound. Generations have intermingled signatures, obliterating precise attribution.

Either of these two choices will place me directly in contact with the old ones and their religious artifacts. It's always impressive looking back across the centuries at human efforts to leave an indelible mark. What were the ancient and not-so-ancient ones trying to convey? Are these effigies and rock art merely graffiti? I would rather believe that these depictions are a sincere attempt at expressing their love for this land, its beauty and the seasons that unfold over this canyon-mesa-mountain country. Whatever the explanation, it's thrilling to walk under the spell of these shadows.

A third choice is to head north to El Rito de los Frijoles and that magical little stream flowing through an enchanted canyon. However, how many times have I made that trip? I've traveled that way so often that I could almost do it in my sleep. Won't that choice be boring?

Then I remember a mystical moment in the backcountry one hundred miles south – the surprise of hiking a trail that I walk scores of times every year. This had become a trail that lost its magic until out of nowhere I found a delicate, but vivid, pottery shard; the lip of a bowl with red and black painted stripes inside. Ancestral shadows reemerged over a once common path. Now walks along this trail sparkle with possibilities and looming apparitions of those who have gone before.

A decision comes easily – the springtime joy of Frijoles Canyon calls. Perhaps Ancestral Puebloans have played their hand in swaying my mind. Who really knows why one route is chosen over two other perfectly fascinating routes? Mind made up, I turn toward the north and the awaiting abyss of Cañon de los Frijoles.

Working up a bit of steam when crossing the intervening mesa, I reflect on the simple pleasure of freedom from work, urban life and electronic intrusions. I'm totally out of it – no cell phone, no CD, no Wii, no iPhone, no body – completely surrounded by breathtaking wildness. Fists unclench and tense sore muscles relax. It's going to be a fine, fine morning.

As the trail drops down four hundred steep feet to the heavily forested canyon carrying the Frijoles River, the atmosphere changes in a tangible way. Vegetation shifts dramatically from Pajarito Plateau's scattered ponderosa pines to verdantly lush shaded canyon. Deciduous trees and occasional fir cling to the southern edge of this east-flowing canyon with pine on the northern side. Long before human-caused fires destroyed the plateau's forest, potent thunderstorms flowing angrily off the Jemez Mountains did their own thinning. Yet, the canyon always seems to have dodged this fatal bullet

Leveling out on a bed of pine needles, the trail weaves through gigantic ponderosa pines with rich cinnamon bark. After a few hundred feet it curves sharply back toward the sun. Sunbeams float down through the dense canopy with light and dust dancing together toward canyon floor. The milky white Frijoles River gurgles around a bend, flowing merrily eight miles toward a confluence with the Rio Grande. White volcanic ash taints this vital ribbon of life. Small fish thriving in the stream dart out of sight toward safety under submerged logs, overhanging brush and mossy river rocks.

In silent forest and hush canyon the river's presence is embracing. Only a couple miles from the nearest road, it's enough distance to be deep in wilderness. Walking along the life-giving river, a profound sense of peace rises up with ghosts of those before shimmering in the background. Amid this solitude, my spirit sings. It lifts a melodious tune to this special glen and life within. Burnishing the moment into deep recesses of my brain I turn down canyon and begin the slow walk back to my other life. Leaving this sanctuary of upper Frijoles Canyon behind, I'll keep in my possession a lingering fascination about ancient paths watched over by ancestral spirits.

Too few of us hear
the clarion bell of silence...
life gets in the way.

A master painter -
Wind froths the grassy ocean.
Elk calf lies hidden.

Jagged granite stones
rumble with tumbling water.
Eek! Eek! warns pika.

TERRYE BULLERS

10
All Roads Lead to Pecos

"What the heck is that?"

Eyes fluttering like a frantic butterfly, an instantly perspiring young Kiowa warrior jerks awake with a start. Left hand grasping desperately for a razor-sharp knife; his right hand sweeps around for tools that made him infamous as the best-of-the-best – a leather sheath holding several lethal arrows and his prized hunting bow. Heart pounding and beads of sweat dimpling his brow, in one graceful lunge he's squatting on the balls of his feet, head swinging from side-to-side like a dog's tail trying to make order out of chaos in gray morning light of this little prairie swale.

A thunderous rumble fills his ears rising in an ominous crescendo. It's as if everyone in his tribe was pounding a rhythmic cadence on ceremonial drums. Fuzzy-headedness evaporates while he urgently gauges the situation. What a horrible way to start a day – wrestled from a sweet dream of Running Deer and thrust headlong into a battle for his life. But, with whom? What?

He breathes deeply filtering a fog of acrid dust that is descending like a shroud over his camp. The Kiowa brave suddenly realizes it could only be one of two things – a marauding band of Cheyenne funneling a coup of horses ahead of them, or, if his luck holds, a herd of buffalo is pushing west towards water. If he ever wants to taste Running Deer's lips again, it had better be buffalo. Some nasty rumors have been flying around the prairie about a bunch of testosterone-laced Cheyenne braves intent on avenging past atrocities to loved ones.

A two-foot wide coulee flush with tall bristling grass runs up the swale's left shoulder. If he can just snake his way forty feet, it'll be possible to see what's happening on the other side. No time to check his pony's tether; it must be tied tightly because the horse hasn't moved. It's just staring to the north, wild-eyed, with nostrils flared and brown ears bent forward, tugging on the reins.

"Stupid Cayuse, don't blow it for me now."

Like a sidewinder on a scorching sand dune the brave slithers toward the swale's crest of waving grasses. How many times has he done this when sneaking up on unsuspecting prey or enemies? Only this time he's trying to swing the pendulum the other way, to go from prey to predator. Two more feet and he will have a view. Pounding reverberations are literally shaking the very ground he's hugging; vibrating like an earthquake. Then, he gently parts the grass and carefully peers out on the other side.

A day in the life of a Plains Indian is always exciting and totally unpredictable. Out there in the immense ocean of grass undulating like swells on an uneasy sea, it's tough to ever reach an unobstructed view into the next gully, draw or arroyo. Little copses of trees and shrubs hunker down, completely invisible with the roll of the land, hiding danger; providing shelter from aggressors.

As the prairie rises toward what years later will be known as the Rocky Mountains, creases and rifts increase like the wrinkled brow of an elder. This discernible ascent and visual heft of mountains on the distant skyline signal to nomadic travelers that their prized destination – Pecos Pueblo – is only a few days ride west. In a piñon, juniper and ponderosa forest along a swift flowing river rests an amazingly magical town. In this part of the world, all roads lead to Pecos – a center of trade where tribal quarrels are momentarily forgotten and excitement fills the air.

Pecos, New Mexico, became a portal for trade and information among the pueblos and high plains tribes. Kiowa, Comanche, Apache and other nomadic tribes traveled to Pecos to do business with the Jemez, Cochiti, Zuni and Taos Pueblos. Imagine the thrill of meeting strange new people, bartering for goods seen for the first time in Pecos, hearing tales of abundant game and fisheries in mountains far to the north, or sharing in gossip about a shaman's premonition of white-faced invaders.

Sitting on a shoulder of the southern Rocky Mountains, Pecos is blessed with a temperate climate, access to plentiful game, fresh rushing water, forest providing fuel and materials essential to life, and centrality to major trails. Pecos Pueblo first gained notoriety in the mid-1300s capitalizing on location as a strategic chokepoint for trade and news. Its market bristled with turquoise and other precious stones; buffalo, deer and antelope hides; pottery; fish; crops; and, a veritable cornucopia of goods flowing up from Mexico.

The Kiowa warrior about to look upon his destiny is bound for Pecos with a collection of premium antelope hides he collected over the last few weeks. This will be his third trip to the Pueblo. He is determined to bring back glittering turquoise jewels for Running Deer and to test his luck with games of chance in hidden Pecos alleyways. Perhaps he can parlay the hides into a small fortune — sufficient lucre to win the hand of this fair Indian maid. He might even double his wealth if buffalo wait over the swale's ridge. A few buffalo hides added to his cache and Running Deer's father would clearly see his value as son-in-law.

Parting the grass, confident that the thunder is from a renegade band of bison stampeding toward water, the Kiowa brave courageously lifts his head above a thick clump of Gama grass and Bluestem. Assuredly the Great Spirit is smiling on him today by sending all these buffalo his way.

The first arrow pierces his back, released by a Cheyenne warrior who snuck up behind the Kiowa brave. Before this arrow's pain can intensify to full-on white-hot, the Kiowa catches his final view of this world — ten Cheyenne herding forty horses along the swale and a terrifying sight of a rider thirty feet away with bow drawn. For a split second the Kiowa sees the incoming arrow as it shatters his cheek and drives deeply into his brain. His final parting thought is of Running Deer and turquoise jewels waiting in Pecos; Pecos that magical town of dreams.

***

Dick slows the battered and bruised Toyota to a crawl carefully negotiating hairpin turns within a narrowing canyon. At this particular moment realization hits that we're unequivocally back home in the high country of the Pecos Wilderness. Why a certain set of bends in the road brings this to mind isn't clear. Perhaps it's a serene black pool of water beneath willows and cottonwoods; maybe it's a glimpse up-canyon of lofty peaks calling enticingly about alpine explorations. Whatever the trigger, mentally and physically we've fully broached wilderness a few miles north of Pecos Pueblo's ancient ruins.

Human use of this road goes back centuries and perhaps millennia. The path may now be paved, but for eons feet pounded a persistent trail alongside the Pecos River. Up here game could be found – sustenance for hundreds waiting patiently back at the pueblo. Like the old ones Dick and I are partly here on a hunt – he for trout and me for wildness. Both can be found in copious quantities throughout this alluring range where high prairies and desert canyons collide with the backbone of our country.

Today may only turn out as a little exploration in the Pecos Wilderness, but it should be rich with adventure and replenishment. Seven centuries ago many at Pecos Pueblo sought the same things. Dick and I will use the old Cowles trailhead located at 8,200 feet leading to Winsor Creek and thence to high country lakes.

Casually pulling items from the back seat and stuffing them in packs, we agree to deliberately saunter. A consciously plodding pace is often maddening when destination-bound, but rushing won't renew; sauntering both renews and enriches. At the moment it's all about setting the right tempo.

Henry David Thoreau liked to characterize his many daily rambles from Walden Pond as sauntering. Hiking implies a planned destination and specific objective to be attained; too regimented for Henry. Walking, in contrast, suggests a deliberately slower pace, perhaps without the spirit of adventure. Sauntering falls somewhere in-between these two approaches. It hints at interest in discovery and willingness to be detoured by something of curiosity. Sauntering also conveys a sense of purpose — to cover reasonable distance when seeking an end such as exercise, or to achieve an adrenaline rush during exploration.

Impetuous folk focus on hiking and covering great distances. The metrics they apply when judging a hike's worthiness are normally mileage and elevation gained. Many of us have used these measures in smug satisfaction after a long day's effort at bagging a peak, reaching a hidden lake or following a meandering river. Rich rewards of sauntering moderate the value of covering vast distances and climbing heroic elevations. Moments outdoors become more introspective and meaningful through the simple act of sauntering.

For some sauntering is an opportunity to smell the roses, or columbine, lupine and marsh marigolds. It's a time for something other than conquering another goal. Appreciating an old growth tree can have more value than hiking fifteen miles. Watching a buffalo calf rollick in the sun attains immensely greater worth than hiking over a distant ridge crest. At its full extension, sauntering becomes a metaphor for blending adventure with the reinvigoration of our lives.

Dick and I are following a primitive path winding along the side of a steep aspen-laced ridge heading toward darkly mysterious forest lakes. A classic Rocky Mountain creek – Winsor Creek – parallels the trail for the first half-mile, singing a wonderfully melodious tune welcoming us to this glen. Lush aspen, columbine and yarrow bracket this creek whose white water leaps over gray mossy boulders and fallen silver aspen. We relax a noticeable degree or two while slowly, intentionally, sauntering up the trail, blending into the mountainside. How we love this country – Colorado hundreds of miles south.

A branch snaps in an aspen copse one-hundred feet above us. Deer, elk, bear? Think of how cautious Pecos Pueblo hunters were when they walked this very trail. Down on the Pueblo's high open mesas spotted with low piñons and junipers it's definitely big sky country with impressively vast vistas. What a contrast to these dark woods where line-of-sight is but a few yards and only question-marks surround an imposing cliff or bend. Today most of the danger is long gone, but back in those days sojourners had to be on their guard to anticipate the unknown.

Methodically hiking, we eventually top out on a 10,000-foot high ridge with a meadow of feathery grasses, lime-green aspen and purple-blue wild iris. To the east a great high mesa of the Pecos Wilderness seems to go on forever covered with shimmering aspen groves, black-green spruce and fir. We'll wind around the western terminus of this creek's valley and then set course along another more heavily forested bowl bound for a small, and very popular, lake. There's no predetermined destination today. We have no goals. We can stop at any moment. The idea is to enjoy the woods, friendship and any excitement that might pop up.

A healthy forest of spruce, pine and aspens delivers signature Rocky Mountain trail conditions – the chance for walking under a comforting canopy punctuated by brilliant blue splotches overhead. In sheltered hollows the forest reaches a tad higher providing tangy cool temperatures and spongy duff as tread. Breathing is a bit more difficult due to the achingly thin air. Dick adjusts by setting a purposefully slower cadence.

Thick stands of conifers parallel the trail exemplifying the Pecos' wonderfully vibrant vegetation driven crazy by huge winter snows and endless summer thunderstorms. Occasionally a jay, thrush or junco flits through the open canopy paying no attention to two intruders trundling along the well-defined path. How many generations of these birds have come and gone through Pecos country since early Pueblo days?

Around a small ridge our path enters a series of forested basins spread like spots on a pinto pony where fir trees grow to tremendous size. The forest seems vibrantly alive with sighing breezes, soothing sounds of rushing creek, and rich humus and resin aromas wafting throughout the under story. Glimpses of dazzling green meadows, overflowing with flourishing grass appear to the north and east. We're nearing Winsor Creek where it meanders through several saucer-shaped fields and fir groves before falling again toward the Pecos River.

Winsor Creek bounces joyously down its granite boulder bed, sparkling in sunlight and proclaiming a bounty of snowfall from the previous winter. Where the creek crosses our path, we plop down and dig into our respective lunches. Out fly bland peanut butter and jelly sandwiches that under the circumstances taste as good as anything we might have had at the best brew pub or deli. Even ordinary tap water tastes pretty good. Dozing in the heat, sun deeply penetrates my green-black plaid wool shirt creating an envelope of sublime comfort. With these conditions it's difficult not to feel connected to this beautiful land and those whose footsteps we're retracing.

After lunch, we wander an eighth-of-a-mile to Stewart Lake relaxing in a shallow bowl at 10,200 feet. Over-used and even abused camping spots litter the area. People simply love a destination like Stewart Lake to death. Mountain water lures them to waved-lapped shores. Subsequent pounding by thousands of boots denudes the lake's outlet. Fir trees, too big to break down as campers search for firewood, have branches unceremoniously pruned to a height of eight feet — the point where no more branches can easily be broken off.

Over-use characteristically began when surrounding community populations soared. The ancient ones from Pecos Pueblo knew about this lake and frequented it as summer boiled over in the lowlands. But, who was the first to follow the twisting stream toward its source? When they reached the lake they must have been pleasantly surprised by its inviting character as well as the fact that it offered another possible repository of food — fish — to be harvested during times of scarcity. Imagine being the first human to look over Stewart Lake's waters.

At roughly four acres, this is a very decent body of water for the Pecos Wilderness. It has a pleasant, almost neighborly, character; just deep enough to be more than a pond and wide enough to offer distance when someone else inadvertently intrudes. Ringed by thick forest, sun sparkles off waves inexorably blowing toward the northern shore as breezes dance through the surrounding forest, virtually failing to move a single limb. Squatting on the shoreline, bathed in sunshine, I have the sensation that I'm melting into the land — like a fallen log lying half submerged in Stewart Lake, reclamation is underway.

Dick runs out of patience as fire-in-the-belly passion overwhelms his longing for a nap. He sets off to fish diminutive streams weaving through the expansive meadows below Stewart

Lake. I can't believe that he'll have much luck. This seems to be an outrageously optimistic move on his part because the stream banks are seldom more than a foot wide, fringed with a heady mantle of vibrantly flourishing grass drooping into the water like tired college students in class who partied too hardy the night before. On the other hand, this grassy cloak delivers excellent protective cover for fish.

Wearing a madman's bug-eyed vacant stare, Dick is determined to thoroughly test this theory and to bring back a plateful for dinner. He's anxious to get his line in the water and without as so much a word makes it abundantly clear that I need to stay away for a while. Even if the fish aren't biting, he'll have a little fishing expedition and in its course wade over this high country meadow, swathed in grass to his mid-calves, negotiating muddy spots, and using every ounce of stealth that he has to creep up on unsuspecting denizens of these clear, swiftly flowing streams.

According to some cosmic rule that can never be violated, Dick will not lower himself to fish in a lake. Some inexplicable inferior standard is associated with lazy fishers who acquiesce to trolling lakes; Dick just doesn't see any worthwhile value in standing around waiting for fish to come to him. He enjoys the chase, stalking elusive trout that use every crafty measure possible to avoid capture from hawk, eagle or fisher. Whatever the motivation, it's always a real pleasure to see him work a stream—intense concentration; eyes flitting about reading the water, observing a fin near the surface, calculating the odds given a bank's undercut; rod, reel and man becoming one in the poetry of fly fishing.

Summarily dismissed, I'll head up-trail to Lake Katherine, taking my time, no rush, just sauntering and with no exact intention of reaching the lake. We turn simultaneously to our adventures. Backtracking to the stream crossing, I begin a slow climb up the east side of Santa Fe Baldy toward this wonderful alpine lake nestled in a rocky basin at 11,750 feet.

Honestly, I don't know what I enjoy most – taking my time slowly climbing up the trail, inspecting everything as I go; freedom from companionship; or aloneness with the mountain. Perhaps it's the combination of the three that adds a tasty sense of exploration in slow motion. Solitude also lets me reflect back on the drive along the Pecos River. Pecos Pueblo is not much more than a dozen or so miles downstream as the crow flies. How much did this forest give to sustain the burgeoning trade center? Did hunters routinely chase elk, sheep and deer on Santa Fe Baldy's upper ramparts?

Almost immediately the trail ramps upward, scrambling ambitiously toward the highest reaches of Santa Fe Baldy, snaking through ancient gnarled fir trees that have stood the test of time. It is slow going as altitude begins to take hold and I desperately suck oxygen like a chain smoker on his last cigarette. Overhead, squirrels chatter incessantly, scolding, indignant about having their peace and quiet disturbed. Their frenzied jabbering lets me know that most people seldom get above Stewart Lake's trail. In times past I bet that many of these squirrels' predecessors made it to someone's communal dinner pot down at Pecos Pueblo.

As the mountain reaches near-vertical and views open up I'm able to get a better appreciation for the lay of the land; of erect mountain peaks rising above 12,622 feet and falling precipitously to forested benches, strewn with lakes. Wooded basins holding Stewart Lake and Spirit Lake to the south look like two distant birdbaths. I can see for miles across the Pecos Wilderness and southeast toward the town of Pecos. This sunny southern slope would have been perfect for tribal members sent out on a vision quest. Their thoughts would have soared in measure with the land flowing below them.

Although I'm crawling along in terms of pace, it doesn't take too long before splotches of snow begin to appear along the trail, laced with fir needles, assorted branches and wisps of moss. A towering rock face rises on the right side of the trail, Santa Fe Baldy's northern rampart, while sun and shade play together in a gentle way at its base. Lake Peak appears across a rocky ridge poking up to just over 12,000 feet. Surely those at the Pecos Pueblo who made it this far into the wilderness enjoyed the same sense of magic. Their travels to this point may have been purposeful – hunting for big game, going through a religious ritual, or defensive patrolling against marauding warriors – but I doubt that their pleasure was any less.

In another quarter-mile, last winter's snow intensifies like an explosion and the outlet stream from Lake Katherine comes into view. At the base of a long frothing white waterfall tumbling down forested slopes, the trail disappears. A good reason for continuing further doesn't surface no matter how hard I search. That's because I've already found what I came looking for – a sweet saunter in lonesome wild lands to sub-alpine country. Lake Katherine will be saved for another day.

With a pleasing splash of mountain water ringing in my ears, wind sighing in conifers overhead, and sun beaming down releasing resins in stately trees, my walk has delivered the right amount of "soft" adventure that I needed. An easy stroll to beckoning meadows hundreds of feet below is all that remains, but first I can't escape thinking about how many others have preceded me to this point. My incredibly great fortune compared to them is leisure.

Unlike prehistoric residents of Pecos Pueblo, I'm not on any specific mission. I have more latitude to simply enjoy this mountain. I don't have to bring back a slab of delicious game, reconnaissance about rival tribes, or lofty insights from the Great Spirit. Nonetheless, even as they worked they also had moments when the mountain spoke to them, the streams sang in such a manner as to drive away lonesomeness, and sun warmed them to the depth of their beings. Perhaps my greatest gift from this trip is realization that the ancient ones and I share a common bond; we both knew the joy of this captivating wilderness.

Spinning away from the semi-waterfall I head southeast and a precipitous drop to Stewart Lake. Big thoughts are finished for the day and ancestral shadows retreat. Like a car set on cruise control, I walk in the warmth of a Pecos sun toward aspens fluttering thousands of feet below. It was a good day to saunter.

An hour later at the trail junction I search for Dick. Where is he? Carefully picking my way east toward an opening beyond the forest's fringe, I eventually spy him in the distance.

Out in a meadow shaped like a huge green leg bone Dick is hunkered over, walking deftly with line outcast, stalking some poor fish. If the old ones had the benefit of such fancy gear it would be difficult to tell them apart from him. There is something decidedly *primeval* in Dick's movements and crouching; a hunting posture honed over the millennia that defies modernity. It's thrilling to watch this dance from a distance, but I'm confused about whom I'm rooting for – Dick or the trout?

Like the best hunters from Pecos Pueblo, Dick knew I was present well before he caught sight of me physically. My intrusion dramatically altered the distinctive spirit of this pastoral setting. It was akin to a major change in atmospheric pressure. Although words escape the phenomenon, Dick *and* the fish felt the moment when I broached the bounds of the meadow. My heft altered the equation and tilted the balance between predator and prey to the trout's advantage. At that split second Dick knew that the chase was over.

With a gigantic grin on his face Dick spins around to say, "This is the most fun I've had in months. Caught three small ones and let them go. No keepers. They're small, but are they ever fun to chase."

Size of fish doesn't matter. Stream volume doesn't matter. This is no San Juan River with its infamous gargantuan trout. This is merely a small set of streams weaving through meadow in the Pecos. It will not be included in any fishing guide. No wealthy anglers will be flying from Texas or Oklahoma in private planes to visit this meadow.

I back off a bit, trying to reset the playing field. Dick has to attempt just a few more casts. His Mona Lisa smile and sparkling eyes tell me everything that I need to know. In his own way Dick has been enjoying a "soft" adventure that places everything else into perspective — trivial problems at work, interpersonal strife with unbridled egos, and frailties of small people. None of these worries matter anymore. Dick has found a small dollop of adventure today — the sort of replenishment that only wildness provides. Nurtured by this fabulous day in the woods, we turn to saunter home past Pecos Pueblo, better people for the experience.

***

Dick and I went to the Pecos Wilderness as a doorway to fishing adventure and renewal. Sauntering instilled a refreshing perspective on the important things in life. Even though we didn't run into other people on this outing, we weren't alone. Shadows of the ancient ones from Pecos Pueblo hovered as I ascended to an aerie high on the mountain's flank. Their spirits reveled once again in the hunt as Dick used primal stealth to connect with elusive trout. However, we aren't the only ones who experience connections with the old ones such as these out in the Southwest.

Terry Tempest Williams recalled similar encounters in *An Unspoken Hunger* while hiking canyon country of southeastern Utah: "Walking in wilderness becomes a meditation. I followed a small drainage up one of the benches. Lithic scatter was everywhere, evidence of Anasazi culture, a thousand years past. I believed the flakes of chert and obsidian would lead me to ruins. I walked intuitively."[11]

Tempest Williams' connection with distant ancestors while navigating Utah wilderness has distinct parallels to the Pecos experience Dick and I enjoyed. Our eyes opened in realization that others traveled these paths years before, navigating the same wildernesses and sharing the same activities. Gone is the murkiness about where we fit in the infinite continuum of time, replaced by something much more substantive. One hundred percent comprehension isn't always needed to understand that we are ineffably connected with those who have gone before.

All roads led to Pecos more than seven centuries ago in this part of the Southwest. Sometimes it's necessary to repeatedly travel those roads in order to appreciate what it was like to live with fewer accoutrements and the most rudimentary technology. A day hike into the Pecos Wilderness brings startling insights into the life of old where people took nothing for granted and rejoiced in the bounty of the Earth; perhaps by spending a couple nights those perceptions can be raised an entire level of magnitude.

***

A flagman swaddled in tawny Carhart overalls signals us to stop in the middle of the trail using a fluorescent orange flag to wave us down. Like back-to-back cars clogging a busy street we almost run into the backside of each other.

"Need you to wait here, there's blasting going on ahead."

I turn to Terrye and Bill who back off a pace or two with a semi-bewildered look. This is the first time we've seen wilderness trail construction that required two people with walkie-talkies to direct traffic. No problem — we know exactly what to do. Any excuse to drop our backpacks is a good excuse, so we slough off these weighty burdens amid a classic stand of huge silvery-white aspen — a Pecos Wilderness signature. Where to set our prover-bial stones is somewhat troublesome to figure out because this path is muddy and rocky, artifacts of recent reconstruction.

Trails in the Pecos are centuries old, the product of indige-nous people who preceded inhabitants of the Pecos Pueblo, trap-pers and early pioneers. Not surprisingly they chose a path of least resistance that gradually was beaten into place by countless feet and hooves. What calamity justified blasting and re-grading ancient trail tread? Isn't it a bit presumptuous to think that af-ter all of these years we know a better way to weave among the Pecos' verdant fields and thick stands of aspens?

No sooner are packs off our backs than the all-clear signal is given. Now the trail crew wants us to hurry up and get past so that they can continue with their work. Picking our way through disheveled earthen mounds we come upon an analog of city con-struction — too many supervisors and not enough actual workers. Clad in worn overalls and filthy jeans, at least the work crew ap-pears to have gotten themselves dirty at some point doing some-thing. We exchange greetings and continue on our way trying to figure out what the big construction project is all about.

We're hiking at 10,000 feet on the side of Round Mountain this soft summer morning. Tatters of menacing black cloud hang over Santa Fe Baldy and the Truchas Peaks, sure indicators of summer thunderstorm activity to be anticipated later this afternoon. Rich grasses and abundant purple-blue iris dot meadows of Round Mountain and speak profoundly about healthy rains the wilderness has received this summer. Across the Pecos River drainage, at Vega Bonito, vigorous stands of aspen flutter in the breeze. Sunlight will soon disappear as yesterday's moisture wells up in anvil-shaped thunderstorms repeating the process which nourishes the Pecos and its waters.

Bound for Beatty's Cabin on the Pecos River just below a confluence with the Rito de los Chimayosos, we're looking forward to a couple nights in the Pecos' mellow wilderness. With only 1,700 feet total elevation gain and loss over just short of seven miles, the walk to Beatty's Cabin is classic and heavily used. By going during mid-week, the number of other visitors we might encounter is minimized and if it all works out perhaps we will have a campsite for ourselves.

Jack's Creek Campground at 8,850 feet was left behind an hour ago; a repository for dusty pickup trucks hauling multi-horse trailers. Packers use the Pecos with utter nonchalance. Most likely trail work on the side of Round Mountain is an effort to remove protruding rocks that are causing aggravating trouble for horses. Those using this path are destined for a Forest Service cabin and corrals. Perhaps it's just a make-work project or training ground for a trail crew. The exact reason doesn't really matter much to us except the potential for attracting more visitors. After Jack's Creek Campground was renovated, more motorized vehicles and people were drawn from the plains to this special corner of New Mexico.

Continuing through luxuriant meadows laced with copses of aspens scarred black up to eight feet from elk rubbing their antlers in the fall and nibbled in spots during winter, we reach a promontory at Noisy Brook. Our view into the canyon of the Pecos River is rewarding. Hamilton Mesa bunches up against Round Mountain. Narrowing canyon slopes give way to black-gray rock as the river forces its way downstream. Steep granite walls bracket the Pecos and create a fishing haven for those who really want to expend extra effort in seeking out seldom-fished pools of the canyon's defile. With plenty of pure water and difficult access, there must be lunkers lurking in those river bends and riffles.

Unlike Pecos trails that climb toward high sub-alpine and alpine lakes, this path to Beatty's Cabin slices straight through the heart of prime elk habitat. Elk are renowned for achieving impressive size in these mellow woods. While we look down the Pecos drainage it doesn't take much to add two plus two together. A fabulous stream provided plump trout and these grass-filled meadows interspersed among protective stands of aspen nurtured herds of gigantic elk. Enterprising Pecos Puebloans could easily have harvested food needed by travelers from the plains and neighboring pueblos. The precise ingredients for favorable trade were located right at the backdoor step of the Pecos Pueblo.

Overhead skies are becoming increasingly overcast as heat and moisture coalesces, forming billowy cumulous clouds laden with replenishment for the vast Pecos watershed. A distant rumble confirms what we know is inevitable – rain is on its way. But, a repeat growl doesn't follow. Experience tells us that there is still plenty of time to reach camp before a downpour arrives. Nonetheless, Bill and Terrye ramp up the pace as we gradually descend towards meadows holding Beatty's Cabin and our campsite.

Eventually a few more ominous growls bark down from the blackening sky. Almost running to beat the rain, we pass several stands of spruce interspersed with aspen – trees that are in the prime of their lives. Thick trunks of both spruce and aspen testify to the overall health of this forest. There are none of those spindly little aspens reaching into the sky that are so prevalent on dry Colorado mountain slopes. These are massively-thick trees in the range of 15-18 inches and well on their way to greater diameters if conditions continue as they have the past winter and summer. Quaking leaves rustle noisily as the mounting storm sucks energy – latent warmth from yesterday and fresh wafts of this morning's sun-enriched air – and moisture from the Pecos.

A peppering shower of droplets pelts us as we enter thigh-high brown grass in a field surrounding Beatty's Cabin. This meadow slopes steeply toward the Pecos River a hundred feet or more down among spruce and fir trees along canyon bottom. We really pick up the pace trying to reach shelter in a grove before things escalate. Racing by the Forest Service cabin, there's no time to visit; we'll have to see what the cabin and corral are all about later in the day. A crack and then boom resonate throughout the drainage as we run for cover. Safe from falling rain beneath huge trees, our concern shifts to avoiding becoming toast by lightning.

This little drama has been playing out each summer across the centuries. Once monsoon season begins, the odds are excellent that each afternoon will bring a refreshing shower or two. In some cases the Pecos drainage becomes sopping and streams rise to overflowing. Indigenous people surely made the connection between lightning and danger in the proximity of exposed ridges or when hunkering down beneath towering trees. They may not have possessed modern lightweight tents, but there always seems to be passable shelter beneath the right tree. Summer huts of bark and tree limbs may have approximated the flimsy shelters we carry today.

Just as suddenly as it begins, the drizzle stops. This is a perfect interlude to actually assess camping sites. We're only yards away from a trail junction leading several miles southeast to Iron Gate Campground. I'll place my tent sufficiently far enough from Terrye and Bill so that privacy is maintained.

Having settled on a prime spot, out come my North Face tent and rain fly with its pencil-thin aluminum poles. Erect in seconds, now I simply have to set up the fly and my little home is ready for a few possessions. In goes a navy blue Sierra Designs sleeping bag gobbling up air as it unfurls, followed by Ensolite sleeping pad. In time the bag will loft into a luxurious cocoon of warmth. Extra clothing and personal items go last before I look for a tree trunk with broken branch from which to hang the empty pack.

Our campsite is perfect. Huge downed logs serve as a kitchen and dining room. There are plenty of places to sit and that provide tables for cooking. The logs also offer a visual barrier from our tents spread fifty feet apart. This is just what the doctor ordered for base camp. The trail to Iron Gate rises on the mountain slope just a bit to our east – the only disagreeable intrusion. Branches and tree limbs under which we camp shelter the view up to Beatty's Cabin. A well-used fire ring is mid-way between our respective sites. Not bad for having to hurry up. The only concern is finding wood in this heavily used site; water is easily accessible with the Pecos flowing right outside our doors.

Rain falls softly that entire afternoon keeping us penned-up in our tents. Go light fastpackers argue that outdoors fanatics should leave all the superfluous stuff at home, such as books. After spending three hours in a compact backpacking tent without a good book, it's easy to see the folly of this suggestion. For me the rhythm of constant drizzle on tent fly is soothing. Snug in an extraordinary down bag, I slow down and enjoy a simple afternoon looking out on pleasing forest through the tent's screen. Like the falling rain recharging the Pecos, I'm on trickle recharge.

While exhalations by surrounding conifers envelope our camp, I'm trying to place myself in the moccasins of Plains Indians that followed the intoxicating roads to Pecos. Their lives were spent out in a big sky and comparatively featureless landscape. What a stark contrast these huge Rocky Mountains must have presented to people more accustomed to a horizontal world. They may have found the forests claustrophobic and spooky; the streams excessively small compared to the broad rivers they knew at home. It must have been disorienting to lose a trail in dense woods and then fight for hours to figure out where to head.

Imagine the Kiowa brave befriending several men at Pecos Pueblo on his first trip to this land. Perhaps he was invited to accompany them on a hunt up the Pecos River toward the sweet meadows of what many years later will be known as Beatty's Cabin. When summer afternoon rains forced the hunting party to hole-up it was likely a welcomed opportunity to relax and share tales, not a menacing intrusion due to the theatrics of thunder, wind and stinging hail. Their precise strategy for avoiding the elements – crouching under a massive fir or building rudimentary shelters to fend off the daily dose of precipitation – is not known. Game was more plentiful than it is today but the flourishing Pecos population may have eroded the ecosystem's sustainability.

Most likely the hunting party would have found the same rhythms that Terrye, Bill and I are discovering on our little expedition. Each day would begin with a breathtakingly fresh morning followed by a welling up of humidity and heat forming towering thunderheads. Depending on available moisture, shortly after noon a deluge or shower would fall forcing them to seek shelter just as the animals they hunted had gone to daybeds. Evenings would begin to clear unless a particularly nasty storm was hovering in the area. The following day this process would be repeated.

We're merely following a long-line of voyagers who visited the Pecos Wilderness and discovered the necessity of bending human agendas to fit what Mother Nature threw at them. I don't doubt that the Kiowa brave spent a good portion of each afternoon engrossed as fat drops of cold rain intermixed with pebbles of hail bounced off the fields surrounding Beatty's Cabin. Weary from hunting and traveling it was a time to enjoy the fat of the land and think about family perhaps hundreds of miles away.

Next day the menu for discovery varies. Terrye and Bill head off on an ambitious hike up Little Jicarita Peak. They'll be gone for the better part of twelve hours, returning very late in the day spent from a long ramble. I have a different plan – I want to become immersed in the Pecos, to know this garden at Beatty's Cabin as an old friend. How can I know a place intimately if I'm always rushing to scramble up this peak or that; or, to touch an alpine lake for a few minutes before rushing back to camp. I'll just hunker down in these meadows and see what treasures unfold.

Exploration begins at Beatty's Cabin before radiating outward. Although the cabin is empty and locked, windows afford an unobstructed view of a rough bunkhouse with disheveled kitchen; its dilapidated wood-fired oven has seen plenty of cooks in its time. Behind the cabin is a well-used corral for tethering horses used by rangers and trail crews. Years of harsh weather have added a rich patina to the cabin and it is beginning to decompose into the surrounding meadows. Somehow the funky structure seems destined for this spot as though it grew out of the land instead of upon it.

Beyond the cabin are pockets of meadows bracketed by aspens and firs spread like a smorgasbord of lakes. Throughout the afternoon I saunter these slopes beneath Pecos Baldy, at 12,500 feet a towering rock monolith. A trail up Rito Sebadillosos toward Pecos Baldy Lake makes no pretense about where it goes or what it takes to reach the Lake. It's a 1,500-foot climb to this high alpine lake, slightly larger than Stewart Lake and equivalent to Lake Katherine. But, the lake doesn't call. I'm just wandering lazily from one copse of trees to the next inhaling musty aspen scents and blending with the land.

Late that afternoon on my third foray into the forest, I lay back on wiry grass below a group of twenty or so thick aspen. It's fascinating how individual pieces of wildness around Beatty's Cabin fit together, a whole that rivets my attention. In aspen groves' shadowy recesses, clumps of blue-white columbine dominate while yellow-red shooting stars are scattered in sunnier spots. The fragile, but huge, blue and white beauties command full attention alongside miniscule damp springs or small creeks.

As shadows from Pecos Baldy Peak fall over meadows and cool the forest, the wilderness exhales, emitting a fragrance at once sweet and musty. Decaying aspen leaves and wet aspen bark bleed a characteristic scent of high mountain gardens. Warm grasses, insufficiently watered by yesterday's showers, shout for more – a bounty that will come two days later in a colossal storm. Lupine long past peak-blossoming struggle to compete against the beauty of rich green grass sheltered under magnificent aspen trees. Rito Sebadillosos trickles pleasantly to the north.

Relaxing in this wonderful park, my city life seems so distant and I wonder whether the Kiowa brave experienced the same sensation? The theater of wilderness around Beatty's Cabin is enthralling. Both the brave and I intended to return to our respective homes – me to Albuquerque and him to endless plains where Running Deer waits. We'll blend back into the comfortable society we left behind. Nonetheless, for a brief moment we enjoyed parallel adventures among grand mountains.

Eventually Bill and Terrye come back to camp after epic miles, lofty elevations and overly ambitious peak bagging. They're sated in an entirely different way than I or the Kiowa brave. Their journey was no better or worse than ours. They knew the Pecos Wilderness from a different perspective having logged dozens of miles rushing from one fantastic peak to another. The brave and I drilled down within a microcosm of the forest. In the end all of us leave with rich rewards, renewed and ready for our next visit to the Pecos.

***

Far off on the Texas panhandle toward the western Oklahoma border a scattering of tee-pees rests alongside a meandering stream. Later this morning the tribe will begin dismantling buffalo hide homes to begin a time-immemorial journey southward toward wintering grounds. A detectable buzz fills the air as families gather to prepare for the journey. It has been a generous summer filled with buffalo beyond their wildest dreams. Sometimes the Great Spirit blesses them for seemingly no reason at all.

As tee-pees begin falling to the ground like deflated balloons, one young maiden wanders forlornly to the edge of camp searching to the west and its fathomless horizon. In her heart Running Deer knows the truth. Her young warrior won't be returning – he's long overdue. Her chief sent out a search party three weeks ago but nothing turned up. The tribe can't afford to wait any longer and it definitely needs all warriors for protection against hostile raids from Cheyenne and Lakota. Even the Comanche, who one day will share these plains with the Kiowa, raid vulnerable parties.

She has never seen the shining snow-covered mountains lying in the west, but she has heard many tales about their grandeur and danger from her long, lost brave. This is little consolation for Running Deer. She doesn't really care that her predecessors lived in pueblos up and down the large river known as the Rio Grande. She doesn't care about the turquoise gems her brave went to fetch from Pecos Pueblo on what was to be his last trip before their marriage.

She's heard other women in her tribe say that all roads lead to Pecos. Could she find the way alone? As her parents call imploring her to help pack, an idea begins to take root in her mind. Either death or her beloved brave are waiting somewhere out there to the west. If she can't have him, then she would prefer the other.

Early next morning she will sneak out of camp and follow that barely perceptible path leading to distant mountains and the road to Pecos.

Magic

Hike up Johnson Creek,
snow swirls yet mountains beckon -
Up? or Down? Tough choice.

WILLIAM I. BULLERS

11

Indian Summer

Topping a slight rise on the undulating blacktop, momentum briefly floats our car toward airborne before it settles down on the other side, but Bill and I hardly notice. We're awestruck by the northern horizon toward Telluride and wondering what all that fresh white stuff is on southwestern Colorado peaks. Consequently, I'm not really looking carefully at the speedometer when a highway patrolman suddenly appears headed in the other direction. He stares at us; we stare at him; and he flashes his yellow lights – slow down – too close for comfort.

Bill and I glance at each other in bewilderment with thousands of questions on our minds. What exactly is going on with the weather? It's the second week of August and things should be predictably hot with powerful afternoon thunderstorms. Colorado's mountain tapestry tells a far different story about a recent vigorous cold front and fluffy high mountain snows. It appears that we are already on the edge of Indian summer; fall has arrived early this year

What me worry? We're veterans at this and a little cold can be expected in these stratospheric peaks. Besides, we'll be camping in a relatively temperate river valley, not extreme high country above tree-line in rocky basins. Persistent warmth from surrounding juniper-laced high desert typically invades these dark canyons throughout August. So, we continue wending toward the Weminuche Wilderness and a historic trail used by Ute Indians and trappers following Vallecito Creek into unbelievably scenic wild country.

Each mile reinforces our earlier realization and adrenaline begins flowing – yesterday a humongous storm blanketed the mountains with a thick coating of brilliant snow. Given clear skies and day-time heating, this unanticipated wintry blast should melt off very soon. Neither Bill nor I give much thought to turning back, but then no one ever said we were blessed with common sense.

***

Indian summer is a popular term describing a sudden flourish – perhaps one or more weeks – of unseasonably warm temperatures in fall. Usually this period of abundant daily warmth coupled with chilly nights occurs in mid-to-late fall, but it all depends on the particular year in question. Indian summer can materialize in November and even December just as well as it does in October. In Colorado's high country these benchmarks have little applicability since summer season is often only fleeting weeks old, preceded by a drawn-out winter-spring and followed by a clearly distinct frosty fall spiraling into bone-jarringly icy winter.

Some claim that Indian summer cannot officially occur until a region has already experienced killing frosts. Again, the applicability to country ranging from 10-14,000 feet is questionable. Most alpine and even sub-alpine plants have adapted to extreme conditions and remain living despite temperatures routinely dipping to freezing and below. Others argue that a profound haziness must accompany Indian summer. But, this criterion best fits lowlands where humidity is typically quite high. The Rocky Mountains are noted for pure, dry air which isn't favorable to prolonged haziness, although dominating high pressure systems have enabled this phenomenon to occur with greater frequency in recent years.

According to Bill Deedler, a weather historian with the National Weather Service in Detroit-Pontiac, Michigan, exact origins of the term "Indian summer" are fuzzy.[12] It may be an early reference to the time of the year when Indians began harvesting game in anticipation of winter. Good weather in fall encourages animals to come out of seclusion, particularly elk and deer as they gravitate toward the rut. This term may also have been derived from the desired calm weather merchants sought for sending cargo on ships crossing the Indian Ocean.

It does not appear that this term arose from any pejorative connotation. Deedler notes that Indians in the Southwest saw this time of year as a blessing enabling them to gather cultivated crops as well as maturing nuts and berries. In this sense, Indian summer refers to a positive weather event and a brief, but enjoy-able, moment before winter's onslaught.

***

Vallecito Creek Trail, paralleling the river of its namesake, be-gins at 7,916 feet. Then, almost nine miles into the Weminuche Wilderness at 9,150 feet, Johnson Creek Trail heads west to-ward 12,680-foot Columbine Pass above fabled Chicago Basin and splendid wildflower gardens that are as good as they get in Colorado's high country – and that's at the edge of perfection. Our plan is to come as close as we can to reaching this trail junc-tion, spend the night, and then hit the high country for a day of wilderness rambling amid fields of mountain laurel, colum-bine, Indian paintbrush, lupine, penstemon and glacial high-land lakes. It doesn't really sink in that a foot or more of fresh snow might cover sky-high meadows.

The Wemiuche Indians of the Ute tribe roamed these moun-tains hundreds of years ago. By 1500 A.D. the Utes were preva-lent in the Four Corners region establishing small communities in desert and mountain habitats. The present-day Ute Mountain tribe located near Towaoc (south of Cortez, Colorado) descended from this Weminuche band.

The Weminuche Wilderness played an important role in hunting and gathering activities of the Utes. Deer, bighorn sheep, and elk along with small mammals are plentiful in the moun-tains. Lush valley meadows offer berries and roots on aspen- and fir-covered benches along throbbing rivers. As abundant bea-vers can testify, the waters are laced with fish. Surrounding hills provide piñon nuts and juniper berries. In all, rich food sources inevitably drew the Utes up the rivers and into high country where they established seasonal homes. Trails throughout the Wemiuche Wilderness hark back to these ancestral beginnings.

We hoist forty-pound packs on our backs and begin walking alongside the freely flowing Vallecito. It's penetratingly cool, but not cold, down in the valley and this trail is slippery wet and muddy in spots. The storm's brunt must have lashed peaks towering two thousand feet higher; we'll know exactly how much damage was done when we reach alpine country.

Bill and I ramble along marveling at Vallecito Creek's frothy white cascades; crystal pure water rushing over shiny granite boulders, pooling in deep blue-green eddies before falling down the mountainside. The conifer forest is dark, casting cavernous shadows along the trail. There is a very noticeable difference in the sun's angle of repose; summer really does appear to be maturing into fall.

Two miles up the trail we run into two forlorn fellows resembling train yard hobos wearing everything they're carrying.

"You two look like you just stepped off a plane from Hawaii," one of the hikers exclaims.

In truth, we offer a pretty dramatic comparison. They're swathed in dark colored high tech rain gear, polypro underwear and fleece. In contrast we're waltzing merrily along in summer shorts and bright t-shirts. But, it's their boots that tell the real story – sodden black and caked in gooey brown mud.

They go on to relate an interminable afternoon and night of frightening anguish. Stinging sleet and then smothering snow followed waves of thundering rain. They went through a survival experience testing their mettle and equipment; but they made it safe and sound. Camped up in Chicago Basin, all hell broke loose in a storm of epic proportions. Gaunt faces tell volumes about little sleep and unexpected cold that took them right to the brink of disaster.

They wish us the best of luck and stop short of warning us not to go up there. Beneath the surface of their casual conversation lurks a bit of passive-aggressiveness – just wait until the cold sweeps over your camp and fluffy white death falls massively from the sky. Then we'll see how comfortable those Hawaiian shorts and t-shirts are.

The next mile is devoid of conversation and nary a whisper passes between us as Bill and I chew on what we've just seen and heard. Still, there doesn't seem to be any valid reason for altering our plans. It's cool, perhaps crisp, but not freezing. It's going to get warmer as the day goes on. The dramatic storm has come and gone. A new day flourishes. After all, summer is only merging into fall, not winter. Confidence from years spent in the outdoors overwhelms thoughts of turning back. We plod along with this hope, reluctant to share concerns lest the other express similar doubts. And, by the way, in case it isn't apparent, we came to these mountains to have a grand time even if that means a little unanticipated discomfort.

Three more miles pass under our boots. Aspen copses dot grassy meadows like spots on a Dalmatian. The meadows alternate with long stretches of crowded fir and ponderosa. Meanwhile the powerful Vallecito roars over riffles before blending silently into the forest when the riverbed levels out. Many generations of Ute moccasins pounded along this path looking for elk or bighorn sheep. And, what did they do when the weather turned unexpectedly nasty? Most likely they threw another log on the fire. By comparison with our high tech gear, we have almost nothing to fear about the weather.

Roughly six miles from the trailhead past a worn wooden footbridge carrying us from the east side of the river to the west, we begin looking for an acceptable campsite. Views up canyon show mountainsides smothered in snow. Conversation lags, anxiety rises and seeps into our thoughts. We're not prepared for winter camping.

With global warming these monstrous shifts in the seasons are becoming fairly commonplace. No wonder autumn has shortened summer. This premature Indian summer may not be any different than what the Utes faced in their own history. We know that hundreds of years ago the Four Corners region went through a massive drought. Their perplexity in discovering significant seasonal shifts was undoubtedly quite similar to what's running through our minds. We prepared for a summer walk in the Weminuche only to experience winter-like conditions.

That night we set up camp on a small forested bluff overlooking the Vallecito. It is classic Colorado with the swift river roaring between huge vertical peaks and a flat little bench hacked out among the conifers. Others have camped here in the past judging by a well-used campfire ring and convenient logs sited close to the fire pit.

As shadows swamp the valley we erect a well-used, but very reliable, tent making certain that its tan rain-fly is solidly staked, able to withstand any downpour. Skies have been slightly overcast, but there doesn't seem to be any sign of deteriorating weather. Nonetheless, as the hillsides amply testify, this is the high country of Colorado and you never know how the weather will turn.

After dinner we walk up valley past our sheltering cove of spruce, pine and aspen to stare at incredible peaks. If these summits were more accessible to the public this wilderness would be a national park. Most of the snow has melted off lower, southern-facing slopes around 11,000 feet with few remnants left in recesses and ravines. However, north slopes tell a bit different story. Too bad we don't have our snowshoes, because we may need them to get much above 11,000 feet. Despite glistening snowfields up high, the valleys appear to be returning to their predictable state for this time of year. It's a perfect mixture of summer and fall all at once.

Walking back to our tent, Bill expresses relief about our good fortune in missing the storm. He's as excited about reaching Chicago Basin as a kid on Christmas Eve. This country is supposed to be the crème-de-la-crème of scenic country in the Needle Mountains according to guidebooks and gossip we've heard from others over the years along trails of the Weminuche. For anyone serious about the outdoors, Chicago Basin is definitely on the life-list. Optimistic about reaching the phenomenal country above our camp, but knowing deep in our hearts that Chicago Basin may never welcome us this trip, we turn in to prepare for tomorrow's promising exploration.

About 2:00 a.m. I wake with a start.

It's freezing – brutally cold. What's the problem? My sleeping bag, made in Colorado I might add, is designed for chilly summer nights with 60% of the down on top. Desperate for warmth, I try to pull on a trusty down parka reserved for moments like this. Problem is the sleeping bag's svelte cut – the early epitome of hyper-lightweight, doesn't make this possible. It only pushes my arms against the bag's fabric crushing down-filling and losing loft. In the interest of saving a few ounces, a lighter bag has sacrificed the protection needed for the extreme conditions. Although the parka provides some cover over my chest, the end result isn't quite sufficient.

Eventually I give up fiddling with the straightjacket of a sleeping bag. There's nothing to do but hunker down and try to get some sleep.

Unfortunately I'm awake every second like a caffeine-crazed insomniac unable to go back to sleep given the bitter chill. I toss; I turn. Cold seeps into my bones, driving a wedge into hopes and dreams of carefree rambling in high peaks above. Throughout the night ghostly images of the two hikers we ran into plod through my mind with gaunt faces and distant, hollow gazes to match. So this is what those two guys meant when they warned us about arctic conditions.

It's beyond frigid and a long, long, four hours till sunrise.

At daylight Bill complains that he hasn't slept as well as he wanted to in his green machine; a combination down and fiberfill bag designed for summer camping. In fact, he's downright grumpy and half awake. Sometimes sleep deprivation is the price you pay for accessing marvelous wilderness and most who explore ragged-edge country have gone through the same drill. You live; you learn and make better choices the next time you're stuffing a sleeping bag.

Despite how grim these experiences seem at the time they also remain much more vivid than trips that are far too comfortable; where your mettle – ability to survive – isn't tested. The two hikers preceding us went through the same kind of hell as we did; only far worse given conditions two-to-three thousand feet higher. Our night probably seems like a walk in the park to them. One thing we all have in common – once burned, prepare for the worst that the Weminuche can fling your way the next time you wander these ancient paths.

Breakfast with hot chocolate and warm oatmeal is over in a flash since we are eager to start climbing into sunshine. In this cold refrigerator we really need something more substantial in the way of calories but back home the planning was light-is-right. Hurrying through frigid purple shadows of dawn toward a trail junction and stairway to heavenly Chicago Basin, meadows sparkle with ice rimed grasses and plants. Temperatures obviously hit the teens gauging from ice covering pools along the Vallecito's edge. My tired old bag rated to fifteen degrees has seen better days; better nights when it lofted efficiently and provided the safety margin necessary in this country. This will be its last outing – tossed out for letting me down.

Stumbling along like drunks from one of Durango's rowdy bars, drowsy from lack of sleep, we turn west toward Chicago Basin. A half-dozen other campers at the trail junction are lounging about in sun swaddled in polypro and fleece – they picked far better camping sites for embracing morning warmth, but more likely than not, the rag-tag band also experienced its fair share of brutal cold. With barely concealed envy and muttering silent curses Bill and I grind upward leaving these slugs to soak up the sun. Lucky bastards.

Rising steeply out of Vallecito's valley, Johnson Creek Trail heads straight up toward a huge rocky basin, a monstrous crescent perhaps a couple of mountain miles across – it's hard to estimate the exact length given the distance and scale of these peaks. Stopping to catch our breath in thinning air and wheezing like flatlanders from sea level, we slowly spiral like sunflowers following the golden orb. Snow blankets the mountainsides and it's not melting off northern slopes – today is just too damn cold. More alarming is the fact that the air has a detectable fall touch to it – hazy rather than clear. Summer is already over in the Weminuche Wilderness. Today appears to be the initial edge of Indian summer.

Back when the Weminuche band wandered these hills, there were no lifelines they could telephone for assistance, no satellite phones to use in calling for a rescue. White settlers encountered the same hostile conditions as the ancient ones who preceded them. For those who forsook civilization's comforts, this bred self-reliance and resourcefulness. If it was cold, you built a bigger fire or froze to death. If it snowed, you had to fight your way back to lower elevations and warmer temperatures or accept your final moments in what must have seemed like an unforgiving, lonely, silent and vast wilderness.

Catching even a modest glimpse of what humanity endured in less technological times has tremendous value in these days where we have access to every feasible electronic assist imaginable. A little hardship along Vallecito River breeds humility, and fascination about the strength of character of those who went before. Sadly, too many in society are buffered from the natural world. We could benefit from getting more dirt under our fingernails after setting up camp; from looking with amusement at a companion whose hair is tossed and matted with fine bits of organic matter after a night sleeping under the stars; or from waking in the middle of the night to an unusual perfume of campfire smoke, stale sweat, and nervous adrenaline after hearing a branch break thirty feet outside the tent.

Bill spins to continue our death march to Nirvana. The trail hardly switchbacks as we gain elevation, gulping down contours as though whoever set this path couldn't wait to reach the magic above. It simply rises upward with the mountainside toward alpine heaven. Nothing much is being said between the two of us. I'm trying to find some reserve deep inside motivating me to go on with putting one foot in front of the other, but it's a losing battle. I feel like I'm sleepwalking and even the gift of warming sun isn't breaking through my mental haze.

The lures of resplendent flower gardens strewn among boulders, tiny rivulets coursing through marsh marigold and penstemon, and phenomenal scenery over picturesque peaks – attractions that normally help to overcome the strain – have quietly been depreciated. Meanwhile an insidious seed begins to form in my mind that this does not equate with having fun. Once such an idea takes root, it's difficult to come up with a rationale to keep plodding along. But, I do, and I will because I love these mountains.

Forty minutes into our trudge upward from the junction at Johnson Creek we stop for a second time to catch our breath. It's so quiet here in the middle of nowhere that the roar of our breathing is almost deafening. Neither of us says anything be- cause it would take too much oxygen. So we bend over slightly with hands on hips gobbling down oxygen molecules from the thin air. Seconds later Bill turns to go higher but I just can't do it. There is literally nothing left to give and as much as I want to continue with a stiff upper lip, it's not going to happen today.

At more than 11,000 feet we are high by most standards in the lower forty-eight. However, in this country, 11,000 feet is nothing; absolutely nothing. We're only in the basement, yet our elevator has stopped working. I'm very sick to my stomach and dizzy beyond belief, my head spinning out of control. Barfing would be a pleasant relief, but it doesn't come. Although I've seldom experienced altitude sickness before, there's no mistak- ing the malaise that pins me down. Too little sleep, too much cold, too little food, too little oxygen; these ingredients coalesce, stopping me in my tracks. It's as though an anchor is chained to both feet.

Bill and I both are devastated. To come this far. To reach the brink of extraordinary alpine country. To have Chicago Basin in our grasp, yet mockingly distant.

Frankly I'm too sick to give a damn at this point. Even the Weminuche's magic is insufficient to prolong this torture. It's hard to mentally override instincts telling me to get the hell off this mountainside and with all candor I'm not real interested in fighting the good fight. Bill is plainly disgusted. Stand up I tell myself. Start walking toward the mythical basin above.

Rather than spoil it for my friend I desperately seek a solution. Perhaps more calories will do the job so I eat another bite or two while trying to compose myself. Think positive thoughts you wimp; you've climbed these rugged mountains for years without any disaster. The Weminuche virtually runs through my veins. But, it's no good. I'm almost too dizzy to walk, to even reach my feet. Reality about this serious predicament finally registers; panic begins to wash over me.

My mind literally seems to be disconnected from the rest of my body. What a most bizarre sensation having your brain completely separated from your body. I feel as though I am outside my physical body looking down on this pathetic scene. I struggle again with another effort, and then give up. Bill is reluctant to turn back, but he's also reticent to go further. Obviously he has a touch of altitude sickness and I can't tell what's on his mind.

Here we stand two people with a burning passion for Colorado's high country, unable to taste the unparalleled beauty of Chicago Basin. But, we're on the slippery slope of danger here. Acute mountain sickness is nothing to fool with this far into remote backcountry. A stupid decision could bring disastrous results. We love this wildness, but we also want many opportunities to share other adventures in the future. So we hesitantly tuck tail and head down. It's not exactly a macho decision, but it's the right call under the circumstances.

The immediate problem is footing and stability because there's no guaranteed connection between what I think and what my body does. Don't try this at home. I can see my feet moving forward, but they don't seem to be linked to my brain. Talk about being spaced-out; it's as though my consciousness is floating slightly above my body and urging it to step around a rock or to take two strides before dodging a depression. When my feet don't quite get it right, my consciousness becomes critical and frustrated about being unable to exert control.

For twenty minutes it's like walking a tightrope over a gaping chasm without a parachute or safety-lines. I have to super-concentrate in order not to tumble down the steep mountainside. Then one thousand feet lower in oxygen-richer air my mind suddenly synchronizes with body. The transformation is startling like snapping your fingers. Things simply click back into place and it's apparent that we made the right choice. We're headed home.

***

When early Ute bands left high desert home sites to spend a summer in the mountains did they tingle with apprehension for the challenges that lay ahead? Imagine the stories that had been handed down over their generations about unexpected snowfalls, wildflower gardens of exquisite beauty, menacing beasts, raging rivers and other natural phenomena that might rear up and challenge them. Certainly their predecessors must have survived an Indian summer materializing from out of the blue like we experienced.

Like the Weminuche band we celebrate wilderness because it brings astonishing splendor, the thrill of danger, often a slight taste of death. Unexpected encounters with summer gravitating into fall, acute mountain sickness and other hazards lurking in the wild have distinct value. These adventures help us leave our doldrums behind; to come alive and to live a full life rich with passion.

***

Some thirteen months later, Indian summer makes a repeat performance by stealing into the Weminuche like a thief in the night. It happens sixty-some miles east of the trail to Chicago Basin along the West Fork of the San Juan River. A little adventure unfolds when a buddy of mine indicates that he wants to find a hot springs tucked away in the distant backcountry. But, before Dick and I can reach the springs we first have to find the proper trailhead.

A gravel road I'm following is becoming increasingly rocky and narrow so this can't be the right way, but there's no place to turn around. Downshift into second as a forty-foot streambed lies ahead slashed out of forest as though a D-9 Caterpillar has lost its way. My car barely makes it across the lively side creek bubbling with white water, flowing over the rutted forest road and down a rough-and-tumble bed of cantaloupe-sized river rock, moss encrusted stones, scattered bark and chunky gravel. Tires slip and whirl spinning off loose gravel and spraying fountains of water before gaining purchase on larger boulders sunk deep in the streambed's bottom, it's just enough momentum to be propelled to the other side.

The trailhead to the West Fork of the San Juan River is supposedly heavily used, but this pathetic two-track road suggests otherwise. Robust spruce and fir line the forbidding corridor almost encroaching right upon it, adding to the sense of being

deep into wilderness. I continue on, creeping like a turtle, wondering if I've lost the way. Around a slight bend in the road a
trailhead parking lot the size of a tennis court suddenly materializes, rough with half-buried cobblestones, chunks of bark, broken tree limbs and troika-shaped gravel. Obviously the Forest
Service doesn't manicure this road and that gives this little hike
some promise because most folks in their expensive SUVs will
turn around. Rolling to a stop, it time for adventure, but where's
Dick — he seems to be late?

That's no big surprise. Dick has a habit of setting meeting
times one-half hour earlier then he intends to arrive, probably
a planned response to my habitual tardiness. There's no big
issue here because the sooner I reach forest, the happier I am.
Who cares if you sit awhile soaking up beauty of the San Juan
Mountains' legendary peaks along the Continental Divide? In
fact, the last time I waited for Dick in the San Juans I was enter-
tained by a bald eagle fishing Big Meadows Reservoir, its success
was aggravating swarms of fishermen lining the lake — that was
time well spent.

It's far preferable to arrive early and simply begin the process
of detuning from the detritus of urban life. Moments lounging
outside my car, munching a snack, or taking a reading on altitude, temperature, wind, sun intensity, and strength of building
thunderstorms are invaluable in reconnecting with the wild. I
slowly ease into a hike that way. An entirely different perspective prevails when I race up, jump out of a car, throw on gargantuan pack and hustle down the trail — that's "A" type behavior
that we're trying to escape.

Eventually Dick rumbles up in his white Chevy pickup —
always a Chevy. Packs stuffed to overflowing, sneakers and water bottles dangling like laundry, it's time to start up one of

the enchanted valleys flowing off the Continental Divide. Our destination lies almost six miles into the wilderness where a narrowing river canyon butts against high ridges of peaks towering 12,000+ feet. Enticing hot springs sit at the base of this ridge, a tantalizing destination and base camp for exploring Colorado's extraordinary high country.

Two miles up the trail, a viscous vee-shaped gash flows into the West Fork of the San Juan from the northeast. This is Beaver Creek, a massive drainage running parallel with the Continental Divide. Beaver Creek eventually rises up to meet the Divide's ridgeline west of Hope Mountain. Having looked down upon the Beaver Creek drainage from over 12,000+ feet on Hope Mountain, this country's remoteness is staggering. The only paths into the valley are from this branch off the West Fork, or alternatively, dropping down from the Continental Divide – most likely both routes were beaten into place by early hunting parties. Elk grow to phenomenal size in the eastern portions of the Weminuche Wilderness.

This is very lonesome country and every time I gaze down on Beaver Creek I speculate about David Petersen's tales in *Ghost Grizzlies*.[13] Doug Peacock, Rick Bass and Petersen advocate that the great bear still roams the southern San Juans.[14] Rough inaccessible country along Beaver Creek might provide the protection the grizzlies need. However, there have been no confirmed sightings for years. This makes me wonder whether Ute hunters intentionally stalked grizzlies; on the other hand they may have purposefully stayed away because of ferocious bears.

The West Fork is a major tributary feeding the San Juan River and infamous trout habitat. Impressive white water rushes down Beaver Creek merging with the West Fork in churning blue pools beset with white foam and swirling agitation. This is serious white water for the San Juans that sends a little shiver down my spine. Make no mistake about it; these mountains are the big time.

Our first major challenge is crossing thrashing Beaver Creek. A stout two-foot thick log perches precariously twenty feet above the roaring creek. We don't know which to be more afraid of should we slip – the whitewater or the fall. Bark on this two-foot diameter log is already soaked black from spray and in spots has peeled away leaving a lighter, shiny cambium core as slippery tread. Normally we would be nonchalant about such a crossing, but this is one where you study the situation very carefully before setting out toward the middle point of no return. A moment of concentration, and then we move quickly to the other side flailing our arms like berserk traffic cops while trying to maintain balance.

On the other side of the creek little passageways weave throughout the undergrowth simulating bark beetle tracks on a fallen piñon. With colossal fir trees providing dense canopy, the valley bottom is very cool with just a tangy taste of fall in the air. It's close to that magical time of Indian summer and for the first time this season the sky has a hazy pall about it. We negotiate a small hillside through stubborn shrubs and find the trail paralleling West Fork. In another half-mile a trail following Beaver Creek is intersected climbing relentlessly upward toward vast lonely grizzly country.

For the next two miles our trail tracks due west following a distinct pattern. The West Fork's presence to the south can be heard and felt, but we are usually far enough above the river that it's difficult to enjoy the rushing, gurgling waters. With each twist around a ravine or curve of the valley we penetrate farther into the Weminuche Wilderness. As an unexpected bonus, despite the trail's heavy abuse we run into no one, thus adding to the remote feeling of this country.

After a couple hours, the trail levels out on a bench approximately fifty feet above the river. Various campsites are strewn here and there along with well-used, in some cases abused, fire rings. All these signs point to the hot springs being somewhere nearby. Another eighth of a mile and Dick thinks he's found it. Peering down the steep bank like a little boy outside a nudist colony, he spies his target. Several buck-naked people are lounging in the springs with full moons on the rise. Although it's tempting to join in the fun, we actually came here to get away from people. We'll hit the springs on the way out. So, we continue along looking for a spot with greater privacy below a hush forest rising steeply overhead.

A half-mile further, the trail suddenly ends its relatively gradual climb at a small creek — this is the West Fork's source bound for a confluence with Rainbow Creek and Cimarron Creek. It's not much more than a tiny side stream splashing raucously in spots and flowing silently along in others. What a thoroughly delightful counterpoint to the West Fork's raging flow lower in the valley. From here our trail rises steeply, sharply up along the stream, seeking the Continental Divide. We've run out of bench and will now have to choose a campsite to serve as a base for further exploration.

Two sites offer pleasant possibilities and possess the requisite distance from the hot springs to ensure solitude. One has a slight ten-degree slope and although a bit more open, has less forest cover than we prefer. The other is perfect, well screened by shrubbery from the trail and level with just the right drainage. An ash-filled fire ring is already well established, but not abused like previous sites one-half mile back down the trail. Two logs cross in an "L" shape forming a natural bench around the fire pit.

However, to our amazement some thoughtless person has left a huge, naked human turd in the middle of the tent platform. It's simply gross. Is this the sort of etiquette that first users of this wilderness followed? I doubt that the Utes trashed each place that they moved through.

We set up camp on the other site.

By deliberately going that extra half-mile we're sufficiently distanced from the sweet spot of why people travel here to the Weminuche. Our camp's most alluring characteristics are solitude and privacy. The main river is just a bit too far away and down slope to be enjoyed, however, the little side creek offers fresh water and melodious river sounds. Surrounded by silence and seclusion, we have the right mix of company and isolation. But what's most amazing is the tingle of excitement about being deep in first-rate wilderness.

That night a dancing red-yellow fire adds just the right atmosphere to a lovely and lonely spot of the Weminuche. Even the stinking turd seems forgivable at a moment like this. As night encroaches no cloud build-up is apparent, just a thin gauze veiling Colorado's cerulean skies. Over bourbon-laced hot chocolate Dick keeps looking up and expecting the worst. The Continental Divide by Wolf Creek Pass is famous for hellacious thunderstorms only this time the pattern has changed.

Dick's anxiety is partly driven by the relatively narrow slice of sky that's visible deep in this canyon. He expects things to alter radically any moment since thunder boomers have been raking southwest Colorado almost every day for the past two months. In fact, he's a little disappointed that we're not being doused.

Given the heavy runoff in all of the streams we've encountered, it has definitely been a wet summer.

Eventually coals go white as our fire dies down and we prepare for bed. We're sharing a tight two-person tent as a measure to save weight so anything that's superfluous has to be placed outside. While stacking pots and pans, gallon water jugs and stove near a handy log that's been commandeered as a seat, a sudden gust of wind blows through camp. It brings a brief chill that's a good ten degrees cooler than the placid, temperate weather we've been enjoying. Without saying a word to Dick, my memory flashes warning signs about the travail Bill and I endured last year.

This time I'm ready.

While Dick is off tending to chores I fluff up the Big Boy. Yes, after last season's little Indian summer surprise, I've brought along the terminator of all sleeping bags rated to minus five degrees. Plus, all of the other reliable accoutrements needed to survive a frigid night in comfort are waiting alongside stuffed in a bag. Dick has brought his summer-weight bag and trusty, but slim, down vest. I can only hope that he ate plenty for dinner because that little zephyr may have been a harbinger of a frosty cool one.

Fast forward four hours. I've been in La La Land dreaming about grizzlies over on Beaver Creek. Nature is calling in more ways than one. First I have to relieve myself and second my ears are freezing. That's to be expected because I haven't cinched the mummy bag up tight. Pulling the bag over my head I hope the first urgency will evaporate and sleep will drown further necessity. Thirty minutes later and it's clear that the only way I'm going to get more sleep is to crawl outside.

Dick is feeling no pain given his roaring snoring; each inhaling rasp measured, and each exhaling growl like a weed whacker engine coughing a bit out of tune. No fear about bears – grizzly or otherwise – with this racket going on. Even my nylon swishing movements getting out of the sleeping bag do little to alter his cadence. I find my camp shoes, unzip the mosquito netting, and step outside wearing a bilious down coat and boxer shorts – must be quite a sight for the owls.

Goodness gracious.

What once was a warm little alcove has transformed into the mother of all industrial freezers. It's almost too cold to do my duty because I want to keep my hands crammed in my coat. I stumble away from the tent past our fire pit and stop momentarily to check out the sky. Indian summer's hazy veil has departed and in its place spreads a blanket of twinkling stars more than a million points of light and each celebrating a phenomenal solar system.

I almost can't move it's so fascinatingly beautiful. I'm probably going through the same exercise that roaming bands of the Ute tribe experienced. They must have endured many premature fall seasons closing like a shroud over summer similar to this night. There's no reason to suspect that they weren't stopped dead in their tracks with almost no clothing and bodily necessities urging them to quickly do the deed in order to slip back under that buffalo skin robe or elk-hide blanket.

One last gaze and then nature can wait no longer. Racing back to the tent I laugh a little bit knowing that this time I made the right decision when selecting my sleeping bag. I anticipated fall over summer and won. There was no way to predict that summer would choose this night to transition into fall unless you had been burned thirteen months prior. Tonight's chill wasn't simply a typical cold night in the Weminuche. In this case the season changed into Indian summer overnight.

Back in our tent, swaddled in down designed for extreme conditions, and with Dick's fail-safe bear-scaring-roar on high, I fall back to sleep with a beatific smile. How close those stars were outside our door. Had I the mind to, I could have jumped up and almost grabbed a handful; they were that close.

And then eternity closes over me like a womb.

Next morning dawns with a razor-sharp chill in the air. Dick is complaining about being too cold – an extremely rare gripe on his part. Even with the campfire snapping and popping we've put on all of our clothes except rain pants and shells. I tell him he's becoming soft to frustrate him, but ice in the water bottles tells the truth. For the first time this season hot chocolate isn't an option, it's a necessity given how frosty it is in this valley.

We search for passing cotton balls through the narrow slit of sky floating overhead – a sure warning of moisture and inclement weather around the Divide – but nothing is drifting past. It appears that dry air will continue to hold sway over the West Fork – a perfect formula for exploring high country. Breakfast chores over, we set our sights on high country using the Rainbow Trail.

Aiming straight up, except for a switchback or two, the Rainbow Trail rises like a Sears Tower stairway above the West Fork. Settling into a deliberate pace, exercise warms limbs, ears and noses as we check off contours. Barely one-quarter mile and two hundred feet higher, scattered mounds of sawdust and sawn logs line the trail. A crew has recently been through here clearing the path, a rare activity that may occur only once every fifteen years or so in the Weminuche.

What lies ahead? This is the big question since we have never walked this path before. The occasional band of Utes would have seen this as remote wilderness; they had no trail guide to let them know about challenges that waited except perhaps for hearsay from other hunters. Yet in many ways we're equally uninformed. Just because a guidebook provides sketchy information does not mean that this is a walk in the woods. No ancient oral history, or contemporary guidebook, can predict what lies around the next corner in deep wilderness.

Silence is eerie and ignites the still air. Except for occasional birdcalls, the ravine is deathly quiet; quiet enough to let our imaginations run rampant about lost grizzlies. A gust of wind suddenly shakes the canopy and then passes. Melodious birdcalls float down from high among the trees. Even with the clear-cut path this is truly the land that time forgot.

The mountainside is comprised primarily of soft volcanic tuff, unusual for the Weminuche. It adds further character to this fascinating land. Meanwhile, our little side stream is quickly becoming lost in dense underbrush and the canyon's very steepness. Uncanny quiet embraces the land as we struggle to gain elevation out of this intriguing pocket virtually lost in a half-million acres of wilderness.

An hour after starting upward, a clearing appears as the trail levels off a bit above 10,000 feet. A long green meadow stretches before us for about one-quarter of a mile. At the end of the meadow, off-white shapes – mules and a canvas tent – signify base camp for those performing trail maintenance. Without the canvas tent it would be easy to confuse the mules as silver-tipped grizzlies sought by Peacock, Bass and Petersen. Not a soul is about and the mules eye us suspiciously from the distance considering how to react. Stopping far short of the camp to give it plenty of breathing room, we plop down on mossy rocks lining this expansive meadow.

Today we aren't looking to bag a peak or to cover lots of miles. There is no first ascent or major ridge to conquer. We have come to find a bit of adventure in the middle of wildness. This is as good point a point as any to turn toward home.

In years of hiking it's doubtful that I have ever come upon a mountain as serene as this; a forest where birds qualify as visitors and where their calls remain whispered; a mountain where even streams sing their songs with quiet, almost apologetic, voices. The knowledge that in several hours of hard hiking we can reach our cars seems immaterial. At the moment it's as though we are the only ones on the planet, a feeling that would intensify if the trail crew's camp was over the divide in a northern drainage.

It's funny how sometimes the least impressive, almost mundane, wilderness settings are the most memorable. There are other areas in the Weminuche that have higher peaks, denser forest, unusual vegetation, more wildlife present, grand vistas, churning water and precarious trails. However, this isolated spot on the West Fork is unforgettable for its seclusion and silence. Dick and I discover that sometimes such seclusion is the adventure; a moment when there is a palpable undertone of danger in a forest that is too quiet, too distant from humanity.

In some respects the Weminuche Wilderness seems to holding something back, but what it is we can't decide. It's a feeling; an atmosphere that warns you to be alert. Perhaps it's just the passing of the season – from summer to autumn intertwined with Indian summer. On the other hand it might be a discernible spirit of place, the personality of the Weminuche Wilderness. For once the intangible seems perfectly concrete, but neither Dick nor I can explain it. Maybe this mysterious vacuum is the adventure after all.

***

On our way back to the trailhead, we stop at the hot springs located alongside the river. Previous visitors have created a rock walled pool in which to soak but exactly how long ago the springs were discovered and by whom aren't known. In my mind I'm certain that the Utes traveled here to get pleasure from a hot soak. Legions of backcountry sojourners certainly enjoyed these waters over the centuries.

In fact a young couple from Pagaosa Springs is already soaking, but they welcome us anyway. That's the unwritten code of the outdoors. From time immemorial wilderness travelers have shared whenever their paths crossed. Our time in the spa is comforting, the sights visually stimulating, but there's a price to be paid. In this case Dick's reward is butt rash from sitting naked with his back to a blazing overhead sun.

Retracing our steps, the trail out is uneventful because it's just a matter of putting one foot in front of the other. The mysteriousness of the Weminuche evaporates a bit with each step toward our vehicles. Any confusion about which season holds sway also vanishes into thin air. Late summer has returned with a vengeance. Bathed in warmth from a cloudless, almost hazeless sky, and thankful for many shaded areas along the trail, our strategy distills to racing across hot spots and slowing at shaded spots. Reaching Beaver Creek, we carefully negotiate the slick log, looking ahead to the trail's end.

An eighth of a mile from the cars, a young man and woman come trudging up the trail – he trudges, she glides. His pack is enormous because he's carrying everything. She carries only her thoughts. The size of his load is impressive – probably forty percent of his body weight. But, what amazes us most is his footwear. He's clad in knitted pink and white slippers. Does it really matter? Having basked in the Weminuche's wild spirit, we're not focusing our attention on some wayward Pilgrims. Our sight is set on the next trip to seek solace in the San Juans.

***

Patricia McCairen mounted the courage to complete a solo river journey down the Grand Canyon – a mighty river fed by the West Fork of the San Juan. In the course of running the river she notes: "Solitude has a sound all its own, a feeling, a special vision. With each stroke on the oars, I draw myself deeper into its realm....The rest of the world has disappeared. It is just the canyon, the river and me. To be here, that is all there is. Nothing more is necessary. Nothing more exists."[15] McCairen captures exactly the experience Dick and I went through in a different canyon – the West Fork.

Solitude in West Fork's canyon was tangible – nothing more was necessary. In the course of climbing to sub-alpine country, where meadow and forest merge and great heights make their presence fully known, senses sharpened. Wilderness was all there was reconnecting us in an embrace. Nothing more was necessary – not a stupendous garden of blue columbine; not a perpetual snowfield cum glacier hidden in a rocky crevice, nor an eagle's view from lofty peaks; not glistening aspens in an alcove of the canyon; and not the whisper of ghost grizzlies. We simply needed to be there where wildness reigned and Indian summer was creeping in; where we were an integral part of the Earth.

We dwelled in the solitude of the West Fork and reconnected. Nothing else was necessary.

Mom, are we there, yet?
Bears, caves, s'mores, rocky forts,
pine cone battles - fun!

TERRYE BULLERS

12

Rites of Passage

ed Fox.
A two-to-three-foot long omnivore with a one-foot-plus multipurpose tail that serves as a warm comforter, warning flag and balancing aid?

A solitary hunter that feeds on pet food and garbage in urban areas; rodents, small birds, frogs, fish, vegetables and fruit in the wild?

Typically swaddled in elegant golden-red fur but also seen in coats of silver, black and reddish-to-light-brown color?

All of the above are accurate statements about red foxes (Vulpes vulpes) found across the world in a diverse variety of habitats. But, the red fox I'm thinking about walks on two legs rather than four.

Red Fox was my chosen name during my membership in the Indian Guides. My father was known as Silver Fox. Together we carved a 6" wooden cube – a cedar block drilled down the middle – with my fox effigy on one side. It took hours to intricately carve the likenesses and then almost as long to precisely paint the background and fox face features standing out in sharp relief. Teepees and my initial, "H", were painted on the other three sides. Whenever our Circle of fellow fathers and sons met we brought those blocks along, proudly stacked them high on a totem pole signifying those who were present.

I still treasure that tribal carving; it's almost as bright and shiny as the day my father and I made it.

Years ago the Indian Guides functioned as a quasi form of pre-Boy Scouts. We met each month to forge a common bond and conduct many, what to me were thrilling, activities and events. One meeting might be devoted to learning a craft, the next to an outdoor adventure.

Our "Chief," Bob Giantvalley, ignited the Circle's thoughts on fire with electrifying tales of adventure. Imagine how he would have mesmerized us with Rick Ridgeway's enchanting tale about Africa in *The Shadow of Kilimanjaro*: "The last time I was in East Africa, several years ago, I had a chance to make a short walk through the thornbrush country with my friend Iain Allan and a park ranger who accompanied us to provide armed protection from dangerous animals. We were following a *lugga* (a Swahili word used in East Africa to describe a sand river that is dry in all but flash floods) when we chased out of the bush a large lioness…The ranger, a six-foot-seven-inch Samburu named Mohamed, raised his semiautomatic rifle to his shoulder and clicked off the safety. We entered the bush...My mind didn't need any academic analysis to tell my body to have every synapse ready to close and open at the speed of light."[16]

Like all of his borrowed tales, Bob would have placed us squarely on the edge of our seats and subtlety helped us contemplate being that close to a very efficient predator. The semi-automatic rifle would seem inadequate in the face of a ferocious man-eating cat. Bob would have enabled us to sense Ridgeway's sweaty palms and perspiration-drenched arm-pits as he went on full-alert searching, smelling, listening, and *feeling* the big cat's presence behind the next bush, over the next rise.

Scrounging stories from great adventurers past, Bob primed us for our own little explorations. By the time he was done telling these tales we lusted for journeys into the unknown. Every magical tour possessed an enthralling combination of spine-tingling challenges and gentle guidance inspiring us to step beyond the safety of home. To walk down a forest path or a convoluted arroyo for the first time was electrifying; as long as someone was covering our backsides.

A perfect example was a Saturday we spent at Southern California's Torrey Pines State Reserve in search of hidden treasure — a huge can of unshelled peanuts. The Circle was responsible for finding that can in what seemed like a vast wilderness — 2,000 acres — set aside to protect the rare Torrey pine (Pinus torreyana), reportedly the rarest pine in North America.

Like most outings we were patiently instructed about safely negotiating these wild lands. Rattlesnakes were rare but possible; as a result we walked thinking that at any step a snake would jump out and slither under our feet. The crumbling bleached orange cliffs of the park had proven vulnerable to rock slides; all were admonished to stay on the trail. Most of these warnings were immediately forgotten after being told about dangers waiting in a tortuously twisting ravine – a highly eroded arroyo – known as "Fat Man's Misery." We could hardly contain ourselves until ensconced in the serpentine labyrinth.

Torrey Pines' damp salt-laden sea air pressed down on us the minute we reached the trailhead. Gray gloomy marine overcast kept sun at bay. A persistent breeze blew cool from the crashing Pacific falling at the base of the reserve. Who cared about the weather? We couldn't wait to begin the search for our treasure.

We were told to look for something, anything, unusual about the land – that was the single clue launching the electrifying start of our unpretentious adventure. Each Guide diligently searched and searched to no avail. Finally somewhat exasperated our fathers patiently led us to an area where the treasure was buried. "Look for something out-of-place." A few minutes later I spied it – tucked beneath an undercut in the orange-vanilla sandstone and hidden from view by a pile of softball-sized rocks was our treasure. What a great moment that discovery turned out to be; busy little hands shoved dozens of rolling rocks away and our long-hoped-for treat surfaced.

Those were innocent days and I relished every second of sharing with my father. I was too young and our parents too naïve to understand that one day Native Americans would protest this quasi-play-acting of non-natives as Indians. Members of the American Indian Movement objected to what they viewed as disrespectful stereotyping and culturally flawed teaching by the Indian Guides program. The YMCA – once known as the Young Men's Christian Association – that sponsored the Indian Guides eventually acquiesced to program revisions.

From my perspective we weren't trying to be Indians. The basic idea was to devote time with your father and other father-son pairs in a variety of activities centered on the outdoors. Hikes, campouts, lessons on useful crafts (e.g., fire building, archery, assembling a pine bough bed, etc.), and the value of camaraderie represented key character-shaping outcomes I learned from the Guides.

Today in responding to objections of Native Americans, the YMCA is more sensitive in its parent-child programs. "Adventure Guides" is the contemporary evolution of the Indian Guides I knew years ago. This new program focuses on four compass points – the family, nature, the community, and fun – while advocating four values of caring, honesty, respect and responsibility. Women and men, girls and boys jointly participate in today's Adventure Guides.

Other than that valuable loving relationship with my father, what I took away most from the Indian Guides were rites of passage. Through campouts, hikes, and similar exciting outdoor activities I learned to love our natural world while developing skills essential to being comfortable and safe in it. That's a pretty good payback and testimony to consider in comparison with the sorry payback kids face today from the electronic world.

That fascination kindled by the Indian Guides has never left; it has only heightened with progressive exposure to wilderness. Intoxicating attractions of physical risk, exotic locations, foreign cultures, or threatening natural forces ramp up the cachet associated with travels to truly wild places. In some cases extraordinarily unusual human rituals or first-ever explorations promise an elixir for my Guide life gone civilized. Gradually I realized that I had to keep exploring and continually seeking new experiences as a fail-safe prescription for maintaining a vibrant and vital life.

Red Fox...my spirit soars when I hear that name.

Silver Fox...the person I owe it all to for successfully guiding me through a child's rite of passage. That sly old fox...he knew how to pass the gift on. From grandfather to father and on to son...every time I connect with the wild Earth memories of those who gave me this life-directing legacy resonate throughout me like a melodious gong gently struck by a velvet hammer.

***

Similar to other cultures the Anasazi followed complex rites of passage as their progeny entered adult life. These rites were designed to help young girls and boys prepare for the vicissitudes and harsh realities of life.

The ancient ones would have understood the well-intentioned nature of the Indian Guides' practices even if they found them a bit amusing. They may have chuckled on observing our lessons in woodcraft. Imagine the mirth they would have enjoyed watching us carefully navigate the vast wilderness of Torrey Pines State Reserve, but a stone's throw from ultra-lux mansions in La Jolla and Del Mar. Undoubtedly rituals surrounding each Indian Guide meeting would have drawn smiles across their faces. But, compared to a backdrop where children are left to find their own way, the old ones would have approved of these efforts most heartily.

Rites of passage.

Contemporary society doesn't do enough to prepare youth for the transition to adulthood.

Inundated by a digitally-driven and electronically-crazed world, our young ones have lost a connection to nature before they even have found it. Their relationship to the environment is most often entirely through human-made means — iPads,

MP3's, iPhones, cell phones, DVD's, television, radios and similar detritus.

Rites of passage encapsulated in old lessons by the Indian Guides seem less humorous when stacked up against generations who have no meaningful bond to their planet.

Fortunately there are still a few courageous women and men who are stubbornly determined to make certain that their offspring know the immense value of wildness and the joy of nature in proportion to how their young ones navigate the web or download a set of favorite tunes. Like the ancient ones, these parents deliberately prepare their children, through rites of passage; to live with the land as opposed to existing in perpetual estrangement.

A few still teach their children well.

***

On a pleasant summer evening as the day's solar power-curve of heat lost ground to encroaching night Don and his six-year old daughter, Molly, called to let me know that they thought it was prime time for a little wild adventure.

The good father, Don wants to encourage Molly's fascination with the natural world around her. He knows that at her tender age, Molly is very impressionable – now is a perfect time to plant the seed of being comfortable in sleeping outdoors on hard ground under glittering stars, eating a tasty meal that doesn't come stuffed in a paper sack, parceling out bits and pieces of ourselves around a campfire, and learning about wildlife that roam outside the border of our camp. Don knows how fleeting childhood can be. He wants to make certain that she understands there is another side to the digital equation overwhelming her evolving life.

Our destination is the broad southern edge of San Pedro Parks Wilderness in northern New Mexico. This wilderness located in the Jemez Mountains is ideal; close to home in Albuquerque yet distant enough to ensure a bit of backcountry adventure. The only downside is a statewide ban on campfires due to tinder-dry conditions.

On the one hand there's nothing quite like a little fire to warm the soul and create contemplative musings about higher things.

On the other a night under the stars is better than a night not under the stars.

I'm ready in a moment's notice.

Hard-core outdoor enthusiasts typically overlook the San Pedro Wilderness because it's largely high mountain parkland – meadows and groves of firs mixed with aspens spread like blankets on undulating hills atop a broad mountain ridge. Lush vegetation is fueled by 35+ inches of precipitation each year — sporadic summer monsoons with their thundering theatrics and crystalline winter snow. There are no 12,000 to 13,000 feet high spires that take your breath away because they dominate the visual landscape; no classic climbs allowing you to cut another notch on your peak-bagging pistol – those are found east in the Sangre de Cristos with Wheeler Peak, Truchas Peaks, Pecos Baldy and Santa Fe Baldy.

Diminutive streams in the Parks harbor multihued native Rio Grande cutthroat trout. This is one time that color trumps size. Their orange-red slashes, black speckled backs and golden patina make up for what they lack in length. They'll fight; but more rewarding is the recognition that these little buggers are the real things that the ancient ones stalked throughout the Four Corners.

Trails crossing the San Pedro Wilderness generally run in the 10,000-10,500 foot range; it's simply not spectacular alpine country. Undulating up-and-down sections like a chaotic rollercoaster can be aggravating for goal-oriented hikers bent on climbing lofty spires. It's possible to hike for miles and feel as though no progress has been made because the landscape hasn't changed dramatically.

Two other dirty little secrets await unsuspecting hikers.

Cattle and sheep graze throughout the wilderness fouling water supplies and detracting substantially from a true sense of wildness. To top it off, local outfitters have chewed up the land with their horses and sloppy camp habits. One would think that those who stand to benefit the most commercially would do everything in their power to protect its pristine character.

Considering these depressing factors it makes me wonder why Don thought of the Parks as a destination; presumably he's thinking about Molly's abilities and her safety. Even if a calamity happened, we would be securely ensconced in Don's Jeep before we knew that we were in trouble.

There's also a very good possibility that maybe Don knows something that I don't know. I can be persuaded to take this trip, but on the face of it the Parks do not send a little shiver down my spine whenever I see them. They have their beauty, as any rich forest does, however a conspicuous distinctiveness never seems to shine through. Perhaps this time will be different; we'll see.

The 41,000 acre plus San Pedro Parks appears to invite neglect in large part due to their accessibility and rich habitat for game. Elk is at the top of the list but hunters also seek deer, bear, turkey and grouse. It's hard to blame residents in adjacent rural communities from exploiting the national forest as a means of sustenance. People scrape to get by economically and whether it's firewood, mineral extraction, guiding services, or timber harvesting, the Santa Fe National Forest surrounding this wilderness receives an extremely heavy hand from humans. This legacy of exploitation naturally carries across vague wilderness boundaries; a pattern of casual over-use that stretches back to the ancient ones.

Generations of families have carved-out a meager but satisfying life from the San Pedro Parks and Jemez Mountains. Many trace their roots back centuries to Spanish settlers. Others have ties with the Zia and Jemez Pueblos as well as the Jicarilla Apache tribe. Far eastern edges of the vast Navajo Reservation are almost within shouting distance of San Pedro Parks Wilderness. Native Americans recognized the bounty of the Parks and its temperate climate compared to weather-challenged northern mountains such as the San Juans in southern Colorado.

We'll be camping in an area which the Anasazi frequented. Their shadows will blanket the paths that we walk, our campsite, and the relatively brief moments we spend in their home.

One thing is certain. When walking mellow trails of this rising and falling wilderness we are following historic paths that date back hundreds of years. We won't be the first to enjoy that punky scent of decaying aspen leaves by an abundant seep at a meadow's edge, that cloyingly crisp morning air making a campfire a necessity, or those stately copses of black Engelmann spruce bordered by wild lavender iris. Spirits of the past embrace and silently protect this wild country in many subtle, yet visible, ways. We just have to look for them.

***

On reaching the main Forest Service road into the San Pedro Parks, Don casually mentions that we won't be heading up the Vacas Trail – a main thoroughfare running south to north along the great mountain's spine. He has another destination in mind — a small almost nondescript canyon, in many respects barely more than an arroyo, off-trail located some distance from the Parks' primary entry point where people typically flock as if they were heading to a busy airport terminal hub.

Very skeptical that we'll find anything in the Parks that most ardent hikers would consider worthwhile, I'm really not in a position to jump ship. Besides, with Molly along I know from the beginning that we won't be hiking very far; this is simply a trip to the semi-edge of civilization.

Are there any parallels between our relatively non-ambitious backcountry jaunt with travel the Anasazi might have made when they called these mountains home? Credible evidence points to the affirmative.

Archeological fieldwork at nearby Chaco Canyon surfaced discoveries such as highly decorated pottery, bird skeletons and feathers (macaws and turkeys), and semi-precious stones (turquoise), as well as other human goods and technologies (e.g., signature building architecture like "T"-shaped doorways that have been found in post-Chaco ruins in northern Mexico) to conclude that the Anasazi at least traded with other people over vast distances. Trips to the Jemez Mountains probably offered a prelude to longer ventures.

Archeologists tend to disagree about the extent of trade and migration between the Anasazi and native populations in Mexico and further south. There is no absolute way of documenting migration of pre-historical people. However, a surprising number of artifacts imply that travel to the area surrounding the San Pedro Parks was a common event.

I believe that the Anasazi possessed an inherent fascination with wild lands beyond their villages. Parents may well have prepared their daughters, like Molly, and sons to survive trips past the pale of pueblo walls; trips that were integral to rites of passage.

Certainly the ancient ones didn't simply plop down in one spot and stay there the rest of their lives. More likely they saw distant mountains as promising abundant game; far-off inviting canyons held sweet meandering streams similar to those that the Anasazi knew in their traditional corner of the world. This curiosity about the unknown and courage to explore the unknown are exactly what Don wants to underscore for Molly; a compelling lesson that the unexpected sometimes brings danger, but it also is counterbalanced by inestimable rewards.

Safety was a prevailing force working against the Anasazi in explorations away from home. Life-threatening risks were beyond the perceived secure boundary offered by tribal sentries such as intersecting hostile bands of unfamiliar people, wild carnivores, or deadly physical challenges. Molly, Don and I face the same uncertainties albeit at much lower exposure. We have absolutely no idea of what dangers lurk in these forests once we leave the car behind. But, we're also intent on teaching Molly that risks can be managed; that security is largely a state of mind. She needs to develop confidence in using her resources in ways that keep her out of harm's way.

***

As we near the end of the paved road, Molly is lounging like a rag doll in the back seat still looking through a few of her books. Almost thirty minutes ago she used up an hour's worth of conversation with question after question about what to expect on her little sojourn to the new world. I like that in a young person – inquisitiveness about where she's going, what will be there, and what to expect. Beneath a façade of feigned bravado just a smidgen of anxiety taints her voice. Normally her mom and dad take her on outings such as these and she hasn't quite reached a decision about me yet.

A New Mexico native, Molly has lived her brief life in an enchanting land nurturing diverse cultures, big indigo sky, majestic forested mountains and multihued high desert. Her birth roots plunge deep into the decomposing granite and limestone foothills of Albuquerque's Sandia Mountains. Like many young folk growing up in New Mexico, she has gained a preliminary understanding about important Spanish and Native American heritages prevalent throughout this vast state. However, what captivates her mind and conversation this soft summer morning is the prospect of wild animals roaming these lands.

"Are there any bears where we're going?"

"Will we see any deer?"

"Will coyotes walk near our tent like they do at home?"

"Are there any bears where we are going?"

Following a confusing maze of dusty, rutted logging roads that devolves into narrow, seldom-used two-track, we plow through an uninspiring ponderosa forest of stunted trees with little girth and less height. No matter where we turn it almost looks monochromatic, the color having been washed out of every-thing – trees, grass, shrubs and ground. Dehydrated-to-the-bone brown grasses blanket the tan-white ground among a tinder dry pale-green forest sitting atop nutrient-deficient soil – not the sort of lush, breathtaking fir and aspen forest that most people seek when they go exploring in the Parks.

Don is weaving carefully among a Velcro tapestry of trees. Around a sharp J-shaped bend several informal car camps appear carved out on this buzz-cut flat-topped plateau. Well-used fire pits heaped with shards of charcoal colored logs leave us wondering how people extinguish their fires before leaving. There's no convenient water source; certainly no springs or small creeks much less something that even begins to resemble a stream. It's a wonder that it all hasn't burned to the ground by this point in our continuing drought.

Eventually we bounce and weave our way to an old quarry pit about the size of a football field and wide-open vistas made possible by this huge scar on the land. Twenty feet deep in places, the pit apparently provided a cheap source of limestone or perhaps served as fill for the main forest road. Withered grasses struggle for purchase, heads flopping to the side, destitute for the smallest smidgen of moisture. There's not the slightest bit of shade for an eighth of a mile on this plateau; trees and shrubs hug the distant periphery.

Don stops and we climb out.

It's one of the absolutely most uninspiring places I've ever visited, on purpose, for a camping site.

What exactly is he thinking? No one is around and for good reason. This place has all of the appeal of camping at Love Canal, New Orleans after Hurricane Katrina, or the outskirts of Victorville along busy Interstate 15 running to Los Angeles. Never an aficionado of National Park Service campgrounds which attract too many people and too much noise, at least those camps are sequestered in locations with redeeming scenic value.

The old ones certainly wouldn't be impressed with our choice of a camping spot.

With great skepticism I hoist backpack and grab a one-gallon jug of sloshing fresh water in each hand. Considering how dry the forest is this summer (made eminently clear while driving here), our prospects for finding potable water are virtually nil.

It won't be a dry camp as far as I'm concerned; these one-gallon life-lines should get us through until morning. Don repeatedly encourages me to leave the water behind. He spreads out a fresh topographical map on the red Jeep's hood and traces his envisioned path to an intermittent stream in a little vale.

I'm not buying into the dream. None of the shaded ravines or gullies that we passed by showed any water or greenery; there was nary a hint of moisture. This mythical stream that he wants to find seems more a hallucination than reality; a mirage in this inhospitable desert forest. If this government-approved map documents a stream as intermittent, then we can be certain it's not going to be flowing given the drought New Mexico has been enduring.

Molly distracts Don by asking for help in tying her shoes. It's a fortuitous break that allows me to escape Don's badgering. The water jugs are coming with me regardless of what he thinks. By the time he finishes helping Molly, I'm already walking toward this small mesa's edge with life-giving water in both hands.

Our self-made pathway down from the dusty plateau requires cutting contours three hundred feet to a sparsely tree-lined canyon. Picking a zigzagging route through hip-high clumps of dull green oak and foot-tall withered brown grass, we're particularly alert for rattlesnakes. Snakes aren't the only obstacle Molly is learning about. Here and there scattered mummified cow pies mark passage of the slow-witted beasts in very early spring when growth was fresh and optimistic. Now the only break in this colorless montage is a jubilant child carrying her pink and multi-floral backpack stuffed with favorite toys and other little-girl treasures.

In less time than Molly normally takes for recess we reach the canyon floor only to confront a mosaic of ugly scars left by off-road vehicles. Years ago this may have been a temporary logging road. Now it's reduced in most spots to foot-and-a-half-wide single-track for knobby-tired motorcycles judging by several ribbons of prints. And single-track hasn't deterred four-wheeled fanatics from taking on the challenge of establishing two-track.

Their efforts have irrevocably defiled what otherwise might have been one of the few beautiful spots in this sorry canyon. What a shame. Without the beaten path, this portion of the canyon would have a large measure of charm — thick forest on northern slopes thinning out to grassy canyon and shrub-covered ravine.

I only look at Don and raise my eyebrows without saying a word. He knows what I'm thinking; and I know exactly what he's thinking: "Maybe we screwed up in coming down here after all." Nothing need be said; what matters most is that Molly see this as a great adventure in the wild woods.

We plod along with our packs, while Don carries on a running dialogue about the insects, birds, and vegetation. He's helping his daughter focus on the fine nuances of this land, to see magic where none exists for old eyes.

Half a mile later we intersect a broader eighth-mile wide canyon which to our amazement has a captivating, gurgling stream running down the middle of it. To the south is a small rustic ranch partially hidden by forest — a private in-holding. The ranch house doesn't look occupied at the moment, but it clearly hasn't been abandoned. With the surrounding invasive web of primary and secondary forest roads; the informal paths beaten by four-wheelers, motorcycles and all-terrain-vehicles; the ranch house; and acres of cattle droppings; the press of humanity is almost more than bearable. This isn't quite turning out like we expected it. Undeterred, Molly and Don continue to walk north along the meandering stream flowing through grassy meadows.

Eventually my fingers and arms cannot take it any longer – the water jugs are just too heavy to go further. Don is hesitant to stop so early, and I can read the exasperation in his eyes. However, we've reached a nice flat bench above the musical stream; it's a perfect place to set up tents. We plunk our gear down on a grassy plot in the eastern lee of a gently sloping hillside sprinkled with ponderosa pines, respectful yards from the whispering creek. The ranch is out of sight a half-mile distant and it appears that we are the only ones around in this small valley.

The rest of the afternoon we take little excursions fulfilling all sorts of deep wilderness explorations that Molly conjures up. She's expert at imagining things that only a brilliant, life-filled six-year-old can imagine. We track deer and elk up and down the valley while helping her to distinguish their scat from that of cattle. But, no animal visitors turn up. She speculates about why a huge ponderosa has fallen down while simultaneously caressing its cinnamon-red bark scented like vanilla. Holes pecked into the ponderosa's bark and that of surrounding pines are examined for acorns and bugs. Molly is like Darwin on a trip to the Galapagos Islands – she can't contain her curiosity, soaking up all the forest has to give like a sponge.

No question is too silly; no topic beyond consideration. Don is transferring billions of bytes from his memory banks to Molly. She's enjoying learning what it means to live *with* the wilderness; to walk through wild land while blending into it. It's a rite of passage that presages her walk to womanhood. A child soon enough to leave her naïveté; a moment both she and her father need to seize.

Hasn't it always been like this from time immemorial, since the pre-historical walk of those past? There are moments that parents need to desperately grab with their offspring otherwise chances evaporate forever. Don is poised at such a moment…it's now or never for him to tip the scales in favor of Molly being one with the land for the rest of her life.

To my great surprise, as an amethyst darkness leisurely descends over our nondescript little wilderness, we have not heard a single, solitary vehicle or seen another person who might unknowingly intrude on this magical rite of passage with an impressionable young girl. This is beginning to seem like remote wilderness after all. Our only regret will be the inability, due to extreme fire danger, to have a little campfire — something to entice a six-year old and fend off fears of the night. But, once this day's final flood of light fades, our little camp undergoes a metamorphosis into a backcountry site seemingly miles from civilization.

A couple of crickets ratchet up their tune by a floppy branched chamisa.

Meanwhile the brook babbles and gurgles a merry tune.

A series of soft zephyrs courses down canyon softly fluttering our nylon tents and rustling the pines.

All is well and the day is done.

Surely the ancient ones melded into the land at moments like these. Perhaps they camped just north of this spot; or maybe they set up a temporary summer lodge in the next canyon over. Wherever their footfalls were heard or their homes nestled down in the San Pedro Parks, we know that they enjoyed moments such as this. Don, Molly and I can feel it unequivocally in our bones. Spirits of the ancient ones come flowing over our camp as if a fog intent on filling our diminutive valley

Molly keeps things active during and after dinner. She has infinite interest in the smallest things we generally take for granted.

Why can't we have a fire?

Why did that tree die?

When do the deer come down to drink?

What do these beetles eat?

Why can't we have a fire?

How do we know there aren't bears around?

What happens if mom needs to get a hold of us?

Why can't we have a fire?

What did Indians eat when they were here?

What bird just made that call?

Why can't we have a fire?

Guffawing to myself at times, I realize how big of an adventure this is for Molly when seen through her eyes – deep in wilderness with her precious dad.

We spend a half hour gazing at stars while Don tells her about various planets and formations. Don really knows his astronomy and with his patient answers even I learn a thing or two. This leads to another long line of questioning about who lives up there among those celestial orbs. Don is on shaky ground but he gives it his best wishy-washy answer.

When Molly finally runs out of gas it's time for all of us to head to bed. An owl behind us in the pines hoots several times creating a scary Halloween atmosphere and sending her off with thoughts of an imminent attack. As Don zips up their tent door I can hear him explaining that bears won't be interested in us because there's no food in our tents. Eventually their soft chatter evaporates and silence shrouds the land.

Stars wink into existence commandeering the pitch black sky and sending an ethereal soft light over the Parks. As I nod off to sleep I wonder if this gentle illumination isn't a cosmic reflection watching over Molly and her two companions; guarding them safely through the night.

Sleep fills our respective tents....

Next thing I know early morning is creeping into camp. Cool, not cold, the day will be sun-filled and eventually hot. I climb out of my toasty sleeping bag, dress warmly and walk as quietly as I can along the little foot-wide stream and above to the plateau in greeting the morning sun.

With the first rays of a new day warming my cheeks, I contemplate the beautiful camping adventure we're enjoying. Reflecting about how mellow, decidedly peaceful and quiet, this whole outing has been, I feel renewed – relieved of stresses that perpetually haunt us back in the city. Come to think of it, it's been a first-rate trip despite this relatively commonplace forest.

Two hours later we're back at the Jeep and headed for home. Molly is dying to get back to her mom and her rite of passage is over for the time-being.

***

Although my excitement meter never rose on this trip, I realize that Molly had a totally different experience. Thinking back to the first moments we left the car, she was jabbering a mile a minute – anxious about what was to come. As we set up tents she scurried back and forth questioning the safety of home for the night. Finding deer and elk scat sent her imagination crazy with speculation about finding wild beasts. To be sure, adrenaline did rise on Molly's rite of passage.

It's all so simple.

We came to a nondescript canyon embracing a gurgling little creek that valiantly fights for life on this pathetically dry mesa. Surrounding thin forest and rough plateau have seen more than their fair share of exploitation by humans from native tribes to latter day residents – the scars are everywhere. And yet, the scars are nowhere. It all depends on how you look at the land and where – a lesson that Molly taught both Don and I in her innocence and marvel at this wonderful world around her.

All of us vitally need experiences with the land in order to keep from being estranged from nature and too set in our ways. By connecting deeply with wild, and not-so-wild, places we gain the solace and peace of nature. In some cases it takes a wizened, and precocious, six-year old on her rite of passage to pry open our eyes. In other cases, only the most pristine wilderness can promote rejuvenation. One thought is clear, we must never, ever, give up the effort to experience these adventures and the corresponding renewal they offer.

Molly will probably never be alienated from nature because her parents have ensured that she knows the phenomenal joy of discovery in the wild. She became part of the solution; the legacy that our society needs to leave for the future. Molly's magical adventure is a formula that all kids should have a chance to experience for in youth is the promise of a better, more humane world.

Naked siren sings
a silvery moonbeam song -
kokopelli love

TERRYE AND WILLIAM I. BULLERS

13

Hidden Hot Springs

Humpbacked and blowing a merry tune on a flute, Kokopelli dances his way on rock art across the Southwest. This joyous little figure delights any who catch a glimpse of him hammered onto stone, etched by surgically precise beatings of stone-upon-stone, or painted in ochre and reddish hues against vanilla backdrops. An uplifted foot signifies his waltz to a tepid beat; or was it more a salsa, rumba or prehistoric swing artists attempted to covey? Whatever the bouncing beat, Kokopelli boogies along entirely consumed in a glorious moment.

His characterization evokes within us a spontaneous sense of mirth and gaiety. We're ready to fall in behind and be-bop across a dusty plaza ringed by dozens of stone edifices while elated on-lookers spill from timbered doorways, miniscule windows and mud-plastered rooftops. It's time to celebrate something – a new season, birth of a child, success of a hunting party returning with fresh venison, annihilation of a marauding band of warriors, or simple revelry after difficult times. Whatever the long ago obscure reason for his lively step, it's easy to read into Kokopelli's skipping shuffle that party time has arrived. And who doesn't want to join in his contagious elation and merry sashaying?

Kokopelli has been dancing his cheery jig for more than two-thousand years according to archeologists. He may have been a deity associated with fertility and good fortune whether as a harbinger of rain, human conception, flourishing crops, or successful hunting. Some weave a mischievous thread into his character aligning Kokopelli with impish tricks such as Coyote might play. Others attribute more charitable temperament and connotations where he represents festivity and whimsy. Almost all authorities agree that he – or an equivalent – was shared across many Native American cultures especially the Hopi, Zuni, and Acoma people.

Kokopelli's hump may have been a sack full of goodies such as seeds, songs, trade goods from Mexico, a bounty of produce, or even babies. His role as a symbol of fertility is confirmed by many depictions of him with a long phallus – a sign that wise young maidens would want to avoid. Emblematic of good fortune, Kokopelli's image was incorporated in pottery and baskets as well as murals. These widespread depictions suggest that Kokopelli was universally viewed in a positive light.

The ancient humped-back Pied-Piper reminds us that not all times facing the ancient ones were necessarily hard. This is a fact we tend to overlook when visualizing those historic harsh days devoid of creature comforts dominating our culture. Despite shorter life-spans, cruel physical toll of daily living, and rudimentary medical knowledge, our ancestors found plenty to laugh about. Their jokes were no less humorous, their celebrations equally rowdy. They took the time to enjoy life and share in laughter when the harvest was better than expected, a cold winter finally gave way to summer's warmth, or perhaps a young scout returned with news of hidden hot springs.

***

Mid-May is a perfect time to celebrate surviving winter and there's no finer spot for making merry like Kokopelli clones than the Gila Wilderness in southwestern New Mexico. This is Aldo Leopold country; the wild country where Leopold's perspective on wilderness changed dramatically after he shot a wolf and regretfully watched the gift of life drain from her emerald green eyes. High desert canyons gouge across the Gila Wilderness draining moisture from peaks 10,000 feet high. In the lower reaches of the Gila along the West Fork and Middle Fork pleasant streams provide respite from furnace-like heat that builds after June first.

Aim carefully to ensure missing the last vestiges of spring's chill and to avoid the trauma of summer's heat. When hitting it just right the Gila provides fabulous country for treks deep into wild and almost inaccessible canyons, along rough rocky ridges, and on top of ponderosa-covered parks. A trip to the Gila serves as a gateway to summer's intensity. And, since it can provide that first extended exploration of a new season, the Gila occupies a very special place in adventurers' hearts.

***

Winding in and out; twisting back and forth; up and down; over and around; wild swaying of the truck is so predictable. Each stomach sloshing turn with its pressing centrifugal pull seems etched into memory from countless trips through these rugged desiccated hills of the Black Range. Drive slowly and time stands still, building a sort of pathetic desperation that it will never end. Take it fast and we avoid boredom, but risk hurling that greasy breakfast burrito and lacquer-tasting coffee from Socorro onto our partners' laps.

A Godforsaken potholed two-lane leaves Interstate 25 by Truth-or-Consequences, New Mexico and heads west over some of the Land of Enchantment's most depressingly brown, stark landscape. Nothing is enchanting about this drive, except the end. From Hillsboro the way goes up and over the Black Range with fluttering aspen and sighing fir forest in shaded glens. Pencil straight pine-covered slopes dominate on sunnier reaches. This is a sweet treat after winding through a scrub oak, scrawny piñon and ragged juniper forest.

The Black Range's highs are rapidly bartered for the downs of intervening valleys in craggy foothill country. Seldom does the road run straight and level. Once again the road twists upward gaining elevation before falling into the Gila Valley. And, just when we are ready to head back home because we can't stand it any longer, a steep drop into the wilderness gateway begins. Gears shift down to slow our vehicle while neck-craning views abound in all directions. Relief – tonight we will be deep within this wilderness.

Out of habit we stop at the Gila Visitor Center seeking information on trail conditions, but the rangers never know anything.

"How's the trail up the Middle Fork?"

"Well the water is high but we don't have any reports from further up yet. The floods of September have scoured the lower section below Little Bear Canyon and the trail has been destroyed."

"How's the trail up the West Fork?"

"We don't know much yet as no one has gone past Hell's Hole twelve miles up. Runoff is down, but picking up within the last few days."

These facts are virtually useless. By glancing at the West Fork we know in a second how high the flow is. Since few are going down the Middle Fork, and like us, typically going up it, what happens below Little Bear Canyon is of little importance. Standing off to the side while friends continue their inquiry, I wonder why rangers don't range. How can they be anymore disconnected from the wilderness they protect? It ought to be mandatory for them to travel on foot or horse at least twenty trail miles each week – everyone else in the world is doing it, why not the guardians?

By now a sort of malaise has set in. Groggy from the drive, hot in early afternoon sun, and punchy from lack of food, Terrye, Bill and I eat a quick bite and throw on our packs. With many miles to go up over dusty tan-white hills toward Little Bear Canyon and then down to the Middle Fork of the Gila River, there's a compelling, almost frantic, desperation to get on with it. In minutes the truck is locked and we're stumbling along with monstrous loads on our backs, blazing sun directly overhead and temperatures rising from the low eighties

Staggering up a rock-infested path toward a crest of short hills defining the lower reaches of the Gila Mountains, we stop often in the meager shade of shabby old junipers and ask why we didn't begin this trip in late afternoon when the sun is going down. But, that question is never answered because the reason is all too evident. Tonight we want to be basking peacefully in the middle of wilderness. We want to forget the big city, and Hillsboro, and road from hell. Tonight we seek the pleasures of being outdoors with few possessions except the treasures of an ancient land, a new moon overhead, and a gurgling stream down from a sandy bank where tents perch.

There's plenty of sweet flowing water where we're bound, but in order to get there, especially with this mid-day start, we have little choice but to bring along two precious quarts of water. This just makes the initial climb that much more burdensome with water's heavy weight, the weight of life.

At a rest stop Terrye patiently sits in the shade, waiting, watching, and knowing that her recess may soon be over. I refuse to sit down for fear of never getting back up. Meanwhile, Bill delves into his pack for some item. Our shirts are soaked with sweat and grease. We're blistered from the shimmering heat, but have made good progress on this mesa strewn with eight-foot high junipers. Ahead are several house-high piñons and the scraggliest pines imaginable, signaling the beginning of oppressive heat's end.

Throwing packs on back, they settle a bit more comfortably as body and muscles begin to remember what this is all about. In an endless panorama, a red-tail hawk rides thermals over the West Fork's expansive valley. Up river is spring's fresh green growth and tucked into a side canyon sits the Gila Cliff Dwellings, an ancient site ensconced under an enormous eyelid of a cliff, too far west to actually see. A faultless pale blue sky speaks of dry air and long wait until July's monsoon rains. I spin and follow the others intent on reaching the hill's crest and release from this toughest part of the hike.

In time our trail begins weaving gradually down into an ill-defined bowl with numerous ponderosa pines and piñons. It only takes a bit more shade of this east-facing bowl to encourage flourishing growth. Evaporating sweat cools quickly now that we're headed downhill – frowns disappear. Winding through stands of leafy oak on top of a cushy brown pine needle carpet, our spirits begin to soar again. The afternoon temperature has dropped to the low eighties; pleasant adventure has returned and we anticipate the Middle Fork ahead.

Little Bear Canyon descends abruptly from this initial bowl. Dry streambed replaces trail and from here boot- and hoof-beaten paths weave through canyons and watercourses. As if to commemorate the change, a profusion of screaming bright yellow monkey flowers obscures a rocky glen's damp east wall. It's a moment like this that has Terrye soaring. She revels in the grotto's refrigerator coolness and vivid blossoms, searching valiantly for hummingbirds typically drawn to this oasis.

How long has this copse of startling beauty been growing on these walls? With the Gila Cliff Dwellings only a ridge away the ancient ones must have taken great pleasure in this pleasing counterpoint – brilliant yellow and jade green against an infinity of earth tones. Mesmerizing flowers recalibrate your thinking and attitude, justifying a sweaty plod across monochromatic mesas. It's such a surprise after furnace-like heat, that even the most callous wanderers discover an unintentional smile spreading across their lips.

Bill and I are a bit more pragmatic as we sense the nearness of the Middle Fork perhaps in increased humidity, overwhelming shrubby vegetation, canyon's depth or barely perceptible sound of tinkling water. Whatever the cues, the attraction is too much and we push onward. In a few minutes Little Bear Canyon flows out into the Middle Fork. Engulfed by yellow-red sandstone cliffs with baton-shaped rock sentinels and needle spires jutting skyward, Little Bear Canyon vanishes as quickly as it starts, lost in the Middle Fork's labyrinth.

Shrugging packs onto the Gila's damp bank, we deposit cares and woes from another life seemingly a thousand miles distant. Guzzling water with abandon now, dripping down the corners of our mouths, we no longer have to carefully conserve each precious drop. The river is strong and clear – it will provide. Birds call loudly in treetops and zoom up and down river. A series of large glassy pools reposes beneath broad overhanging sycamores and other riverine canopy. Rich, dank scents of decay from small stagnant green-black pools waft downstream along with a thousand other odors tucked away in our memories. The Middle Fork of the Gila flows purposefully, never rushing, down canyon bends towards the Visitor Center some six miles distant.

It's a vastly different complexion on my comrades' faces, yet we don't know how to express our feelings in words. To conclude that we're having fun somehow doesn't quite capture it because this is more than just a good time – we're celebrating a little backcountry exploit. I don't say anything except pick up my pack with a smile– those are words enough – and commit the act we've been waiting for; adventure's ultimate beginning. Splashing across the river I seek a sandy shore and obscure path through trees and bushes.

For the most part route finding is extremely easy in this river canyon. White-red rock walls soaring several hundred feet bracket the Middle Fork so it's not as though explorers can lose the trail – the trail is the river. But, paths generally cut the meanders saving distance and seeking solid ground – a euphemism for wading through sand. After the first river crossing our trail is nothing more than river rock and sand pits along one bench or another. It's amazing how laborious it is to wade through sand with a heavy pack on your back.

With sodden socks, and boots filling with sandy grit, we trudge along slipping in dunes that mock our progress. It's just as well that our pace slows down because it's time to be especially alert for rattlesnakes along the river's edge. Sudden movements are the precise recipe for unknowingly stepping on one of our friends. A mouse, lizard or other small creature rustles through the underbrush and we jump ever so slightly while adrenaline courses through our veins. Eyes and ears alert to movement we scan the path ahead for the big picture and then drill down focusing on the next five yards, especially trailside, watching for the unexpected. Get bitten down here and you're in for some big time trouble.

Laboring along this ancient path under full backpacks evokes a very comical image. Physically we resemble so many Kokopelli figures, stooped from weight's oppressive hold yet dancing a light step from the joy of wilderness exploration. Even banter among friends is full of mirth and good tidings. We have no flutes, but the Middle Fork plays a soothingly pleasant tune.

A reprieve from sand and river rock lies ahead at the next crossing. We pause to select the best line and then cross on wet marbles that roll precariously underfoot. By now we're relishing each dive into water that refreshes — water with temperatures surprisingly cool considering how warm the country is cradling this flowing ribbon of life. For many crossings, it only reaches mid-calf. But, in spots you begin plowing water that's past your knees or higher. Water aerobics place an added strain on tiring muscles. It's not the distance that makes the difference in the Gila, but terrain.

Plunging a little more recklessly when trying to maintain a fast pace, I almost lose balance on slippery algae-covered rocks. Dripping gallons of water I crawl up a dirt bank that's the fore-runner of relatively level walking and firm tread for a half-mile. Our path weaves through a deteriorating orchard evoking memories of hardy pioneers who lived in – rather than visited – this captivating canyon.

No sooner have my sopping, dripping boots dried out a bit than another thirty-foot stream crossing appears. These fords are one of the Gila's endearing features that ramp up the fun and challenge. No two crossing are ever alike. When the gentle rolling Middle Fork spreads out, they distill to nothing more than a virtual skip across a wide spot in the canyon. You barely get your feet wet. Others where the Middle Fork gathers, canyon walls narrow, and the resulting channel forms a "vee," require an altogether different approach. The second you step off the river bank you tense-up as rocks rolls underfoot and water rises up your thighs. Still others are bi-modal – you splash down into one pool, claw you way up a gravel bar, and then splash down again.

Watching Bill or Terrye cross the Middle Fork in front of me does little to ensure a smoother crossing. In most cases they end up disturbing the riverbed. Then the mossy rocks become a slick bed of instable marbles intent on bringing me down to their level. If ever there was tailor-made time for trekking poles, this is it.

Another crossing comes up. How many has it been since Little Bear Canyon connected with the Middle Fork – twelve or fourteen? I'm losing count. We'll have at least twice as many crossings before leaving the Middle Fork drainage.

Plodding along with canyon walls rising ever higher, spruce and fir trees sprout from rocky ledges virtually inaccessible from along the river. Eastern slopes are less steep and wear a cloak of oak, pine and juniper on higher sunny reaches. Could these slopes be climbed to escape from torrential rains and occasionally horrific floods scouring the Gila in late summer? We could easily scramble out of harm's way, but once on a mesa top it would be difficult to determine how to reach a road given the undulating nature of the country. Such a decision could be more hazardous than simply waiting for high water to subside.

At several bends in the canyon a multitude of red rock spires and tent rocks or hoodoos appear – cones of soft rock wearing hats of much harder substance – pinnacles resembling a defective Velcro strip. Standing in a grove of ponderosa pines with warm rich sappy fragrance enveloping the canyon, several spires beckon, calling us to explore. Unfortunately we still have many miles to go hike on our planned route. Besides we're getting very hungry. It's time to find a nice camp.

*** *

Sun disappeared from the canyon an hour ago and cool breezes begin flowing in cadence with the river. For the last half mile the canyon narrowed and few attractive camping spots could be found. An acceptable site appeared in the open ponderosa forest, but it was a relatively long way from the river and a fire ring looked dangerous among the thick bed of dry pine needles. Now I'm having second thoughts. My friends are back there somewhere, perhaps I should backtrack?

No; the idea is to gain ground, not lose it. Growing impatient with my inability to find a spot, hungry and increasingly weary from the miles, only one question dominates my mind – where's a good campsite?

Emerging from a thicket of shrubs and small trees, the path drops to the Middle Fork. Looking upstream the canyon curves off to the left and two possibilities present themselves. With two fords there is a copse of ponderosa on a flat bench at the river's bend – a campsite is visible in the distance. On the other hand, the first ford will bring me to a bench on the east side of the canyon and there appears to be a camp behind a screen of cotton-wood, elder and locust. Look backing, there's no sight of Terrye or Bill. I hope I haven't gone too far for them.

The Middle Fork's channel has funneled into a "vee" shape a bit deeper than other spots but it presents no significant problem and I sway across on slippery algae-covered rocks. After crossing and shucking pack on a sandbar, it's possible to see the trail behind me – a better vantage point to determine when Terrye and Bill catch up.

Free of the nylon stone on my back, walking with palpable buoyancy, I'm thankful that the hard work is finished. Having lost forty pounds, I virtually float when walking. Entering a shady alcove offered by large sycamores and cottonwoods, I discover a nice fire ring and logs. Perfect camp. Far enough from the river to assuage ecological concerns yet close enough to access water for cooking, drinking and extinguishing fires. In fact, the camp is so perfect that there's no need to cross and explore the ponderosa flats. Here we have privacy from any passersby on the trail; over there we'll be exposed in the open – not that there are hordes of people out. We've seen no one since leaving the Visitor Center.

After fifteen minutes of sitting on my pack, restlessness bubbles over. Where are they anyway? Walking down to the river over a fifty-foot bar of sand, gravel and round river rocks, I poke along drilling down on the river's microenvironment. A brown-black spider rushes out of a clump of flourishing parrot green weeds at my feet, scurrying for new cover. Squatting at the water's edge I look upstream.

Why are so many clumps of green algae growing at this particular spot? It's open to plenty of sun, but the swift current should keep things under control. Why is there so much sea green vegetation just up from our campsite? Sauntering along the riverbank I notice a ribbon of flourishing growth with a tiny stream dissecting it. Aha, there's a diminutive creek entering the river.

This is pretty peculiar. There's no side canyon, so it must be a spring. Along a brilliant swath orange-yellow flowers are blooming in profusion – an enticing glen. Bending down to feel the spring water's coolness, I'm shocked. It's very warm, almost hot. There must be a hot spring further up.

Following the stream through thick brush and climbing uphill, several crystal clear pools lay ahead; one is probably thirty feet across, an oval shape. Decomposed granite lines the bed of this pool; a hot tub in the wilderness. No wonder the river has more algae and moss than in other spots. The spring brings nutrients and warmth to encourage growth.

Now there's no question where we will camp. I begin setting up my tent and in due time Bill and Terrye mosey in dropping their packs with relief. I share the news of my little side exploration while showing them the coveted site, a grand discovery after all of those muscle-sore miles. And then we turn to the time-honored duties of setting up camp, building a fire, purifying water and making dinner.

How many times in the past have we walked right by the hot springs completely oblivious to its sweet waters? We almost feel foolish for having missed this unexpected treasure in the past. Surely the Mogollon band occupying the Gila Cliff Dwellings came to know these springs. Their ruins are sited above large hot springs on the Gila River so they were familiar with naturally heated water. Who among the Cliff Dwellings' inhabitants made that eventful first discovery? Picture how the telling of the story poured from their lips while others stood around possibly disbelieving the tall tale.

When a larger group went back to scout out the supposed discovery did huge stupid grins adorn their faces – like Bill, Terrye and me – as they positioned themselves in the full flow of 98 degree water? Gloriously warm water – not too hot or too cold – poured over their bodies easing countless aches and pains. Sitting in the therapeutic waters we relax and share a bit of mirth about sliding on moss covered river rocks, unrelenting packs that grow heavier each year, and tall tales from Gila trips past. As dusk yields to darkness we sit immersed in the embracing waters.

Listen! Was that a flute player rustling nearby shrubs, or just a downstream breeze?

After a yummy dinner made more comfortable by our lucky discovery, we enjoy a delight that only backcountry exploration delivers – a crackling campfire. Standing around dancing flames, drinking hot chocolate, and weary from miles but eased by a long warm soak, we toast the Gila Wilderness and good fortune to do that which we love most. Our sleep that night is sound; very sound except for light footfalls and an almost indiscernible plaintive flute-born melody emanating from a mirth maker who guards these precious springs.

***

Crisp morning air envelopes our campsite as blonde-white sunlight dapples canyon margins where soaring walls fail to block the sun. A robin calls lustfully upstream proclaiming territory in this wonderful canyon. I rise quietly from a cocoon of down, pulling on a light jacket to ward off chill, and walk softly to the campfire ring. Glowing red coals remain hidden in ashes. With a fistful of woody twigs laid on the fire pit's center, I blow a mini gale to raise flame and warmth. More smoke than flame responds to this call, but patience pays off. Sputtering ignition and a light crackle signal a growing blaze.

Next chore is to light the Svea, a stove that makes a horrible racket even on low. But, it always starts. Water is heating and well on its way to boiling by the time two sleepy heads crawl out of their tent with loud groans. We're stiff from exercising muscles that atrophied over winter. Our bodies cry to stay put while relishing the campfire and hot springs in this enticing grove. Some senseless discussion ensues about remaining one more night, but we all know what the answer will be. To complete our planned circuit we will hike the remainder of the Middle Fork up to The Meadows. The debate doesn't last very long after breakfast is finished. We'll explore the rest of the Middle Fork today.

Our packs are a little bit lighter, but our bodies have lost energy, so things just about balance out. Able to carry less water I'm elated that my stone is reduced to something more tolerable. Tightening straps and belt, packs settle into place. Now we face the biggest challenge of the day — our first ford of the Gila. Dipping into the swift-flowing stream and rushing up on the opposite bank, goose bumps the size of pebbles protrude on legs and arms. Ten minutes of swift walking will take care of the chill.

Middle Fork canyon continues to narrow with ever-higher walls reaching hundreds of feet to plateau rim. It's very cool as we enter a cathedral-like section of the river and we're able to see our breath while walking along, hunched over like the flute player. In spots soft yellow sun beams down on the river and light plays over its surface with a fresh sparkle. Fords are shorter, but deeper, and water rushes up my thighs when plowing through the swift flowing stream. Large spruce trees cling to each bank, shading river from sun. In hushed tones the Main Fork takes on a wild quality characteristic of high country.

At various bends and diversions where rocks and tree trunks are jumbled high from past floods, the Middle Fork undercuts the opposite bank. Hanging over rushing waters, red sandstone cliffs mottled with green-gray moss rise thirty-to-forty feet before curving back into mountainside. From there steep forested hills rise a good five hundred feet or more. I'm thinking about how few people are fortunate to see this lovely spectacle, thankful that we continued hiking rather than altering our trip for the spa's comfort. Winding through the canyon, we're keeping a tepid tempo to ward off chill and to cover miles through this quiet wilderness.

Our trail climbs uphill for about one hundred feet – an unusual distance from the river – and bisects a curve. At the end of this transect a straight stretch of river, perhaps one-quarter mile long, flows at the base of the west bank. Emerging out of tall pines and spruce, I hear the screech of an eagle – no three eagles. Two fledglings are being taught how to fish along this straight section of the Middle Fork. I try to blend back into the trees while watching this little training exercise.

The fledglings perch high in an enormous spruce tree overlooking the river. Their parent flies parallel with the river before swooping down to its surface, and then returns to the tree with outrageous shrieking calls. This causes a chain reaction as the young ones emit a great hue and cry. Next, they take turns flying the same vector, but remain twenty feet above the river fearful of going lower. Parent eagle tries it one more time before Terrye and Bill finally catch up with me. Unaware of the eagles they step out from under the cover of tree limbs. I usher then back but it's too late. The lesson is apparently over as long as we're in the vicinity.

Walking past several bends in the river, the Middle Fork's canyon opens slightly, almost imperceptibly. Sloughing of rocks on an eastern cliff face may be the key signal of this alteration in topography, or perhaps it's the river slowing, widening along a sunny channel. Fascinating red-white rocks penetrate swirling waters; waters forming deep pools of translucent green against shadowy cliff faces. Ambling along sandy banks and forest trail the character of river and canyon seem to change every half-mile or so as morning disappears.

With my stomach serving as alarm clock, it's time to look for a rocky perch in the river where the mix of sun and shade is tempered. A long languid stretch turns up around the next corner and I try several boulders before nesting down. Greasy salami and long-horn cheese taste fabulous after expending so much energy to keep warm and to safely negotiate river crossings. Sun heats to the bone.

Bill and Terrye soon catch up and pull out their own snacks. We aren't keeping time. There's no schedule other than to reach The Meadows before nightfall. Glancing up river we all know what's coming because the canyon's slopes are more gradual and flush with juniper and piñon on the east. Pines dominate on the cooler, higher western slopes. The Meadows is undoubtedly around the bend.

This is both good news and bad. On the one hand the physically demanding mileage is about done for the day. On the other hand, The Meadows means that we will be sharing the wilderness with other people before too long. These are concerns that the Mogollon band also carried. For them other people usually implied enemies and threats to personal safety. How much more cautiously they must have trod these ancient paths; anticipating danger around every bend and never really free to relax in the park-like surroundings they called home.

With some regret we stow meals and continue up river. In a mere forty minutes the Middle Fork's confluence with Indian Creek is reached. This spare creek tumbles down from the east mesa, pausing repeatedly along its boulder-filled course. From high on the west cliff side looking into Indian Creek it appears that rock – not water – flows down this watershed. Among the jumble of rocks an angler balances on Ottoman-sized boulders stalking elusive Gila trout. He's the first person we've seen since leaving the Visitor Center.

Fifteen more minutes of walking and a broad gap in the Middle Fork of the Gila opens up with huge fluorescent green cottonwood trees towering over grassy parkland. This is our campsite for tonight. Compared with the Middle Fork's narrow confines, this space is liberating, but at the same time melancholy. We will have to choose an open, less private site for camp. But, there is an undeniable scenic allure to The Meadows with its verdant floor and almost boundless space.

Terrye and Bill comment on how beavers have changed the landscape since our last visit. Many huge cottonwoods have been felled leaving less shade. It's not as enticing as when an immense canopy of lime green fluttering leaves shaded dark emerald meadows, but it's still better than any car campground we'll ever experience. Finding a campsite isn't difficult in The Meadows given all of the relatively level ground. Tents are erected before each of us goes off exploring the upper Middle Fork in late afternoon seeking unknown treasures such as hidden hot springs.

***

Like many who preceded us, we found this little jaunt on the Middle Fork of the Gila River to be ripe with new discoveries – new to us, but undoubtedly well chronicled in the history of human habitation across this region. We shared a fulfilling camaraderie that enhanced our adventure despite rugged conditions. Mutual respect grew for each other during this journey adding to the pages we have read about each other during past trips. So it is for many folk who fellowship with others when they do what they most love to do. This kind of sharing works best when the parties involved know how to allow space for the others – time alone without constant interaction – a workable formula simultaneously nurturing friendship and solitude.

David Petersen in *The Nearby Faraway* commented on a friend's habit of seeking aloneness after dinner each night during a camping trip: "After a feast of dehydrated noodles, crackers and water, feeling rested but talked-out for the nonce, we go our separate way. Branson wanders off to take pictures, while I just wander. Strolling (you could say care-less-ly) through a patchwork of onion-scented meadows and juniper-flavored woods at the edge of night, I'm suddenly bushwhacked by an inexplicable sense of well-being. What's going on? I stop and stand in silence, smiling like the happy idiot I am, and eavesdrop on the evening chatter of bluebirds, nighthawks, robins and an anonymous assortment of little gray singers: lovely wild voices twittering amongst the bushy trees. In full darkness I trail the scent of juniper smoke back to camp – Branson has already returned

— and retire to the haunting calls of poorwills, the maniacal music of coyotes."[17]

The innocent joy of being in the wild — "well-being" in Petersen's words — is best when shared with others and also when there are opportunities to achieve solitude. When Bill and Terrye return, *separately*, from exploring the upper Middle Fork of the Gila, a palpable joy of adventure accompanies us that is shared during dinner around the campfire.

As our fire dwindles to red-hot coals and a slight chill moves downstream, a whippoorwill begins to call. It is the call of the wild and adventure; of being outdoors among friends and in land that few travel due to the exertion required to be there. It certainly isn't base camp at Mt. Everest, the Tsangpo Gorge, the African plains or Antarctica. But the Gila is the embodiment of wildness; the first designated wilderness in the United States.

Taking the warmth of fire, friendship and the embrace of a rugged yet beautiful land to bed, these small but significant adventures ensure that I will continue to pursue this passion for living life outdoors; a life that many think untenable due to dirt, sweat, heat, cold and exertion. As I snuggle under generous-down-filled fabric a silent, but persistent, melody wafts over camp.

Night's cooling air rushes downstream stirring fragile cottonwood leaves overhead like thousands of tiny cymbals in an ebb and flow of gentle percussion. Occasional bursts of aggressive wind act like a tympani booming across the park-like meadows. Meanwhile the Middle Fork gurgles with joyous laughter, momentarily freed from the confines of the upper canyon, bound for the narrow defile up which we walked the past two days.

My eyes grow heavy as contentment with wildness lies like a blanket over our camp. It's hard to nod off as rich panoply of scents smother smoke from our dying campfire. Although no moon brightens the night sky, starlight shines in gentle beams through the cottonwood canopy overhead. Straddling blessed sleep, a faint sound reaches my ears and then momentarily blows away with the breeze only to return again.

Was that laughter mixed with the gentle sound of a shrill flute that I just heard? Senses well up as I strain to hear more, and then sleep collapses over me as visions of Kokopelli dance in my head.

Future Past

*Suddenly, the dark's
a-glitter with diamonds.
Can we touch a star?*

TERRYE BULLERS

14

Driven from the land

Massive vanilla-capped fuzzy cotton balls masquerading as thunderheads are the signature weather feature people remember most about the Southwest. Ballasted by deep plum purple undersides from which yellow-white etched lightning spears the land, these storms are terrifyingly feral. Torrential downpours, sleet, hail and plummeting temperatures are only a few of the dramatic theatrics accompanying the monsoon season in early July.

Early July....

Wait a minute....

Isn't that the same time that those cathedral peaked mountains are opening up for family explorations along wave rippling shorelines of forest lakes? Haven't high country snows melted off allowing the more adventurous to penetrate deeply above tree line? Doesn't early summer mark the very moment when folks set off to camp for a few days in the outdoors, to enjoy a leisurely picnic around a smoky fire, or to saunter at the edge of beautiful country while taking in grand vistas?

Paradoxically no sooner are backcountry paths clear of snow, glacial temperatures are beaten back by sunshine that lingers forever, and then from nowhere spring up massive thunderstorms. How does that work? The second after winter's largesse is overcome I'm immediately put in a position of contending with a daily onslaught of rain, sleet, hail, and freezing-temperatures?

Scientists offer deeply intellectual explanations regarding how land over the Southwest warms while moisture is funneled up from Mexico. But, they don't seem to comprehend the absurdity of it all. Winter's remains are barely gone and then another set of depressing weather factors must be addressed.

It starts with lethal lightning and boisterous thunder rolling over ridges like some gigantic bowling alley.

SSSSnnnaaappppp.

ZZZZzzzzaaaaappppppppp.

BBBbbbbbaaaaammmmmmmmmbbbbboooooommmmmm.

An innocent-enough little crack, a dazzling flash and then tympani drums echo on and on. If I or the spruce I'm standing next to weren't flash fried, then I'm about to be doused with a potentially lethal concoction of the worst that cranky weather gods can throw at me.

If my juju is grooving just right I've got nothing to worry about. However, go often enough to worship those cathedral peaks in the Southwest and eventually Las Vegas' probabilities catch up with me. Even those who possess the luck-o-the-Irish better watch out. The Law of the Monsoons has the final say. I should know; I finally tested that law one too many times.

***

My friends and I have only been hoofing it fifteen short minutes along Archuleta Lake Trail before the first ominous growling rumble of thunder rolls over this lofty mountain basin like books falling off a shelf.

Our spirits sink in proportion with the clatter. *Looks like another miserably wet summer afternoon on the way.*

This is one time we should have started the trip a little earlier in the morning, stopped fewer times for junk-food goodies, or speeded with reckless abandon; we would already be at the campsite. Instead, we took our sweet time because that seemed right – to let go of life's frenetic pace. We bartered for mountain time where there are no big agendas or deadlines. Glancing behind me, Dick and Luther are nowhere to be seen. Their goal on this trip is fishing, not hiking, and they definitely won't be rushed.

No problem – I'll press forward with the intention of setting up camp. Besides; it simply feels good to be out here in the wide open with no one else to answer up to except myself.

Our destination is a modest conifer strewn bench in southern Colorado's Weminuche Wilderness where Gibbs Creek flows into the South Fork of the Rio Grande. There's no trail up Gibbs Creek so we're speculating that it will offer superb fishing for native trout. My compadres are, after all, fishermen extraordinaire at heart. Fishing isn't my immediate worry. I'm only trying to place camp where everyone wins – hikers to reach Archuleta

Lake hunkered down 150-or-so feet below a 12,000 foot pass on the Continental Divide and fishermen to access an untrammeled stream birthed by springs and seeps almost two miles high on the divide's eastern face.

Although this trail's destination is named for a former Colorado politician of Spanish ancestry, the Utes coveted this land in the summer. The Capote and Mohuache bands laid claim to the southern San Luis Valley of southern Colorado while the Weminuche band typically remained west of the Continental Divide. Before the Utes commandeered this exceptional territory, plains tribes of Kiowa, Arapaho, Cheyenne and Comanche periodically made forays to these slopes.

It's probable that we will be following faint paths the Ute and other native bands beat along the Rio Grande as they fished and hunted for wild game. Even today these slopes nurture robust herds of elk and antelope; we've seen them from a distance as well as bear.

We'll be sharing another impressive legacy that confounded the Utes and other indigenous people throughout the Southwest – horrific weather.

Almost every summer gi-normously great gobs of moisture are funneled up through Mexico. Eventually humidity, cloud cover and a generous wealth of precipitation reach past Colorado toward the northern Rocky Mountain States. In some instances – usually a prelude to spectacular displays of rain, lightning and cloud build-up along the Continental Divide – the moisture freight train heads directly north into Texas while spreading to points east. As amazing as it seems, this seasonal weather pattern mimics the same monsoonal phenomenon observed in India and southern Asia.

From a climatologist's viewpoint, seasonal rains flooding from northern Mexico form the North American Monsoon System, also known as the Southwest Monsoon or American Monsoon. The monsoon typically appears in July – on average July 3 – but in some years it begins to form in late May or early June if conditions are favorable. Once the monsoon triggers with daily cloud build-up followed by scattered but intense rainfall, it lasts through July until early August and sometimes as late as mid September. The National Oceanic and Atmospheric Administration (NOAA) claims that the most intense thunderstorms associated with the monsoon occur from July 20 to August 20.

Climatologists and weather observers are drawn like rock band groupies to the spectacular displays of lightning and drenching downpours emanating from the American Monsoon's massive thunderstorm cells. Cumulous clouds progressively build skyward as if reaching for space itself to 40,000-60,000 feet before leveling off with rushing jet stream wind. These high altitude currents help artistically form the anvil shapes so characteristic of large, independent thunderstorm clouds. Resulting storms grow in intensity sucking every last drop of moisture passed up from northern Mexico with baking heat from the high plains and desert. When these ingredients coalesce along the Continental Divide cells are spawned that gradually travel eastward often growing in proportion with additional moisture and heat.

Along the Rocky Mountains the North American Monsoon System translates into intense daily thunderstorms that build very late in the morning or in early afternoon. Skies become obscured by black-purple rain clouds that rattle into each other until they glom together. The result is a weather phenomenon equivalent in ferocity to tornados and hurricanes. These storms are very dangerous because they are accompanied by sudden dramatic temperature shifts, pelting hail, torrential showers, hurricane force winds and stinging snow at high altitude. Only fools tempt fate by being near the Continental Divide when such storms pass over. There's no better way to be miserable than to go into the high country at this time of year with subpar gear.

Another thunderous roll rockets overhead from the west, similar to outrageous bowling pin thuds at your local alley when a pro shows off. We're definitely not going to make it to camp before rain falls, particularly with the trail climbing persistently uphill like this.

Crack – KaBoom!!

Great; just great. Here it comes; first a gauzy drizzle and then a flat-out downpour. It's time to change plans before we go much higher. I quickly spin around and head down-trail, practically running. I need to intercept Luther and Dick before they start this climb. We can camp somewhere down along the 113 acre trailhead lake where it's almost pancake flat. There must be sites where we can hunker down in case this isn't merely a passing shower.

SIZZLE; *Crack*; **KaBoom!**

Good night. Am I going to be forced to stop and pull on my rain parka? I really don't have the luxury of even a few seconds if I want to intercept them before they struggle upward.

PLOPPP; Pitter; PPPPLLLOOOPPPPP; Ping, ping, ping, ping, ping. A curtain of raindrops destined for the Colorado River fall like a vaporous veil into my face and over this hillside.

Minutes later I run into Luther and Dick. They're only steps away from beginning this steep grade. Thank God I intercepted them. A dark thought flashes across my mind: imagine the verbal abuse I'd be pummeled with if they had clawed their way up only to lose that elevation again. Gentle rain shifts to fat, wet gum-drop-size pellets hammering the forest around us.

Rumble-**Kaboom**!

Hugging a not-too-large fir like a long lost relative, we cringe when another timpani roll is followed by a zap signaling more frenzied electrical activity. We're too exposed standing this close to a tall tree. Adding to our dilemma, dry ground underneath the branches suggests that this tree is clearly substantial enough to serve as a lightning rod. After hurriedly discussing options, we decide to flee back a quarter mile where a path that circumambulates the lake splits off.

I'm running, but the trail's inevitable stones and roots make our flight a sure recipe for a fall. Everything is wet enough to challenge our footing. We have to pick our way carefully, but quickly.

Good news, 40 yards ahead is a copse of spruce offering some protection without sticking up like the Eiffel Tower. We duck under the branches and slough off our packs trying to gauge what's next in store from this hammering tempest that swooped down from out of nowhere.

A few more minutes of pandemonium unfolds before the storm ends as quickly as it started. Now we can collect our thoughts and reconsider the most promising strategies in a world gone gray with drizzle mixed with huge dollops that splat everything in sight – find a cozy spot nearby; continue in these questionable conditions higher up the mountain; go back to the truck and drive to a nearby trail where we often camp only minutes from the trailhead; or, head for town.

The decision is made for us. At the lake's far southwestern end we find a passable spot to erect tents. We've seen better camps; and worse, but this will do. Next time we'll reach the trailhead earlier.

Today's first explosions won't be the last because it is late summer in the San Juan Mountains. Monsoon season started more than a month ago and probabilities favor rain almost every day. The Swiss-like predictability and ensuing regularity of rain becomes pathetically monotonous. However, when a big hunk of moisture streams up from the south, storm frequency and intensity increase. Such is the case today and profuse thunderstorms can be anticipated each afternoon for the next several days. The die is cast for this trip.

These aren't any of those downstream run-of-the-mill thunderstorms with a smattering of lightning, a few brief downbursts and then a steamy departure. This is the thunderstorm *BIG TIME*. The vast desert Southwest funnels cauldrons of heat toward Colorado's high country and cool air aloft over the Continental Divide. When the two collide it's an intimidating sight especially along the two-mile plus high divide.

Experienced mountaineers know that Rocky Mountain storms can be lethally wicked. Above tree-line there's no shelter from the elements. Even within the forest risk is high for lightning-induced casualties. A fried elk, big horn ram, black bear or other crispy critter isn't a pretty sight. Some gamble and die. Others show respect and live to climb, hike or fish for another day.

What's the probability of being killed by lightning? Most authorities cite 1 in 600,000 as the odds that a person will be struck by lightning. According to the National Oceanic and Atmospheric Administration there are 7.7 casualties for every 100 million lightning flashes.[18] These numbers seem big; the odds of being struck infinitesimal. Further assuaging our fears is the fact that 90% of those struck by lightning live to tell about it. The probability that a person will be struck twice is smaller still – 1 in 360 billion. Facts of this caliber nurture a "What me worry" attitude that can be fatal.

These figures may explain why some outdoors recreationists go boldly where others fear to tread. But their boldness can leave them wrong; dead wrong. The fallacy in thinking a hiker only has one chance in 600,000 of being hit relates to the statistics themselves. Most of the 600,000 people are sequestered indoors, driving cars or in locations where lightning doesn't occur with great frequency. Those climbing mountains or heading into the high country dramatically raise the probability that they will be hit because that's where lightning often begins – with clouds nurtured by warm moist air being funneled upward along mountain ridges.

The innocent act of climbing a mountain enhances a person's exposure level. Lightning tends to seek tall objects when coursing to earth. Any time hikers enter sub-alpine or alpine zones, they increase their vulnerability by becoming one of the tallest objects in the vicinity. Furthermore by scaling ridges and peaks their exposure level intensifies.

So the next time you raise the odds that you will be hit by lightning think twice. Protect yourself by keeping low to the ground. Crouch on the balls of your feet to minimize the amount of electricity that will be conducted upward in the event of a nearby strike. Although rubber boots are as ineffective as automobile tires in insulating from a strike, nonetheless do everything to become as small as possible and to minimize the extent to which lightning will find you. Stay away from tall objects such as trees and rocks. Do not lie flat. Better yet, retreat from high ground before thunderstorm activity begins.

Only you can protect yourself from lightning in the high country.

An interlude in the pesky showers gives us a chance to carefully place tents. Space is tight and Luther's old Walrus tent is the largest; we relegate the venerable tent to a cushy spot between firs. Dick's solo Sierra Designs, spare as can be, is placed next followed by my two-person Mountain Hardware tent. Camp chores unfold – gathering wood, setting up a kitchen and campfire, hanging a line for food, purifying water – before serious fishing gets underway. While Dick and Luther head off it's my chance to wander up trail toward Gibbs Creek.

An afternoon of exploration evaporates before I know it. Further thunderstorm theatrics fail to materialize. It's surprising that the early storm folded so easily before moving on; a lucky break in monsoon season. Nonetheless it's still cloudy with sunny moments lending a remarkable tranquility to this drainage. Perhaps we will dodge a bullet this time.

Several hours later, Luther comes striding into camp. Anticipated trout didn't rise to his flies – not enough allure in the lure or perhaps this stream has already been fished out this year. Not far behind is Dick. Like Luther he's sopping wet from dancing among wet willows bracketing the South Fork. These two masters in fishology have been soundly skunked.

No fish from these two pros is quite a noteworthy event. They aren't amateurs by any stretch of the imagination. The paradox of fishless fishermen is accentuated by the conditions they were facing. Normally it's very hard to nigh impossible to land trout in flawless weather. Cloudy and rainy weather usually brings hogs out to feed. There's protection in those rain drops that wise fishers know to take advantage of. Yet, even the best-of-the-best also have their mortal moments. At least the fishing gods were compassionate by not favoring one over another; neither Dick nor Luther was chosen to figure out the intricate trout puzzle.

Luther hugs the fire while fiddling with his reel. All of that trash talk earlier – the bravado and pride – has been replaced by silence. Standing next to him I can see gears going furiously a mile-a-minute in this head.

"Let's see; first I tried the Royal Wulff and never had a rise."

"Then I switched to the Blue-winged Olive Emerger, but that was as successful as a spinning rig."

"Maybe I should have gone longer and deeper with a Pale Morning Dun?"

"The old tried true and tested Adams let me down."

"Crap, I think I left the Wooly Bugger at home."

Dick sidles over; unusually quiet and deep within brooding thoughts paralleling Luther's about what, if anything, went wrong when everything else was perfectly lined up. He's not talking smack anymore. He's more than a little perplexed that he hasn't a clue about what caused this unexpected spanking the South Fork has dished out. But, he's not about to carry on a running discourse with Luther about more promising fly selection in fear that a little insight may slip out that gives Luther the upper hand; a keeper of heroic proportions.

Neither says a word to me. Fortunately I read the dilemma and keep my mouth shut. There's high worth in a fellow that knows when to go to ground around a campfire. Silence makes a pretty fair companion at moments like these. Once Luther and Dick get their next strategy sorted out in their minds then they will become the gregarious fellows that I well remember.

Ten minutes later and they're chatting up a storm. From here they'll talk their heads off, but not one word will seep out about fishing strategy. This is, as we all know, about upholding honor.

Our campfire is smoldering along, not a big blaze because any wood we can find is fairly damp from the recent rain. Flames struggle to add cheer as clouds progressively begin to block out the feeble sun. Conversation almost stops dead still as the sun winks out behind a cloud the color of an overripe plum – no one says a word because they don't want to jinx the situation.

Dick is passing hors d'oeuvres around when a low growling rumble is followed by a dull crack like a broomstick snapping in two.

Here it comes again.

A light patter of raindrops follows several more thunderous crescendos making our hearts sink a bit. It would have been nice to finish our meal before being hammered by rain again. However, Mother Nature doesn't exactly care what we want, when we want it, or why. As far as she is concerned, it's time to generously water these dry forests and replenish trout habitat that are shriveling in a lingering drought that's sucking the life out of this land.

For an hour or so we huddle pathetically beneath huge white fir and spruce surrounding our campsite, offering fairly decent shelter. A mattress cushion of dry duff beneath the sheltering arms of these old giants – short dark brown needles, gray bark, black twigs, yellow-green-pink seed cones detonated by squirrels and wispy moss – feels like it's been fluff-dried on high using a gigantic gas dryer. A real honest gully-washer hasn't occurred this season and quite possibly hasn't passed through here for several years. Everything is parched beneath these ancient specimens towering 60-70 feet or more.

Dick does a little jig back-and-forth from the sheltering trees to fire cooking up mouth-watering green chilé cheeseburgers wrapped in huge floppy flour tortillas. He's sopping wet, oblivious to it all. Luther and I clinch the trees while saliva drools in huge waves down the sides of our mouths. We can smell them, but they're not ready yet. These tortilla-burgers will be a comforting remedy since we're famished. Furthermore, we desperately need high octane calories to fuel our bodies; the temperature has dropped some twenty degrees after a chilly rain began falling lightly over this valley flowing off the divide.

Dick puts gourmet finishing touches on our burgers cum burritos – medium, moist and juicy – and begins serving them up. Luther folds his lips around a tortilla pocket of heaven; greasy droplets splashing out one end. As I sink my teeth into the heart of my burger the miraculous plays out. GGggggooooooooodddd. I can't decide what I love best: flavor, warmth or fill?

With inspired timing the storm abates almost precisely to the second as we finish dinner. Clearing skies seem to imply that the rain may be over for good.

Of course only a fool would count on this because if there's enough heating left another round could easily unfold. Sometimes a particularly nasty thunderstorm cell spawned far to the northwest over Monument Valley drifts in like a thief in the night; that's happened more than once to us. This is the magic of summer that spontaneously materializes along the Continental Divide. Expect the worse and you won't be disappointed.

While Dick and Luther wash dishes and tell lies about fishing I saunter down trail a bit. Dusk is beginning to smother our valley, muting color and building long protective shadows. Everything is dripping in this forest so I head east toward a large meadow with thigh-high grass and dotted with copses of fir. Entering the meadow's edge, a slight series of movements by a stand of two dozen stately spruces catches my eye. I focus; trying to discern the source.

Elk!

Six horse-sized brown shapes are moving cautiously like ghosts through the mist. I duck back under cover of a convenient fir. My heart is pounding like someone knocking on a door. Elk are prolific in the San Juans, but I always feel blessed by their presence. Imperially regal as they carefully edge into the meadow, they are alert for any danger. These elk are very healthy. No ribs are showing, their coats are as glossy and slick as a high-maintenance Kentucky Derby racehorse.

They've come down at twilight to feed on lush grass in this lonesome meadow. Translucent-white clouds of vapor mimicking today's thunderheads pour from their snouts, rising in the meadow's heavy damp air. Our storm has dramatically lowered temperatures above tree line chasing them down to these lowlands harboring better prospects for grazing. The lead cow is as nervous as a sinner entering church. Her head is swaying back and forth; radar on full alert. I remain absolutely still watching their graceful promenade before deciding to reverse direction — they don't desire interaction with me. Best to leave them alone.

How many generations of elk have come and gone since the ancient people came calling in search of food? That's what makes these mountains special. They are connected to a long line of backcountry travelers. It's a rich legacy that I share at an unsuspecting moment like this. For all of the changes that have transpired over the centuries, these elk are just as wary of humans. Thank God we haven't lost that wildness. It matches the geology and climate of the surrounding forests.

By the time I make it back to the campfire it's apparent that nothing has changed as far as Dick and Luther are concerned. Liars are still telling tales about fishing exploits. It's all part of the ritual, wholesome entertainment and camaraderie that makes backcountry camps such fun. However, this time it won't last long because cold breezes sweeping off the divide drive us to ground and a cocoon of warmth in our sleeping bags.

Thirty minutes after settling in my bladder decides the time has come to leave behind this pocket of comfort under high-tech fabric. Cursing slightly, I zip down the bag, fumble back into enough clothes to keep from freezing and then tip-toe from camp to a far clearing.

I'm a little surprised that I don't need my flashlight to point the way. A huge crescent moon guides the way. And, as I stop to do my duty I tilt my head back and gaze on the cosmos looming silvery large overhead.

Snappy crisp air floods my nostrils.

Eyes adjusted to the darkness, millions of stars drill down, seemingly drawing closer to me in a celestial hug. I'm speechless and simultaneously ebullient that this beautiful side of camping has unveiled itself when all factors pointed otherwise. I never thought I'd get to see the stars like this given such cloudy skies.

My ears open to sounds of the night. It's supremely quiet except for a soft rustle of wind surging down off the peaks and the melodious sounds of the South Fork gurgling toward canyon country hundreds of miles away.

There are many brief moments that make a trip; this is but one.

Returning under the floodlights of heaven I snuggle back into my womb and shut off the lights. My sleep is sweet.

Next morning dawns soft and quiet in the high 30's. Resinous smells blanket our hobo campsite from a damp forest reviving after a healthy dousing. With the fire crackling, first Dick, then Luther, plods over from the warmth of their down-filled tombs to greet a splendid new day. Main topic for discussion is where they will fish today. With water boiling on the stove, we're easing into breakfast and basking in a clear mountain morning. Dick and Luther will fish downstream among a mass of willows while I head up-trail.

As the day matures into afternoon there is nary a cloud in the sky – quite a departure from yesterday. After sauntering up trail and off, I decide to walk a mile-and a half back to Luther's Jeep for tomorrow's breakfast that's cooling on ice. A spontaneous thought fills my mind that I ought to bring back a tarp with bungee cords for shelter over our kitchen area. There's no hint of rain, but sometimes it pays to play it safe. A tarp could provide the insurance we need to stymie further monsoonal activity.

By early evening the fishermen return from their exploits. Both tried to reach an expansive pool below a forty-foot cascade after climbing up precipitous South Fork drainage. It was much steeper than they anticipated and obstructed by ankle-wrenching moss-covered boulders and downed logs piled like giant sticks. They caught a number of relatively small keepers – Browns – despite throwing every lure, fly and nymph at them. Dick adds a sorry note of disappointment that if we had made it farther up to Gibbs Creek fishing would have been more successful on that trail-less creek. What does he want – me to control the weather as well?

Water begins boiling for pasta – it's symbolic of what's happening in the atmosphere as this cloud-free day suddenly changes in a big way. Bruise-colored clouds scud over the Continental Divide and descend on South Fork.

Here we go again.

Several impressive thunder rolls and claps ensue, but for the most part we're treated to a persistently steady, cold rain. Fortunately the tarp enables us to cook up a somewhat soggy, but longed-for meal. Our hearts are still light enough to enjoy this little wrinkle on our dinner. All this dampness is aggravating, but it's not enough to sour the mood.

At least not for another ten minutes.

Half-way through dinner the rain suddenly picks up an order of magnitude. Rain is pelting the campsite leaving us to push bathtub size indentations filled with water off the tarp. Even resistant dry spots at the base of conifers are a thing of the past. The South Fork's forest and this camp are drenched. Temperatures plummet as the rain whisks away all that solar radiation absorbed in the course of the day.

It's beginning to look worse than ugly.

Another hour goes by. Twilight approaches as we huddle beneath the tarp hoping the torrent will taper off so that we can at least enjoy a flickering fire. For a moment the rain slackens and spirits begin to soar. A few more pieces of dry wood are thrown on the fire, but it's only a guarantee for the inevitable. Rain intensifies, pounding our camp. Drops are hammering everything in one of those moments telling your intuition that you have broached that safety margin. This is shifting from serious to calamitous. Desperate for someplace dry, we retreat to our sopping tents.

Darkness descends over this mysterious South Fork basin. We're silently hunkered down in our respective tents, rain-flies pulled taut to disperse a flood from above. It's a bitter-sweet time. We know how much this forest needs moisture after several years of drought, but we also want to enjoy each other's company around the campfire.

Thirty minutes later almost complete blackness covers camp. Raindrops are beginning to tail off a bit. Is it over?

No.

A deafening rumble of thunder floats down from the Continental Divide like bad news delivered by the IRS followed by a brilliant white flash making it seem as though I've just turned on a 150 watt bulb in my little tent. That was a monstrous strike but only a hint of what's to come. This first huge boom is child's play compared to what will transpire over the next two hours. A storm of almost epic ugly proportions is drifting directly east with tumultuous hovering clouds. We are square in the middle of its path.

In my mind I can see the weather channel warning flashing across television screens in Alamosa, Pagosa Springs and Durango: "Severe weather warning. A brutal thunderstorm with accompanying winds exceeding 60 miles per hour, golf-ball sized hail and flooding is progressing at 30 miles per hour over the Wolf-Creek Pass area of the San Juan Mountains. Avoid all streams and low lying areas as flash floods may occur."

A few minutes later all hell breaks loose as a mega thunderstorm cell implodes with fireworks and canon-like explosions over the South Fork drainage.

We're seasoned campers who have spent more than a fair share of years enduring bad weather. Rain, hail, snow, thunder and lightning, frigid temperatures, sleet and various combinations thereof have pelted us in the backcountry. So, a bout with a wicked thunderstorm is about par for the course. Plus, we have the necessary high-quality equipment along to survive a bad storm above 9,000 feet. Nonetheless, this time we're in for a real treat.

This decade's mother-of-all-summer-thunderstorms is hitting the San Juan Mountains.

Lightning flashes once every 3-5 minutes followed by monstrous blasts and detonations. It seems like the Army is running field exercises using artillery on the divide above. From beneath a paper-thin rain-fly it appears that lightning is striking somewhere just shy of the Continental Divide, on surrounding 13,000 foot peaks, and along descending ridges of the drainage. Only occasionally can I see the outline of a specific strike. Mostly it's just a brilliant illumination of the entire sky that floods over our tents. At this point I'm thinking about the potential for really big hail or massive flooding – both are a distinct possibility.

After half-an-hour the tempo *picks up*. As the cell floats over our basin lightning is striking every thirty seconds. There's an almost incessant symphony where the lead instruments are timpani drums – huge galactic drums. I can now see the outline of specific strikes in addition to dazzling bright light inundating camp. I've seen darker overcast days than tonight, thanks in large measure to this unanticipated light show.

There's no alternative but laying there in complete awe of nature's power. I'm stunned; shell-shocked; and yes, even a bit frightened. How long will this last? How bad is it going to get? Will the rain intensify to flooding proportions? Will hail descend and if so in what size and volume?

Another crack ripples the air and white zigzags course above.

This time we're lucky. Rain and hail to match the thunder and lightning never materialize. Gradually over 45 more minutes, the storm slowly drifts east after being hung-up for almost two hours on the Continental Divide. An hour later when I finally get up to take an adrenaline-laced pee the dismally black basin lightens and a few stars appear. For the moment it's over. But tomorrow we'll wake to heavy cloud cover and the precise recipe for another extravagant display of energy and celestial forces nestled among the headwaters of the Rio Grande.

***

Up-close-and-personal, in-your-face confrontations offer the most memorable backcountry experiences possible. It is one thing to casually lounge in a cushy threadbare recliner with libations in hand watching "Storm Stories" on the Weather Channel® and quite another to be out there in the chaotic melee. From inside a building, life-threatening hail the size of golf balls – and larger – carpeting the ground several inches deep is traumatically frightening; that is, until you're forced to survive such a storm out in the wilds. Hail takes on an entirely different meaning under those conditions. Pelting rain jumps from a minor nuisance to widow maker.

Crazy weather is a frighteningly special gift accompanying summer in the Four Corners. It is an energy that we can't control, testing our mettle and commitment to roam back alleys and hidden nooks of this vast land. Such power forces us to tap character hidden deeply in ourselves – patience to wait out peppering hail under a forlorn fir; endurance to battle persistent rain day-after-day; wisdom in selecting a camp protected from lightning bolts; prudence in carrying more essentials than you expect to need – more accoutrements, more clothing, more food; courage to laugh at ugly conditions; and spirit to keep from being a pain-in-the-ass to companions by complaining endlessly about the misfortune of miserable weather.

Nature's power in the Southwest is definitely awe-inspiring; but perhaps even more impressive is its flat-out inconsistency. There's no reliable ability to predict when the monsoon season will start...or end for that matter. Some years the rains well up in mid-May. In other years July 4th comes and goes with still no sign of moisture pouring toward the north. As if to underscore all of this absurdity, recently monsoon rains have failed to make an appearance.

Weather vagaries aren't limited to summer. In many respects the entire special spectrum of year-round weather patterns has gone screwy. Winter snows reach 30 or 40 percent of normal; less in some unlucky spots; more in spots that for some reason are blessed. There's always hope that things will be better in summer, but that's not guaranteed anymore.

Magic of beguiling weather in the Southwest seems to have disappeared.

So...what's new?

The Anasazi lived with these very same conundrums. However, it was worse – far worse – for them. They couldn't drill down to tap precious subterranean water supplies. They were unable to twist a spigot and quench their thirst. It's amazing how easy we have it by comparison with modern plumbing and intricate supply systems that bring west slope water to eastern cities along the Rocky Mountain front.

The old ones and we may not be all that different when considering what's happening to the environment. We watch the ecosystem change in radical ways. They did too. Fir and spruce are decimated by beetles. Ponderosa and piñon pine are drilled to oblivion. And like those who passed on, there's nothing we can do but watch the forests come and go while shaking our heads. Wagging tongues can't replace the moisture that plant and animal life need.

We can transport water around, but only to a point. This technological skill enables modern society to avoid whole-scale migrations that the Anasazi endured. When things dried up in the thirteenth and fourteenth centuries, Ancestral Puebloans were left with no choice but to move on.

Unblemished lands waited for them.

We don't have that luxury.

Perhaps we need to drill down more deeply to commiserate with the Anasazi and learn from their experience.

They were driven from the land, but they had other places to turn to.

That leaves me pondering: "Where will we find succor?"

Past. Present. Future.
Harmonize? Break asunder?
Life's conundrum.

15

What Would the Old Ones Say?

oft creamy half-light of dusk pours down on Canyon Road, that super trendy avenue of art galleries and restaurants for which Santa Fe is internationally known. Last-minute shoppers spill out onto this narrow crooked street, forced to promenade on pot-holed asphalt; sidewalks are virtually non-existent given that paths hearken back centuries ago. Our power-shoppers don't really care about on-coming cars because this moment is, after all, only about them.

Or, so they think.

A beer-crazed local driving a faded and severely dented black beater roars up the constricted defile slightly weaving from side-to-side thanks to his favorite nectar's kick. Through a cracked and partially shattered windshield a blank stare warns those catching a glimpse of his face about total obliviousness to anyone, anything. An ever-so-slight shit-eating-grin reinforces that he *will* run over anyone with the audacity to get in his way.

Street theater in the Holy City is well worth the price of admission and something I'm enjoying immensely while stumbling over century-old pavers on the way to historic El Farol Restaurant. Two trophy blondes (by bottle and surgeon, not birth) almost wake up too late to the oncoming black sedan. He has them smack in the middle of his radar. Pricey Ferragamo sandals pay a terrible price as they dance toward the faux sidewalk faster than their last shopping-fest to Houston's Galleria.

The local flips back thick greasy gray locks with a wave of his hand, one finger pointed prominently in the blondes' direction. Of the two, a slightly chubby one jumps on the curb, glasses askew, shouting his anatomical nickname. She's wasting her breath. He figured that out years ago.

A quarter-mile further up Canyon Road Gestapo valets at the world's finest restaurant – Geronimo's – make certain that casual evening strollers don't intrude on *Geronimo's* sidewalk. We weave back onto the street anxious as a mother goose with young goslings about being in harm's way. Guests seated in Geronimo's cheap seats – virtually in the street – carry on conversations without missing a beat despite the fact that the blondes were nearly terminated. Deep in shallow discussions, several throw quick furtive glances our way –checking us out, or checking to see if we notice them? These are the time-honored rituals of the Santa Fe scene.

One hundred feet more and we reach El Farol's front porch. Last chance to breathe in wafer thin mountain air – laced with

a quixotic scent of New Age/New Mexican cooking at its prici-
est. Cloudless skies are fading from azure to deep indigo and soft
purple on the eastern edge of Santa Fe. How I hate to leave this
tableau for the cramped innards of an ancient hacienda cum styl-
ish restaurant.

Duty is calling – dinner reception for a sweet young couple married earlier today in a sparkling green aspen grove three
thousand feet higher on the mountain. Turning toward the host-
ess as we enter the restaurant-proper a potted mosaic of alyssum,
petunias, marigolds and violets slaps me in the face with showy
color and perfume. Ah, the memorable sights, scents and spirit
of a magical town.

A decrepit adobe, El Farol is a serpentine maze of dark little
rooms; hallways headed nowhere, low ceilings and variegated
flooring. Weaving toward the back we snatch quick glimpses of
a highly populated bar, a multitude of chic diners sequestered in
tight corners, an industrious wait station and ultimately several
long rooms overflowing with guests and friends. It is unbear-
ably hot, almost stifling, and loud. All that happy conversation
is bouncing off hovering mud and plaster walls. But, the mood
is celebratory, so much more embracing than whispered conversations in Geronimo's where diners don't dare show too much
exuberance – that would be bad form.

We make obligatory rounds extending congratulations to the
buoyant couple and beaming parents. It's been a long week for
them; exhaustion commandeers their eyes if you look closely.
Fortunately, truly excellent sangria is being passed around by
El Farol's attentive wait staff helping to mellow the celebration.
Just the right balance of dryness from red wine battles sweetness
from Cointreau, and tartness from orange and lime. It creates an

intoxicating flavor, pleasing to the palette and perfect for slaking thirst rising with the temperature in these cozy little quarters.

The groom's proud mother, a talented artist who is truly at home in Santa Fe, issues a command for all to be seated at their assigned tables. Her lilting Judy Collin's voice harmonizes with the mellow vibe surrounding this festive occasion. Hors d'oeuvres are about to begin.

Tonight we're sharing with two other couples who hail from Austin, Texas. They're guests of the bride; we're guests of the groom. There's trouble brewing here that could easily pass unnoticed. Chance encounters between Texans and New Mexicans are always interesting due to their unremitting deprecation of anything not-Texas.

Our first few minutes of stilted conversation unfold fairly predictably. For their part, Texans usually gush appreciatively about how beautiful New Mexico is compared to other states — heretically, even more beautiful than Texas itself (Imagine!). They swoon about majestic mountains overflowing with aspen, fir and pine. They wax eloquently about Santa Fe's thrilling uniqueness and normally summarize sights and places they've enjoyed – the Plaza, O'Keefe Gallery, Canyon Road shops and galleries, treasured restaurants they've discovered, and outlying destinations such as Bandelier National Monument or Taos Pueblo. In all, they sit there taking pleasure in their sangria with smug little smiles reflecting their good life.

New Mexicans can't stand the patronizing attitudes of Texans. An underlying current of superiority electrifies this intersection of two different cultures. One state is impoverished and the other aspires to the cutting edge of economic, educational, political and cultural supremacy. All of their praise sounds a bit too bogus. They hark from real wealth – deep pockets. New Mexico is merely a playground; they really wouldn't want to live here. When all of the stars and planets align perfectly they might acquiesce to a vacation home. Nonetheless, get a life; New Mexico is a developing country without the sorts of refinement they think represent Texas.

It's going to be a long night, but we're determined to take the high road and get past this initial skirmish and status mongering. To help matters a waiter brings one of El Farol's signature hors d'oeuvres — a deep fried avocado sitting atop several delightful sauces.

Perfect timing.

With food in our mouths it's difficult to continue the wooden conversation. Besides, now there are precious moments for the sangria to kick in with full force. Our table is suddenly quiet while we munch the taste and texture of an exquisite avocado made wholly exceptional.

After dribbles and drabs of small talk, conversation turns to what people do for a living and the education they've attained. It is part of a bizarre status dance designed to help us understand that we're blessed to be sharing dinner with them. All of the Texans have graduate degrees, some of them at the doctoral level. One couple boasts of offspring who are finishing their M.D. degrees. Make no mistake about it; they are definitely upwardly mobile and all working with impressive high tech firms.

It's this last tidbit of information that really captures my attention.

With a bit of mirth I observe that New Mexico seems intent on becoming a Silicon Valley wanna-be. "New Mexican business and public leaders are adamant that high tech is the righteous answer to the state's beleaguered future. The state only needs to capitalize on the national laboratories in its midst — Sandia

National Labs and Los Alamos National Lab – while using various aspiring commercialization engines such as Albuquerque Economic Development, Next Generation Economy Initiative, Technology Ventures Corporation (part of Lockheed Martin) and Science and Technology Corporation at the university. It's all so simple – exceptionally vital components are present and accounted for. Certainly New Mexico is poised to take-off one day like an Apollo rocket before soaring to the success Austin, Texas has already enjoyed."

I glance over at our guests. Three are sitting with mouths wide open and parrot-green mushed-up avocado dancing on scarlet tongues. An image of roast pigs comes to mind but I wipe it away while carrying on with my little sermon.

"Consider some of the leading investments in technology that have been made around the Rio Grande corridor. Intel has built the world's largest chip manufacturing plant in Rio Rancho. Eclipse Aviation came close to bringing a super-low-cost, highly technological private jet to market. Sandia and Los Alamos have expanded their missions encouraging scientists to take inventions to market. The university has literally poured millions of dollars into intellectual property commercialization. Federal research grant funds are rising rapidly as university scientists catch high tech fever."

One of the Austin foursome about chokes on his sangria when laughing out loud, "You've got to be kidding."

His companion snorts, "High tech is already dead."

In unison the other couple blurts out in an ostensibly rehearsed and syncopated beat, "New Mexico is too late, the high tech heyday happened fifteen years ago. Biomedical offers the only prospects for profitable technology ventures these days."

All four of them chortle a bit and slap back another slug of libations. Drawing in a deep breath, one of the Texans from a semi-conductor firm admonishes, "Tell your political, business, university and national lab leaders to get a life; New Mexico is not the next Silicon Valley – never has been; never will be."

Having baited them a bit to this reaction, I share the good news being bandied about throughout the Rio Grande corridor – Albuquerque's and Santa Fe's coveted predisposition for technological take-off according to Richard Florida in his books *The Rise of the Creative Class* and *The Flight of the Creative Class*.[19]

"Who is this Florida guy?" one of the Ph.D.s asks, committing a major faux pas. She just tipped her hand that perhaps Texans don't know everything after all, and I'm certain she would give anything to take back that question.

"At the time he wrote his book, Richard Florida was a professor of regional economic development at Carnegie Mellon University – impressive credentials. He argues that thirty percent of all employed people form a so-called 'creative class'. These individuals are at the cutting edge of innovation in their fields. They tend to be highly educated, young, computer savvy, allergic to bureaucracy, and drawn to bohemian lifestyles. Technology, talent and tolerance characterize creative class members who eschew anything manufacturing while tuning into everything that is remotely avant-garde. These technology geeks, artists, intellectuals, and contrarian thinkers would rather bike to work, resonate with live music, eat vegan, and live down to a lower standard of material consumption. Here's where Albuquerque and Santa Fe fit into Florida's thinking."

Pausing briefly to catch my breath I glance longingly across the room at the enraptured bride and groom surrounded in a mosaic of vivid colors worn by guests, reflected off El Farol's earth toned walls. Will they be able to maintain this loving embrace over the decades, this delightful couple?

"Using Florida's rating system; Albuquerque is the number 2 city on the creativity index among regions with a population between 500,000 and 1,000,000 people. Santa Fe is ranked number 4 on the same index among regions with a population less than 250,000 people. In short, the Rio Grande corridor should be ripe for harvesting as far as innovation is concerned. New Mexico possesses underlying preconditions and distinctive spirit of place needed to encourage creativity and innovation. When adding up the enormous resources at the national labs with the inherent creativity-laced populace, assuredly New Mexico is primed for explosive growth among historic communities lining the Rio Grande."

"New Mexico nurtures a fond dream deep in its bosom that it will soon become the next Silicon Valley. All of the necessary ingredients are present – the labs, universities, sunny climate, energetic young populace, bohemian lifestyle – everything. It's bound to happen any second; virtually any minute now." And with that final statement I turn back to what's left of my sangria.

Eyebrows soar on the Texans and their eyes roll as they look at each other with massive incredulity and disbelief.

One guffaws under her breath before saying, "Let me put this to you as politely as I possibly can. New Mexico is a total blast to come visit. We love the quaint mud huts – excuse me, alluring adobe trophy homes – melding into the high desert hills, pretentious restaurants offering passable fare at impossible prices, and ambience – Santa Fe style – on the twisting narrow streets of this ancient city. The mountains are spectacular and such a welcomed diversion. Native arts and contemporary artwork add stunning exclamation points on shelves and walls back home."

"We truly do enjoy your rainbow-colorful International Balloon Fiesta in Albuquerque. It's a comforting delight to stuff ourselves with fatty Mexican food after looking through charming tiny shops in Old Town or strolling through your first-rate Rio Grande Zoo. Best of all there's no humidity. It's so dry that it feels ten degrees cooler than the thermometer actually reads. Yes, New Mexico has many blessings, but please get a grip on reality — it's not going to be the next focal point of the technology revolution."

Her compatriots' heads nod vigorously in agreement — a gathering of bobble heads — as they swap knowing glances with each other.

A companion pipes up, "Let me make a few observations that may hurt a bit and that render Florida's predictions as groundless as a fortune-teller's hollow visions. First, New Mexico is almost illiterate. It constantly ranks among the lowest in K-12 test scores. It's not that New Mexicans don't try. I've read about the millions of dollars invested to improve education in this state but it isn't working. The drop-out rate stinks. High school graduates are ill-prepared for either college or the workplace. Look at all of the expensive private schools that have cropped up."

"Second, no matter how nice the climate is, no one in the high tech field wants to live where the crime rate is so high. Admittedly every city is confronted with the occasional violent crime and widespread petty burglary associated with drug trafficking. But, New Mexico is unusually inept at resolving these problems. Driving under the influence of alcohol seems to be a commonly accepted social practice here; violators receive virtually no retribution as habitual offenders. They don't do time for doing the crime. The people who pay the price are the innocent — and dead — bystanders."

Our monologue spouting Texan tilts his head up slightly and glances out of the corner of his eye toward his compatriot. Wordless encouragement is communicated when their eyes meet. They think they are giving me a spanking. In fact I couldn't agree more with this razor-sharp criticism.

Another sip of sangria is in order.

"Third, leadership of technology commercialization remains an oxymoron. Public and private organizations seem to be continually bickering about who is leading economic development. Sunday's paper ran an excellent exposé on the matter – petty politics and tiny egos blocking any forward progress. It's all just the same old tired jargon and no results – nothing – for investing tons of resources. Leading through rhetoric leaves top officials feeling proud about future prospects. Intellectual property never becomes commercialized because somewhere along the line someone drops the ball or puts up barriers. Initiatives atrophy and die or simply become passé."

By this point his partner yawns like a 15 pound bass taking in a healthy trout fry. She slowly swirls a swizzle stick in her glass while staring off at another table whose revelers are deep in jovial conversation. Methinks she has heard one too many of his lectures before – or is she simply jealous that she doesn't have the speaking spotlight?

"Finally, like-it-or-not, New Mexico has an entrenched reputation as a center for low tech jobs. With an under-educated workforce, New Mexico can attract plenty of low paying jobs because few other communities want them. Intel's presence is a perfect example. Intel's research and development arm and corporate headquarters are located in other states, not in Albuquerque. The Intel plant is staffed by good people, but definitely not Richard Florida's creative class. Savvy high tech firms are looking for people with a strong work ethic – that simply doesn't match with New Mexico' laid-back and mañana lifestyle."

Pleased with his little soliloquy, he grabs another jagged hunk of onion-laced bread, spreads a bit of seasoned red pepper and goat cheese before stuffing it down his gullet. All eyes stare at me – it's time to defend the Realm, but I'm not about to be rushed. And, much of what they have shared in the way of criticism is justified. Their ranting and raving have simply focused on the downside rather than looking at this from a more positive, enlightened perspective.

"Couldn't agree more with your comments," I begin in response. "New Mexico may forever be a Silicon Valley wanna-be. It's entertaining to fantasize that 20+ years after a fad has blossomed, somehow, someway, New Mexico is suddenly going to emerge as the next high tech center – a place to which the rest of the global economy will turn for the next generation of technological wonders. In many respects it is complete utter fantasy. Business, community and public leaders may want it to happen; they may invest precious resources trying to make it happen; but, it's just not going to fly. And, here's why – but, for an entirely different set of reasons."

As I launch into a retort the groom suddenly turns from a table across the room and migrates to our table for a chat. Kevin is always the gentleman I would expect nothing less. His eyes are dancing and he can't quite wipe that beatific smile off his face. "How are you folks doing tonight? I am so happy...."

While Kevin showers polite consideration on his guests I turn over a number of thoughts in my mind about New Mexico and it's maniacal obsession with economic development.

The Land of Enchantment is justifiably renowned for its diverse culture, a simpatico interrelationship among Hispanics,

Native Americans and Anglos. Ancient civilizations lived here before Europeans arrived. Over the years this history has substantially influenced how local communities and society evolved, particularly in terms of enduring values and world view. Unlike so many other states straddled with bland homogeneity, New Mexico sparkles because of its multiculturalism.

Who can deny the scenic grandeur of this supernatural place? Topography and vegetation vary as much as the cultural context. Sky-high mountains serve as visual reference points and massive collectors of precipitation. Ultimately snow transforms into rivers that incise rough canyons as water seeks access to distant seas. Altitude is a prevailing common denominator. Deserts are found more than a mile high. They lead to dry forests and eventually to fir-covered slopes two-miles-plus in elevation. High thin air lends a sparkling quality to sunlight for which New Mexico is famous. All of these natural splendors vastly influence inhabitants' perspectives.

New Mexico has certain distinctive qualities or assets – multicultural society, scenic beauty and a wealth of natural resources, ancestral traditions, and vibrant idiosyncratic communities. None of these strengths is particularly conducive to high tech or building the next Silicon Valley. In fact, many of them are essentially inimical to such a goal.

Kevin has genuflected enough and charming Ramey is pulling on his sleeve to join her in the other room where their parents are waiting. As he departs I reengage my friends from the "Friendship State" in our skirmish.

"While business and public leaders may espouse the desire for economic development and growth, others in New Mexico are content with less. But, they don't see it as less, they see it as *more*."

Our fearsome foursome seems totally perplexed. Their eyes belie an indwelling confusion about a concept that is unthinkable – doesn't every person alive want to consume more? It's absolutely un-American…no…un-Texan…*not* to want to live in a bigger house and drive fancier cars!

"A large percentage – perhaps a majority of New Mexico's citizens – don't want to see natural resources trashed merely to put up more subdivisions of MacDonaldized southwestern theme homes. They don't want congested traffic and the problem of building further infrastructure to take care of additional people simply because it means that someone is going to make a quick buck. They rather cheer for the threatened Silvery Minnow and protect water it needs from being sucked out of the Rio Grande by some insensitive manufacturing plant that's producing dubious goods of doubtful quality."

"In effect, blind-less pursuit of high tech is equivalent to ignoring New Mexico's societal context. It is an insidious trend threatening the state's future. New Mexico could lose its very *soul* if developers and public officials have their way. For centuries New Mexicans knew who they were, how they got here and where they wanted to go. This spirit of community and place is beginning to evaporate. Pursuit of high tech means that New Mexico is just part of the global industrial complex and many citizens don't want to go that route. Excuse me for saying so, but New Mexicans would rather leave that dismal prospect to undesirable places like Dallas."

The Texans recoil as though I belched in their faces. What heresy. Here is a bumpkin with the audacity to suggest that their gi-normous state stinks? Suddenly the atmosphere at our little table became very chilly. Once again I have overstepped common decency by telling the truth. When will I ever learn to keep my big mouth shut and opinions to myself? Well, they asked for it and now the truth is staring them in the face.

Frigid silence covers our table like a light-filtering shroud. They conveniently munch on a piece of pasty pasta, a limp zucchini or errant shrimp from their entrees. Hatred fills their eyes and they try to contain a mounting desire to fling dinner's remnants in my face. Oh, if looks could kill.

Texans have a very difficult time listening because they prefer to monopolize conversations, not listen. And to be honest, I had been dominating this tête-à-tête since the very moment they tried to demean this state.

Just as I am finishing my last word, in a moment of inspired grace, the groom's father saunters over to our table and interjects by introducing himself. How perfect. It was that precious moment I needed to stand and walk away from my Texas friends. Undoubtedly they want to respond; to debate the matter and share their wisdom gleaned by living in the greatest state in the union.

Unfortunately I had far more important matters to attend to; I ask the groom's father to direct me to the restroom.

***

How do you build a great community in which everyone wants to live while simultaneously retaining compellingly distinctive qualities that make it unique, a star gem among many jewels? This is an issue that countless cities and states constantly tussle with although success usually eludes them in the end.

An enlightened answer for New Mexico and the Southwest can be framed by asking another question: *"What would the old ones say about this matter?"*

Almost from the sanguine moment that a town receives national notoriety as one of the top ten, top fifty or top one-hundred places to live, play, do business or retire to; insidious forces conspire to make it less. The very press of humanity eventually overwhelms something that worked, in the process diluting the joie de vivre of an extra special location.

Encouraged by a voracious media looking to sell vast numbers of magazines and newspapers because of the trite rankings, those within favored communities tend to develop a myopic view. The good news of making the rankings severs them from reality starring them in the face. Such is the case for many Southwestern communities, especially Albuquerque and the Rio Grande corridor.

Rather than recognizing inherent strengths in the Land of Enchantment, public, business and community leaders seem obsessively intent on recreating – redefining – New Mexico. They want to be like San Jose, Rochester or any other city that has enjoyed a modicum of high tech success no matter how ephemeral it might be. They fail to see that like other fads the high tech bubble can easily burst leaving tattered shreds and confusion behind.

Barring some miraculous transformation Albuquerque and Santa Fe – *as well as hundreds of other aspiring hamlets, towns and cities in the Southwest and elsewhere across this country* – will probably *not* become the next central focus of national and international attention for high technology. More likely they will evolve in fairly predictable directions building upon inherent strengths while being constrained by natural weaknesses.

Although the Rio Grande corridor may relinquish economic growth over the long run, it could possibly regain something of immeasurable value that has gradually evaporated – its *soul*. The ancient ones would certainly tell us this.

Rather than trying to make a silk purse out of a sow's ear, New Mexico could rejoice by celebrating its many blessing and building upon its distinctive assets. The visiting Texans hit the nail on the head after all. It's tough to eat crow, but admittedly they recognize the Land of Enchantment for what it really is – a fabulous travel destination laced with art, Native communities, pristine scenic areas, trendy shopping, haut cuisine to die for, historic places, diverse recreation and so many other attributes created by a centuries-old multicultural population.

The bottom-line: New Mexico has so much going for it that it doesn't need a high tech boom.

Building a tourism-centered economy based on magnificent scenery, mysterious Pueblos and historic Spanish settlements may not seem as sexy and glamorous as discovering the next ultra advanced micro-chip or electronic biomedical wonder. However, it's all a matter of perspective and values.

Although it may be heretical to suggest, perhaps leaders in the Land of Enchantment represent a minority viewpoint. Their vision of greatness isn't really shared by a large portion of the populace that would rather trade-off a bit of economic success for clean water, air, contained commercial development, less traffic congestion and limits on urban/suburban sprawl. Unfortunately, those that ascribe to this view don't wield the power.

This jostling of priorities continues each day while an unspoken backdrop unremittingly influences those living along the Rio Grande from Tesuque to the Santo Domingo Pueblo and down to Albuquerque's South Valley as well as all manner of nooks and crannies in-between. It is the spirit of this land intertwined with ancient cultures that over the millennia have called this place home. Contemporaries may fail to openly acknowledge this presence and even deny that it exists, but they are only deluding themselves.

Ancient ones hover up and down the Rio Grande.

They are ever-present in the background, overseeing windswept sage-covered mesas, Bosque thickets brimming with cottonwoods and bountiful bird-life, red-yellow arroyos flooding into the Rio Grande with its life sustaining waters, and heavily-forested mountains reaching to the Heavens. In the same sense their ghostly apparitions can be found wandering twisted alleyways hemmed in by massive adobe brick walls, within the asphalt canyons of downtown Albuquerque and gliding over the sprawling national lab complexes.

Yes; the old ones do care enormously about how their ancestral lands are being violated in the name of economic development and an insidious grab for money. Whether glitzy Pueblo casino, dominating silicon chip manufacturing plant, or rambling housing development with cheap look-alike faux pueblo-style homes, those who have passed can only feel deep remorse for the desecration of what to them are sacred lands. They are probably even more perplexed by the propensity for these trends to have accelerated in blind pursuit of high tech development – the means to an end; the end of a distinctively spiritual landscape and extraordinarily special place on this Earth.

At one time Los Alamos, New Mexico was the cutting-edge center of sophisticated high technology, yet almost no one knew about it. In Quonset huts, non-descript barracks and Spartan laboratories, this nation's preeminent scientific minds figured out how to split atoms. In a bizarre twist of logic, they created an apocalyptically destructive device as a means to achieve peace. These scientists clearly understood the appallingly dark implications of their work – in finally ending World War II they were simultaneously crafting a means by which any misguided mis-anthrope could literally destroy our planet.

Los Alamos was chosen as a national laboratory site in part due to its remote location in a nearly unknown state. Sited on ponderosa and piñon pine forested mesas at 7,500 feet elevation, Los Alamos was virtually undetectable given surrounding forest, deep canyon cleavages spilling toward the Rio Grande and rela-tively uninhabited Indian reservations and rural Spanish-origin farming communities bracketing its flanks.

A more beautiful location for a laboratory is hard to imag-ine. Each morning scientists could watch New Mexico's fabled magenta-orange sunlight ignite distant ridgelines of the Sangre de Cristo Mountains above Santa Fe — an inspiration to continue their path-breaking intellectual discoveries.

The irony of Los Alamos is its sinister presence in a sacred land. Hundreds, even thousands, of years before, pre-Puebloan ances-tors gravitated to the mellow canyons in what now is Bandelier National Monument. Pumice stone ruins, pictographs, petro-glyphs and stylized emblematic icons of stone lions are found throughout the monument. They testify to the powerful spiri-tual presence emanating from this land. How the ancient ones must have recoiled when leaders in the mid-Twentieth Century decided to place that evil laboratory in such a hallowed spot.

After the war ended Los Alamos lingered for a brief time as the center of cutting-edge high tech development. However, even while New Mexico was reaching this epitome, science in-exorably drifted back to traditional coastal centers — Berkeley, Massachusetts Institute of Technology, California Institute of Technology, and similar labs — accessible to business acumen and large populations hungry for new technology-based prod-ucts. New Mexico simply wasn't viewed as *the* place where future technology would evolve. For one thing, Los Alamos was niche-bound around the atomic bomb and bad vibes associated with this tool of Armageddon-destruction. For another, Los Alamos was simply too far in the middle of nowhere to become a center of commerce-based technology.

Not surprisingly, New Mexico did not evolve into a Mecca for high technology after World War II. The national labs remained – Los Alamos and Sandia – while continuing a narrow focus on defense missions. True to its inherent assets, the Land of Enchantment returned once again to a renowned tourist destination. Quaint adobe villages, mysterious Indian pueblos and the endless Navajo reservation, soaring alpine spires, high desert mesas strewn with rocky canyon defiles, the muddy Rio Grande twisting through tree-choked Bosques, and countless other enduring symbols of New Mexico's legacy dominated the minds of those outside the state when they heard the term "Land of Enchantment."

And, so it will persist in the foreseeable future because of New Mexico's magical character. Silicon Valley wanna-bes will continue to be just that – dreamers of a vision that doesn't fit with this special land or its spiritual essence. There's nothing enchanting about becoming a third-rate imitation of Austin. New Mexico's destiny, and that of the Southwest, is much loftier than this; its future sparkles with imposing potential when the scale of economic ambition is harmonious with the soul of this land and heritage of people comprising historic communities – and ancestral shadows – along the Rio Grande.

References for Additional Reading

1. Annie Dillard. *Pilgrim at Tinker Creek*. New York: HarperPerennial. 1998, p. 36.

2. Diane Ackerman. Deep Play. New York: Vintage. 2000, p. 156

3. Henry David Thoreau. *The Maine Woods*. Princeton: Princeton University Press. 1974, p.71.

4. Philip Caputo. "Alone," *Wild Stories: The Best of Men's Journal*. New York: Crown Publishers. 2002, p. 71.

5. Robert V. Taylor & Stephen Albert. "Human Hunting of Nongame Birds at Zuni, New Mexico, U.S.A." *Conservation Biology*, Vol. 13, No. 6 (Dec., 1999) pp. 1398-1403.

6. Craig Childs. *House of Rain*. New York: Little, Brown and Co. 2006. pp. 83-83.

7. David E. Stuart. *Anasazi America*. Albuquerque: University of New Mexico Press. 2000. pp. 107-124.

8. SueEllen Campbell. *Bringing the Mountain Home*. Tucson: University of Arizona Press. 1996. p. 70.

9. Stanley Crawford. *The River in Winter*. Albuquerque, University of New Mexico Press. 2003. P. 106.

10. Robert Michael Pyle. *The Thunder Tree*. New York: Lyons Press. 1993. p. xv.

11. Terry Tempest Williams. *An Unspoken Hunger*. New York: Vintage. 1994. p. 55.

12. William R. Deedler. "Just what is Indian Summer and did Indians really have Anything to do with It? National Weather Service Detroit/Pontiac MI, Fall, 1996, at http://www.crh.noaa.gov/dtx/stories/i-summer.php

13. David Petersen. *Ghost Grizzlies*. Boulder: Johnson Books. 1998.

14. Rick Bass. *The Lost Grizzlies*. New York: Houghton Mifflin. 1995.

15. Patricia McCairen. *Canyon Solitude*. Seattle: Adventura Books. 1998. p. 47.

16. Rick Ridgeway. *The Shadow of Kilimanjaro*. New York: Henry Holt & Company. 1998. p. viii.

17. David Petersen. *The Nearby Faraway*. Boulder: Johnson Books. 1997. p. 188.

18. National Weather Service Forecast Office. http://www.srh.noaa.gov/mlb/ltgcenter/ltg_facts.html.

19. Richard Florida. *The Rise of the Creative Class*. New York: Basic Books. 2002.

www.ingramcontent.com/pod-product-compliance
Lightning Source LLC
Chambersburg PA
CBHW022101280326
41933CB00007B/218